DATE DUE

NO 26 '03			

VIRTUAL INSTRUCTION

Issues and Insights from an International Perspective

Carine M. Feyten

Joyce W. Nutta

1999
Libraries Unlimited, Inc.
Englewood, Colorado

Libraries Unlimited, Inc.
P.O. Box 6633
Englewood, CO 80155-6633
1-800-237-6124
www.lu.com

Library of Congress Cataloging-in-Publication Data

Virtual instruction : issues and insights from an international perspective / [edited by] Carine M. Feyten, Joyce W. Nutta.
xvi, 262 p. 17x25 cm.
Includes bibliographical references and index.
ISBN 1-56308-714-6 (paper)
1. Distance education--Computer-assisted instruction.
2. Telecommunication in education. I. Feyten, Carine M.
II. Nutta, Joyce W.
LC5803.C65V57 1999
371.3′5′0785--dc21 99-25018
CIP

To our grandmothers,

Madame Hippolyte Limbourg

and

Mrs. Jerome L. Watson

Contents

List of Illustrations

Figures

Tables

Preface

This story began in two areas of great contrast and far apart, northern Belgium and Florida, when the co-editors of this book embarked on two journeys whose paths led them to the same destination. Carine Feyten, an associate professor at the University of South Florida and a native Belgian, was a visiting professor at the Leuven Institute for Innovative Learning (LINOV), a European think tank that coordinates research and projects related to distance learning and technology in education. Joyce Nutta, a native Floridian, was an assistant professor at the University of South Florida, creating and offering a series of distance learning courses to meet the increasing demands of a high-growth area with a high ratio of "non-traditional age" students. It is striking how each editor's process of research and development was so clearly influenced by her cultural contexts. The Belgian approach was studied, guided by theory developed at an international think tank. The Floridian approach was a swift response to an expanding need, developed through empirical application and refinement of commonsense instructional design and delivery.

The authors' experiences are perhaps a metaphor for the global phenomenon of the development of virtual instruction. In all parts of the world, virtual instruction has been a theory-driven as well as an empirical response to the call to apply new, barrier-removing technologies to education, retaining and expanding upon the best qualities of instruction offered through more conventional means, while exploring new approaches to learning that exploit the inherent properties of the technologies used. In addition, throughout the world virtual instruction has been developed in ways that were culturally situated, and the finished products show the stamp of their cultural context, yet clear universals have emerged that mark each product as virtual instruction. This is the focus of *Virtual Instruction:* to explore and explain how these technologies are adapted within cultures around the world to reach the same goal of providing increased access to learner-centered, interactive, communication-focused instruction through computer-mediated distance learning, and in doing so, to provide theoretical and practical guidance for educators.

Many people have contributed to the development of this book. First, we would like to thank the international authors who contributed chapters. Betty Morris and Cheryl Eckl of Libraries Unlimited have provided patient guidance and insightful encouragement. Many thanks to Professor André Oosterlinck, Rector of the Katholieke Universiteit Leuven, for inviting Dr. Feyten to spend her sabbatical there, and to Professor Georges Van der Perre and the whole LINOV team for providing a stimulating environment and allowing her to participate in their exciting work. Special thanks to Tony Scully for his wit and assistance in the revision process. We are indebted to our bright and talented graduate assistants Gregory Taylor, Michelle Macy, and especially Annette Norwood—without her patience, attention to detail, and perseverance we could not have finished this book. We are grateful for the support that we received from the University of South Florida for developing a paradigm for virtual instruction. Carine would like to thank her parents, Edgard and Viviane, and Joyce would like to thank her family, Giorgio, Francesca, and Marco, for tolerating and appreciating their demanding work schedule to complete *Virtual Instruction*.

Contributors

Chen Ai Yen
Instructional Science
National Institute of Education
Nanyang Technological University
469 Bukit Timah Road
Singapore 25, Republic of Singapore

Christel Claeys
LINOV—KU Leuven
200A Celestijnenlaan
3001 Heverlee, Belgium

Jan Elen
Katholieke Universiteit Leuven, DUO
Naamsestraat, 98
3000 Leuven, Belgium

Carine M. Feyten
College of Education, EDU 208B
University of South Florida
Tampa, Florida 33620-5650

Han Fraeters
Katholieke Universiteit Leuven
Audio Visuele Dienst
Groenveldlaan 3b3
3001 Heverlee, Belgium

Graeme Hart
Whirligig Technologies Pty. Ltd.
7 Carlton Street
McKinnon 3204, Australia

José Lambert
Katholieke Universiteit Leuven, CETRA
Blijde Inkomststraat, 21
3000 Leuven, Belgium

Joost Lowyck
Katholieke Universiteit Leuven, CIP &T
Vesaliusstraat, 2
3000 Leuven, Belgium

Azam Mashhadi
Instructional Science
National Institute of Education
Nanyang Technological University
469 Bukit Timah Road
Singapore 25, Republic of Singapore

Jon Mason
Education.Au Ltd.
178 Fullarton Road
Dulwich SA 5065, Australia

Joyce W. Nutta
College of Education,
EDU 208B
University of South Florida
Tampa, Florida 33620-5650

Sally Reynolds
Katholieke Universiteit
Leuven
Audio Visuele Dienst
Groenveldlaan 3b3
3001 Heverlee, Belgium

Takashi Sakamoto
National Institute of
Multimedia Education
2-12, Wakaba
Mihama-ku, Chiba, Japan

Jef Van den Branden
LINOV—KU Leuven
200A Celestijnenlaan
3001 Heverlee, Belgium

Georges Van der Perre
LINOV—KU Leuven
200A Celestijnenlaan
3001 Heverlee, Belgium

Elizabeth Wellburn
CLN, Open School, B.C.
1016 Verrinder Avenue
Victoria, B.C., Canada V8S 3T7

Introduction

WHAT EXACTLY IS VIRTUAL INSTRUCTION?

Virtual instruction takes place through computer-mediated *communication,* typically at a distance; it can be, but does not have to be, synchronous, that is, the instructor and learner don't have to be engaged at the same time in the teaching/learning activity. We also include in the definition of virtual instruction the notion of *interaction,* such as the kind taking place in active learning. This is an essential component of virtual instruction that differentiates it from other types of distance learning such as correspondence courses. The key elements of virtual instruction are (1) computer-mediated communication, (2) active-learning type interactions, (3) instruction taking place from a distance, and (4) synchronous or asynchronous communication. The instruction can be of a more conventional synchronous nature or as convenient as virtual office hours, where the teacher doesn't have to be there physically with the students. Class anywhere at anytime!

HOW IS VIRTUAL INSTRUCTION SIMILAR TO/DIFFERENT FROM DISTANCE LEARNING?

Distance learning encompasses correspondence courses, one-way satellite television; videotaped instruction; or television courses, such as closed circuit or educational TV that broadcasts university courses over television channels in the service region of the university at specific times. These types of courses do not classify as virtual instruction. They do indeed take place at a distance and some of them are asynchronous, but they lack the key element of interaction and active learning. In addition, virtual instruction is characterized by computer-mediated communication such as e-mail, Web-based instruction, Internet relay chat, CUseeMe, two-way videoconferencing, or any combination of these tools.

WHAT IS THE PURPOSE OF THIS BOOK?

This book attempts to make connections and ground the concept of virtual instruction in current theories in the fields of education, anthropology, communication, sociology, and economics to offer a blueprint for instruction of the future. Because virtual instruction is such an international phenomenon, emerging from around the globe, we need to examine linguistic and cultural factors that affect computer-mediated communication. The book offers perspectives and insights from experts around the world and gives guidelines for implementation of successful programs.

CHAPTER 1

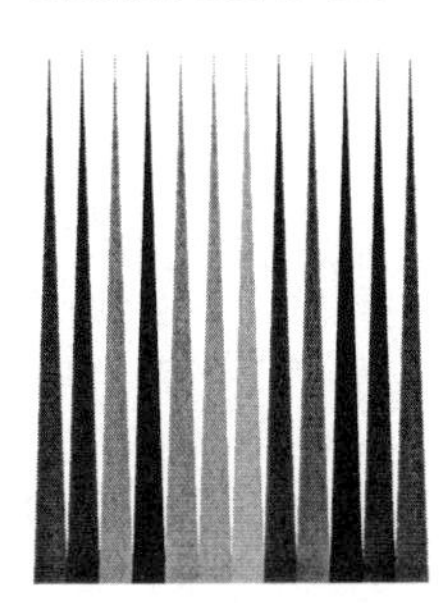

Mapping Space and Time

Virtual Instruction as Global Ritual

Joyce W. Nutta and Carine M. Feyten
U.S.A.

Around the world, in every type of profession, there is an air of excitement fermenting into a bold intention, shaped by rational and empirical influences, a well-founded conviction to exploit the potential of "virtual instruction." As this embryonic area of inquiry is formed, educators have relied not only on the extension of theory from established disciplines to virtual environments, but also on practical trial-and-error experience with these new technologies. Although virtual instruction promises to be one of the most significant contributions to education as the new millennium nears, educators are only beginning to grapple with the intricacies of this new approach. As with any novel and powerful force, the challenge is to apprehend and apply virtual instruction in a productive way.

Through exploring international and multidisciplinary perspectives, *Virtual Instruction* provides a conceptual framework for this global movement and offers specific guidelines for implementing various types of virtual instruction. The chapters in *Virtual Instruction* help to clarify the predominant theoretical issues pertaining to this area of almost uncontrollable expansion, while offering distinct practical suggestions based on the experience of pioneers in the field. The reader will be challenged by the exploration of new questions and the consideration of different answers to old questions. Ultimately, the reader will possess a foundation from which to apply virtual instruction in various settings and for different purposes.

CULTURAL UNIVERSALS AND PARTICULARS OF VIRTUAL INSTRUCTION

Although the chapters in this book describe virtual instruction programs in diverse societies throughout the world, they include striking commonalities that transcend cultural contexts. Notable examples of these universals include the shift in the role of teachers from knowledge communicators to supporters of student learning (which can conflict with certain cultures' views of learning) and instructional activities that focus on using collaboration to solve real-world problems. Multiple factors have converged to create these common features of virtual instruction, including:

1. The development of powerful information and communication technologies (ICT). The properties of the technologies lend themselves to reflection, collaboration, and research.

2. The emergence of transnational communities. Certain activities, such as requiring students to collect and organize specific information from the Internet in their own language, can better accommodate different languages and cultures than disseminating one source of information to all students. Also, experts from different countries may contribute specific information to a student's overall experience with a topic.

3. The change in skills required for the modern work force and international economic interdependence. Higher degrees of education are required for many jobs, requiring more heterogeneous populations to enroll, and most jobs now require workers to be able to solve problems as part of a team and to think creatively and critically.

4. The establishment of a global information society. Students must know how to access, evaluate, organize, and apply information.

5. The results of new research on learning processes. The learning theory known as constructivism has indicated that students should not be passive recipients of knowledge but rather active constructors of their developing understanding of a subject.

Despite the presence of these universal factors, the global implementation of virtual instruction has also evolved in varied, unexpected, and culturally influenced ways. As noted in the following chapters, from Japan to Australia, Belgium to Singapore, program details differ. For example, certain cultural contexts seem to foster the use of particular media, emphasizing text/image-based or face-to-face instruction. As the ICT take root in different areas of the world, they are adapted to fit the relevant characteristics of the culture and needs of the society, a situational appropriation of resources rather than the reception of a commodity.

COMMUNITIES AND COMMUNICATION

More than simply making education more accessible and efficient, virtual instruction contributes to the realization of a new paradigm of learning. As mentioned above, this new model recognizes the culturally mediated nature of constructing knowledge and emphasizes student-centered active learning. Of even greater consequence, however, is its placement of interactive communication at the heart of the learning process.

A repeated theme in the chapters presented here is the connection between the view of communication and education. The precepts of the transmission theory of education are closely linked with those of the transmission theory of communication. In the transmission view, the purpose of communication or education is to transmit information. According to communication theorist James W. Carey (1988), the transmission model views communication as a way to distribute knowledge farther and faster; its purpose is to control space and people. In contrast to the transmission model of communication, Carey proposes the adoption of a ritual view of communication, a symbolic process whose purpose is to create, maintain, repair, and transform culture. In the ritual view, communication is not the act of imparting information to a recipient. Instead, it is a symbolic activity between individuals that creates community.

A clear parallel can be drawn between the ritual view of communication and the constructivist approach to learning. Both view the exchange of information more as an interactive, negotiated process than as the delivery of a commodity, and both avoid valuing the message (or outcome) above the process. Beyond the methodological issues of teaching and learning, however, lie even greater concerns. If communication is viewed as a means of creating culture, then those who are engaged in virtual instruction are involved in creating a virtual community, one that extends beyond physical borders and cultural distinctions. In this sense, virtual instruction can create multicultural learning communities, unlimited by space or time. What might a multicultural, global learning community look like? Perhaps it would resemble a forum that

- collectively creates knowledge, using computer-mediated communications and global resources;
- enables individuals, regardless of their race, gender, or class, to produce, access, and interact with information in ways that are compatible with their needs;
- embraces the characteristics of each culture represented and includes them in the new cultural fabric;

- respects different perspectives and promotes diversity of thought;
- seeks and develops commonalities in experience and purpose.

This is a portrait of virtual instruction and the focus of the chapters that follow.

REFERENCES

Carey, J. W. (1988). *Communication as culture: Essays on media and society.* New York: Routledge Kegan Paul.

CHAPTER 2

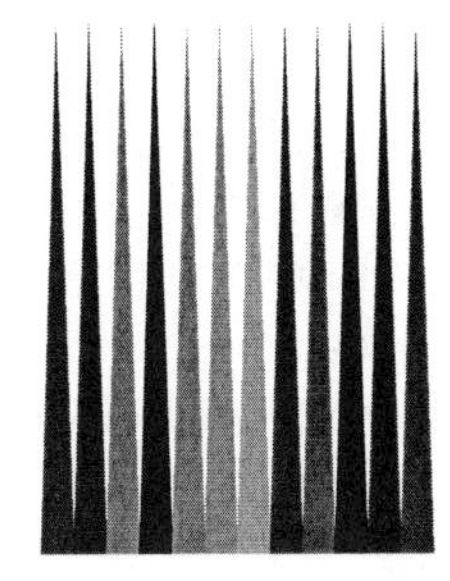

Assessing Cost-Effectiveness for Virtual Learning and Instruction

Why and How?

Christel Claeys
European Union

INTRODUCTION

Differing ideological points of view on societal issues may be irreconcilable; however, raw figures may often force a consensus in the short run. Given the ongoing debate on the desirability of introducing information and communication technologies (ICT) while the educational world faces a financial squeeze, it would be helpful to have valid research documenting that ICT not only results in enhanced performance but moreover achieves this at an equal or even lower price. It is therefore quite surprising that there is very little convincing material about the cost of using educational technology. Although there is a substantial body of literature on the learning achievements of ICT, the evidence produced is contradictory and therefore cannot be used to argue persuasively against or in favor of its introduction in education.

These findings justify efforts to continue developing methodologies for evaluating ICT investments in education. Such methodologies should encompass a meticulous analysis both of costs entailed by ICT and of the types of effects encouraged by its use. This should lead to a framework allowing rigorous cost-effectiveness analysis in education, which this author believes does not yet exist. This chapter does not provide a clear-cut solution for conducting cost-effectiveness analysis, but rather puts forward some important questions and issues that need to be addressed before engaging in this kind of research.

COST ANALYSES: SELECTING A TOOL

Analyses dealing with costs, benefits, efficiency, and effectiveness are tools that were originally developed in the field of economics for analyzing the desirability of social investments (e.g., in health and transportation). However, interest in the economics of education is increasing, and these tools are applied (with the necessary modification or adaptation) to investments in education.

Unfortunately, conducting a cost analysis is not a simple task. A literature review of current research on cost analyses of ICT quickly reveals that (1) research is scarce, (2) there is confusion about the concepts of ICT and their operationalization, and (3) different analytic frameworks have been used to evaluate the use of ICT in education. For the sake of completeness and for a good understanding of the remainder of the discussion, the different methods of evaluating educational investments will be briefly explained.* There are two basic forms of evaluation: *external* and *internal*. External methods refer to evaluating educational investment in terms of payoffs to the individual in the form of higher productivity, hence higher wages; in the form of a monetary benefit for the society that outweighs the costs; or

*For a good introduction to the different methods of evaluating educational investments, including their strengths and weaknesses, see Levin (1983) and the *International encyclopedia of economics of education* (Carnoy, 1995. sec. VII).

both. External methods are represented by, among other things, cost-benefit analysis, rate-of-return analysis, and manpower analysis. Internal evaluations aim at evaluating the payoff to alternative educational investments in improving educational outcomes (measured in quantitative or qualitative terms) and are carried out primarily by means of cost-effectiveness analysis.

An important question in the development of a framework for evaluating ICT investments is: What is the most appropriate tool to use? Literature on evaluating ICT in education shows that cost-benefit and cost-effectiveness analyses are the most commonly applied; however, the concepts are often used interchangeably, although they have distinct meanings, as described below.

Cost-benefit analysis is an external method and requires that the costs and the benefits of a particular intervention be explicitly and numerically valued: Both the cost and the potential or actual benefits of a program are expressed in monetary terms. Cost-benefit analysis enables a direct comparison of the costs and benefits of alternatives or a comparison of their magnitudes with those of other types of social investments in education or in other sectors (Levin, 1995; Sikorsky, Niemic, & Walberg, 1989).

Cost-effectiveness analysis (CE) is an internal method whose major feature is that it acknowledges that most educational interventions are dedicated to improving achievement and learning or, in other words, to outcomes that cannot be easily converted into monetary terms. Hence, CE requires a careful consideration of how the effects of alternative educational interventions will be assessed. It is, however, related to cost-benefit analysis in that both represent economic evaluations of alternative resource use and measure costs in the same way. It is important to emphasize that in CE the evaluation of costs is separable from the evaluation of effectiveness (Levin, 1995).

A comparison of the essential characteristics of both methods suggests that cost-benefit analysis is primarily designed to investigate more general problems, such as deciding whether the cost of investing in ICT in education outweighs the monetary benefits of having a computer-literate society. By contrast, CE appears to be more appropriate to analyzing the various options within a particular area of decision making because it deals with precise issues such as which ICT investment, under which conditions, achieves desired (learning) objectives at the lowest cost. One might state that cost-benefit analysis could precede CE, and that once it is decided that an ICT investment in education is desirable, CE can help in making an optimal selection among alternatives. This author argues that CE bears most relevance to the issue of evaluating investments in new technologies in education, as further illustrated in this chapter.

WHY SHOULD WE CONDUCT COST-EFFECTIVENESS ANALYSIS?

Good Reasons for *Not* Engaging in Cost-Effectiveness Analysis

Let us reverse the question, and ask "why not?" Although, as previously stated, a good analysis of the costs and effectiveness of technology investments in education might be very useful, this is difficult and time consuming. Therefore, the question, "Do we really need CE to decide on the desirability of computer-mediated learning?" is not gratuitous. Indeed, a number of "beliefs" can be put forward that appear to make CE redundant:

The emergence of the Information Society stipulates a widespread integration of ICT in education

Very few people would deny that economy and society are shifting from the (post-) Industrial Age to a new Information Age. The present and future are described in terms of the Information Society, the Knowledge Economy, and so forth, and established institutions, paradigms, power relations, and current driving forces for creating wealth are questioned and challenged about their power to survive (Cox, 1997). It is claimed, then, that while we have admittedly entered the Information Age, the locus of control of formal education is still the same as it was in the Industrial Age. Educational institutions seem to be caught within an inappropriate model of teaching and learning that is failing because it is designed for an economy and society that no longer exist. Therefore, it seems reasonable to argue that education has no other choice than to face a major paradigm shift; it has to move beyond its Industrial-Age conception and design if it is to be successful in the new society and economy. Adoption and full integration of ICT are considered to be of the utmost importance in such an educational reform. First, the core of economic activities resides increasingly in information technology and its spin-off industries, and it is therefore desirable that education should focus on skills and abilities that are competitive in the job market. Second, ICT has become part of the daily life of youngsters; they grow up in a media-rich environment and are comfortable with and adapt easily to each innovation in technology (Lever-Duffy, 1993). Education should respond to their cultural expectations and use their language. Failing to integrate ICT into the education process would further widen the gap between real life and education (European Round Table of Industrialists, 1997).

In summary, because the continuing diffusion and use of new technologies in education appears to be the only way to keep up with the evolution in society, why bother with tedious CE? In this context, Herman (1994) raises the question of whether dramatic technological breakthroughs in the past met the test of (short-term) cost-effectiveness, for example, whether it was cost-effective to move from slates and chalk to pencil and paper, and in the next stage to printed books. It is doubtful that anyone has actually bothered to calculate the cost-effectiveness of previous shifts. One could claim that regardless of the relative cost, students' preparation for the future requires that they acclimate to technology.

ICT is the only way to educate an increasing number of people

The second belief holds that computer-mediated learning, in particular at the level of higher and adult education, might well be the only way to educate an increasing number of people in the future. Whether we like it or not, the Knowledge Economy not only demands more individuals with college or university education, but due to the rapid technological changes and continuous upgrades in the knowledge available in particular fields, lifelong, continuous, and perpetual learning is becoming mandatory for most people. Can the residential colleges, assembling all learners on campus, and the brick-and-mortar classrooms, cope with this type of challenge? The answer is clearly no. As pointed out by Twigg (1994), classroom-based residential institutions were developed to serve a relatively small and homogeneous student population. In the United States at present, higher education has turned into a mass phenomenon. Whereas only 3.2 million students attended college in 1960, the total number of students in colleges and universities is expected to increase from the 1995 level of 10.3 million to about 13.2 million full-time equivalent students by 2015 (Commission on National Investment in Higher Education, 1997). This growth is fueled by a growth in the U.S. population, but also by a phenomenal increase in the percentage of students pursuing college education. We have no reason to believe that trends in Europe and Asia would be different, given the standardization of the world's economy and culture. Referring again to the U.S. example, we can conclude from the figures that in 20 years' time the higher education sector must be prepared and equipped to educate (at least) an extra 3 million students.

ICT serves the needs of an increasingly heterogeneous student population

The student population has shifted from being quite homogeneous to becoming exceedingly heterogeneous. More and more adults, at different ages and with differing amounts of prior education, enter the education market for various reasons. Some want to upgrade their knowledge to survive in the job market; some stopped their education at high school and are trying to obtain a college degree at a later stage of their lives; some are unemployed and desire to be reeducated to find a new job. For many of these people, it is almost impossible to travel to a set place to be taught and to stay there for any length of time. This learning mode is incompatible with a job and family life. Hence, residential education alone cannot serve the needs of today's students. Increasing access to learning is indeed one of the major issues in the design of the education of the future.

Technology is usually seen as an excellent means of providing increased and easy access to education, overcoming barriers of time, space, and even cultural and social issues. Although this change has already been partially achieved by traditional print materials in distance learning institutions, more and more educators, both in traditional universities and open universities, are capitalizing on increasingly advanced ICT and methods (e.g., the Internet and the World Wide Web) to offer courses for distance learners. Technology allows for more flexibility in the learning process, broadening the scope for multimodal learning at the individual pace and place of the learner, while offering more effective interaction with the teacher and collaboration with peers than traditional distance learning (e.g., correspondence learning).

Especially in higher education, the dominant paradigm of residential education is challenged by the emergence of a "virtual university" that provides universal access to off- and online courses, preferably individually tailored. By doing this, the virtual university is responding to very acute market needs. Implementing (costly) strategies enabling society to educate more and more people at a higher level in the long run can be considered more important than short-term issues of cost-effectiveness.

ICT is the first medium genuinely to support constructive learning

As stated in the first "belief," the Information Age calls for a paradigm shift in the teaching and learning model. A series of in-depth interviews conducted with 65 European experts in the field of using ICT in education (Claeys, Lowyck, & Van der Perre, 1997a) revealed that interviewees perceived the implementation of the constructivist model of education as the core mission for an educational system preparing for the Information Society. The premise that learning in the future will be more student centered and project based, requiring more self-regulation, self-discipline, collaboration, communication, and creative and critical thinking, was widely accepted. The idea of organizing education in a way that enables students actively to shape their own understanding and that enables teachers to facilitate that process is not new. As pointed out by Starr (1996), "progressive" educational reformers are, in fact, reviving an old and worthy tradition. What is new, however, is that a growing body of evidence suggests that ICT might be the first medium that actually fosters the model of constructive learning. Using technologies in education increases the possibility of transforming into reality the objectives of constructivist education. Means and Olson (1995), for example, observed in a study of the performances of technology-rich schools that technology supports improved instruction by adding to students' perception that their work is authentic and important, increasing the complexity of learning with which students can deal successfully, dramatically enhancing student motivation and self-esteem, instigating greater collaboration, and giving teachers additional impetus to take on a coaching and advisory role.

If technology, through its potential to turn a passive learner into an active participant, and by means of its appealing format and broader opportunities for stimulating the acquisition of those skills valued by the Information Society, helps to bring about a necessary educational reform, then again one might ask what the relevance of CE is.

This section concludes by presenting a pragmatic reason, rather than a belief, for not conducting CE. Information technology is at present by no means stable. On the contrary, it is subject to ongoing changes in technological developments, rapidly declining prices in hardware and software, and uncertainty about the evolution of communication tariffs. Under these circumstances, it seems obvious that CE is prone to swift obsolescence, which diminishes the potential value of conducting tough research on the cost-effectiveness of ICT in education.

Good Reasons for Conducting Cost-Effectiveness Analysis

Although the "beliefs" discussed are accepted as valid, engaging in CE (in particular as opposed to cost-benefit analysis) can be justified. The main reason for doing CE can be summed up in terms of its quality as a powerful decision-making tool and its inherent demand for a very rigorous analysis, which is bound to increase our insights into the nature, magnitude, and causality of the effects produced through the use of educational technology. The usefulness of CE is discussed below.

In most countries, education is facing a financial squeeze, and financial investments in ICT almost inevitably imply budget constraints in other parts of education or in other aspects of the social service system. Therefore, the educational system has the social obligation to account for its expenditures and preferably to do so by making optimal use of the resources at hand. Indeed, the taxpayer has the right to know and demands evidence that the money spent on ICT results in an effective and fair educational system. Hence, clear information about and undisputed demonstration of the importance of technology are essential to secure funding, which taxpayers are reluctant to provide, and to ensure continued growth in technology use.

In these times of cost consciousness and conflicting interests and opinions about education's role, making decisions in a framework of contradictory evidence about the costs and effects of ICT in education is untenable for educational policymakers at all levels (from the governmental level to the level of the individual principal). To design and choose among educational strategies, good mechanisms for analysis and choice are needed. Cost-effectiveness analysis might offer a solution in this respect. It is a decision-oriented tool, in that it is designed to ascertain which means of attaining particular educational goals are most efficient (Levin, 1995). CE can reveal the cost implications of an educational reform, assess its financial feasibility, provide diagnosis of past and future educational resource utilization, and project future educational cost requirements (Tsang, 1995). Optimally, it does so in conjunction with providing an assessment of the effects of the proposed intervention. In addition, cost-effectiveness analysis holds the promise of allowing comparisons between alternative educational policies or interventions. In this way, CE can function as a powerful tool to guide the decisions of educational policymakers.

Another advantage of using CE as a decision-making tool is that it helps to clarify costs and benefits of different components in different models or methods. To the extent that it is financially impossible to implement a complete innovation design, CE affords us the chance to select the features of the planned educational ICT intervention that will best achieve the desired outcomes. For example, student support services are known to be very expensive; however, if it turns out that a successful implementation of ICT is closely tied to the provision of such services, the decision maker has valid motives for not cutting these technologies from the program. CE offers the possibility to make the links between costs and effects explicit.

Profound and meticulous research on the costs and effects of introducing ICT in education will shed light on the complex issue of how and under which conditions technology can improve learning, and what other, possibly less expected, outcomes are produced by its use and why they occur. CE will allow us to find solutions optimizing effectiveness at minimal cost.

Finally, and from a more theoretical point of view, establishing that schooling can be made more effective and efficient, for example by the use of ICT, is seen by educational economists as one of the great challenges of our time (Levin, 1995). Again, CE is put forward as a tool that can prove this point.

HOW SHOULD WE PROCEED?

In the contemporary literature dealing with technology in education, the issues of cost-effectiveness or cost-benefit analysis are dealt with quite marginally. In those cases where references are made to these topics, the authors in general do not move beyond the level of identifying trends in CE, based on their own perceptions of determining factors and how they will evolve or on beliefs that are to a large extent supported by one-sided arguments. Evidence relying on defined numerical data is scarce. Moreover, the terminology used is either not defined or only vaguely defined.

As an illustration, following are some arguments used in the literature to justify either that ICT is cost-effective or that it is not. Over time, ICT will turn out to be cost-effective, because the initial high cost of producing multimedia or online courses will be offset by the fact that in a telematic (a contraction of "telecommunications" and "informatic") environment there are low maintenance and updating costs, and the addition of course material or alteration of existing text is a relatively simple process (E. L. Davis, 1997; Jennings, 1995). In addition, reproduction of computer-based learning material requires only a tiny fraction of the cost of printing and distributing textbooks (E. L. Davis, 1997). This cost-reducing factor will be strengthened by economies of scale that are bound to arise, given the greater access to education for a wide variety of learners (Rumble, 1992). The substitution of falling technology costs for expensive and rising labor costs is another factor in the debate about cost-effectiveness analysis of ICT, but it is advanced quite implicitly because it touches on the very delicate matter of the role of the teacher in the future (Claeys, Lowyck, & Van der Perre, 1997b; Educom Review Staff, 1996). Finally, E. L. Davis (1997) remarks that information technology has generated dramatic cost-benefit gains in virtually every other sector in the economy and, hence, could be expected to produce similar results in education.

Less optimistic views about the evolution of the cost-effectiveness of ICT come from Bates (1995), who argues that ICT is not a tool that will shift the costs of education downwards; from Pournelle (1994), claiming that ICT is not cost efficient; and from Cambre (1991), who predicts that using ICT in education will be subject to continuously rising costs in the years to come. It is striking that warnings against a positive evolution in cost-effectiveness are often framed in the short term. Several governmental documents express concerns about the huge investments needed in the short term to set up the information infrastructure. It must not be forgotten that the traditional educational structure cannot be abolished overnight. Hence, from a societal point of view, a positive evolution in CE is impeded by the fact that two parallel educational systems have to be maintained (in particular when one chooses to adopt the evolutionary approach to reforming education, as described by Van der Perre in Chapter 5 of this book).

We do not make the claim that this opinion-based type of thinking about costs and effects is worthless; rather, it contains elements that might prove valuable in the development of a rigorous framework for conducting CE. However, the state-of-the-art research on CE, documenting contradictory outcomes, underscores the necessity to elaborate on the question of how to proceed if one is aiming at conducting an analysis reliable enough to function as a decision-making tool.

Before engaging in CE, two initial problems have to be solved: the identification and measurement of relevant costs and the conceptualization and measurement of effectiveness. Next, it is necessary to link costs to effects, input to output.

ON COSTS

This section addresses the question of how to account in a comprehensive way for the costs of ICT-based education. Studies dealing with this issue so far have shown that the computation of costs incurred by educational technology is not a simple matter.

There are two broad categories of research on the cost side. Attempts have been made to look at the *macroquestion* of how much it would cost to achieve different levels of technological penetration in the whole nation/continent (Rothstein & McKnight, 1995; Task Force "Educational Software and Multimedia," 1996). Other studies have tried to estimate the total costs associated with equipping individual educational institutions with advanced technology, with transforming them into virtual schools, or both; hence, dealing with the cost issue at the *microlevel*. In both cases, however, analysts have followed Levin's (1983) method of estimating the costs of an educational program. Levin's procedure is called the "resource" or "ingredient" method and aims at identifying and detailing every resource (ingredient) involved in the program and, in a second step, placing a value or price on each of them. From the contemporary literature, we derive the most common categories of costs that are included in cost analyses:

- hardware
- software
- teacher training or staff development
- technical support of the system, including maintenance and upgrading costs
- student support

- retrofitting
- infrastructure for networking
- personnel and management costs
- material costs (disks, papers, telephones, wires, and other materials for keeping the technology program going)

At first sight, one might think that it should not be too difficult to assign prices to each of these cost categories. However, besides the very basic observation that detailed administration costs are often simply unavailable, there are a number of conceptual problems complicating the estimation of costs. First, assumptions have to be made on the useful life of each cost category. Second, given the necessity of amortizing costs over a certain period, assumptions have to be made about inflation rates. A third component of these time-related problems is that costs of hardware and software and telecommunications tariffs are subject to extreme fluctuations, changing almost continuously. Fourth, a cost model requires a host of assumptions on the configuration of the technology being established in the educational institution.

It is not surprising that, depending on the cost categories taken into account and the assumptions made, various studies result in a broad range of cost estimates. Keltner and Ross (1996) attempted to shed some light on the issue by setting up a study, the objectives of which were to obtain a deeper understanding of the costs involved and to identify the main causes of cost variation in educational technology programs in K–12 schools. Their analysis suggests that the two most significant determinants of annual cost variation are (1) computer density, the ratio of computers to students, and (2) the additional personnel needed to support the technology program. Software and staff development costs represent a relatively small proportion of the overall cost. The results from a macrostudy (Rothstein & McKnight, 1995) focusing on connecting schools to the information infrastructure are slightly different. Rothstein and McKnight's study corroborates the viewpoint that support is one of the largest annual costs educational institutions face. However, it also contradicts Keltner and Ross, stating that equipment expenses are deemed not to be of much importance in the overall cost.

These contradictory findings emphasize that any estimate of costs should be treated with caution. Comparisons between different scenarios of technology implementation are meaningful only if the assumptions underlying the cost models used are similar; thus every attempt should be made to make these explicit.

The problems mentioned above do not cover all potential difficulties in the process of assessing costs of ICT in education. Without intending to be exhaustive, the following discussion points out additional cost aspects largely neglected until now but worth considering in an attempt to optimize the evaluation of educational technology.

First is the issue of *hidden costs*. For example, the time invested by teachers and professors to (1) acquaint themselves with ICT, (2) integrate computer-based learning material into their lessons, and (3) develop appropriate course material for an ICT environment is generally not taken into account. Another hidden cost generally overlooked was mentioned by Watson as early as 1972: How do we account for downtime, or time when the computer network has crashed and all computer activity is suspended? The integration of such hidden costs could be amenable to a more accurate CE.

Second, the use of ICT might entail *unexpected costs* (Collis, 1994). Indeed, Merrill (1995) claims that evaluating technology in education poses special problems, because additional educational changes, beyond the technology, are needed to reveal the technology's full promise. It is hardly possible to separate an economic analysis of new technologies from an analysis at the pedagogical, organizational, and institutional level, where we can expect changes to occur that evoke expenses initially not thought of. Interestingly, Hiltz and Turoff (1978) itemize a number of considerations pertaining to the fundamental utility of computer conferencing that actually might be interpreted as *unexpected savings* of an ICT application. They observe, for example, that computer conferencing results in conciseness of the information exchanged: Material is presented in a more word-economical manner in the written form than in the oral form, and as a result more complex material can be conveyed or exchanged among the group than is otherwise possible. In addition, they observe that computer conferencing increases the quality of the decision. It goes without saying that the quantification of savings associated with these rather intangible benefits, as compared to a face-to-face environment, is difficult. Accounting for unexpected costs/savings undoubtedly is a very difficult endeavor. Experience from case studies and possibly some controlled experiments might be helpful in quantifying these differences.

Finally, from a classical economic point of view, *opportunity costs* should be brought into the picture. Opportunity costs are defined as the value of the input in its best alternative use. For example, when brick-and-mortar classrooms are empty half the time because learning and teaching occurs to a large extent in a virtual environment, an opportunity cost of not using the buildings is incurred. At the macrolevel, due to investments in ICT, society could, for example, incur foregone opportunities to invest in social welfare initiatives that could lead to such benefits as decreased criminality. The question remains, however, to what extent the identification, measurement, and quantification of this type of costs improve the ability to conduct meaningful CE.

From the above discussion, it might be inferred that the computation of the costs of an ICT intervention in education is complex. CE would certainly benefit if efforts were made to be more explicit about the purpose of cost analysis and the assumptions underlying the cost model. Assigning hard numerical data to each cost category mentioned is difficult, and it is perhaps worthwhile to consider whether the efforts required to quantify all costs incurred outweigh the usefulness of the final cost estimates. To sum up, it seems necessary for the research community to deal with the question of whether we are willing to accept including only those costs for which accurate estimates can be obtained or need to take a more holistic perspective on the cost side of ICT by allowing scope for subjective estimates and values on those cost aspects that are more elusive. Moonen (1990) argues that the latter approach is preferable because it strengthens the discussion about the future value of technology in education.

ON EFFECTIVENESS

The literature on the effectiveness of educational programs making use of technology provides mixed evidence. There is a growing body of research demonstrating the "no significant difference phenomenon" (Russell, 1997), showing over and over again that there are no significant learning benefits to be gained from employing different media (from simple textbooks to fully interactive, online broadband material) in instruction. This stream of research encompasses comparative studies of ICT-based education and traditional schooling, concluding that there are no measurable differences in learning effects (often expressed as achievement scores on traditional tests).

On the other hand, more and more empirical studies make broad, inclusive, and consistent research-based statements on positive effects produced by integrating ICT into the curriculum. To give but a few examples,* from the student's perspective, it is shown that technology (1) produces increased motivation and self-esteem (Barker & Franklin, 1996), (2) improves technical skills (Peck & Dorricott, 1994), (3) results in more collaboration with peers (Software Publishers Association, 1996), (4) increases the quantity and quality of the student's thinking and writing (Means & Olson, 1994), and (5) increases the tolerance of ambiguous information (Tella, 1995). From the teacher's perspective, it has been found that technology (1) increases communication and collaboration among teachers within the school (U.S. Department of Education, 1994), (2) induces professional growth (U.S. Department of Education, 1994), (3) increases the productivity and efficiency of teaching (Peck & Dorricott, 1994), and (4) banishes preconceived notions of what students are capable of (Mikropolous, Kossivaki, Katsikis, & Savranides, 1994).

Following is an investigation of the potential reasons for these conflicting results on the effectiveness of ICT, beginning with a list of problems faced by researchers trying to evaluate the

*For an extensive bibliography of studies devoted to assessing the effectiveness of multimedia at all levels of education, see Kotlas (1998).

impact of technology. This list provides a sample of potential difficulties to be solved but is by no means exhaustive

1. There is a considerable degree of confusion about concepts and the way in which they are made operational: Cost-effectiveness, cost-benefit, efficiency, and cost analysis are used interchangeably, or different authors define and measure the same term differently. It goes without saying that these studies are bound to produce dissimilar results.

   In agreement with the position advanced earlier that technology needs to be introduced in the educational system, CE is the most appropriate tool for evaluating new technologies in education. This perspective renders redundant the concern typically addressed by cost-benefit analyses, "whether a social program such as investing in educational technology is more beneficial for the society than an alternative investment in any other sector." Conversely, CE analyses focusing on questions such as, "Which are the right conditions to encourage and improve well-specified educational goals for a certain type of student in a certain type of institution in the most efficient way, this at the lowest cost?" fit into the framework of opinion that ICT is necessary and justifies claims that CE has a great potential as a decision tool.

2. A great deal of research examining "cost-effectiveness" of alternative educational interventions simply compares costs while assuming the same or equivalent outcomes. We believe that this assumption is flawed with respect to the use of ICT. The literature has shown that technology produces unexpected results; outcomes are obtained that are overlooked in the traditional approaches and, hence, are initially not incorporated in an overall evaluation. For example, some studies indicate that computer-based instruction is not really doing better than traditional schooling in terms of acquisition of basic skills, measured by traditional assessment methods. However, the same studies provide empirical and unforeseen evidence that there are significant effects on students' complex thinking

skills (Herman, 1994). In addition, in-depth research investigating the performances of technology-rich schools has found that many indicators other than achievement scores are necessary to describe the outcomes; increased student and parent engagement, better job placement success, strong support from students and parents, and improved attendance have all been cited (Glennan & Melmed, 1996).

3. The fact that many studies observe that technology produces outcomes that cannot be captured by traditional accountability measures implies that traditional ways of assessing the effectiveness of educational programs might be deficient for the purposes of evaluating the contributions of technology. Means and Olson (1995) agree that traditional assessment methods are poorly aligned with the curriculum and pedagogy of educational institutions investing heavily in educational technology. Therefore, it might be argued that the causes of conflicting findings are not the technology-based innovations but rather the evaluation methods used and the nature of the effects measured.

4. A fourth reason for contradictory evidence is that the assessment of the effectiveness of technology most often takes place in imperfect research environments, where variables other than the technology being implemented can affect the outcomes. Research showing improved learning or other beneficial effects from technology is, therefore, vulnerable to rival hypotheses concerning the uncontrolled effects of potential confounding variables. The literature suggests that observed effects may be artifacts produced by, among other things,

    - noncomparability of the experimental group and the control group (Herman 1994);

    - noncomparability of teachers (Teachers volunteering to use technology are prone to be more enthusiastic, dynamic, etc.; hence, teacher effects are fully confounded with effects of technology; Herman, 1994);

- differences in the instructional methods (Technology often prompts teachers to develop a better instructional design; Clark, 1997);
- uncontrolled novelty effects for the new media used (Clark, 1997);
- a more effective structuring of the learning material used in an ICT-based environment (Moonen, 1996).

Moreover, comparison between studies is impeded by the use of different data resources and of different measurement methodologies (Herman, 1994).

The problems mentioned above are partly solved by meta-analysis, a technique designed to overcome the possible shortcomings of individual studies by aggregation and to quantify and render comparable the results of various studies aimed at proving the effectiveness of an intervention. According to Kulik (1994), meta-analyses have on several occasions yielded the conclusion that programs of computer-based instruction have a positive record in the evaluation literature. However, this author believes that meta-analyses are fallible in that they create a composite picture of the individual findings and thus do not reveal why and how an effect is produced. Chances are that the conglomerate of studies actually balances out a potential technology effect if the application, for instance, facilitates learning for one type of student and inhibits it for half of the other students who possess different characteristics. Kulik (1995) acknowledges that meta-analyses should be subject to closer investigation because they differ somewhat on the size of the gains obtained, and it is necessary to know which factors caused the variation in the meta-analytical results.

5. An interesting difficulty discussed by Herman (1994) is that the effective implementation of technology requires time, so that one can anticipate a time span between implementation and the occurrence of the actual effect. Moreover, it is not until teachers reach a comfort zone with the technology that they may engage in genuine instructional innovation aligned with the potential of ICT, and in doing so further increase the probability of achieving positive effects. The problem is thus in deciding when to measure, as measurements at different points in time are liable to produce different results.

6. A final problem is that researchers have attempted to quantify the achievement effects of ICT in isolation, whereas the actual use of educational technology does not and should not occur in isolation (Software Publishers Association, 1996). Evidence has shown that technology triggers additional educational changes, for example, at the organizational level (Merrill, 1995). Therefore, simple outcomes concentrating on learning improvement will not do. A complete analysis of changes at the pedagogical, organizational, and institutional levels might be warranted so as to reveal the full impact of technology.

The reasons itemized above appear to converge toward the conclusion that effectiveness of technology should be studied, taking into account the full context in which the program is implemented. The question, "Is technology effective?" is essentially unanswerable. Identifying the right conditions under which a technology-based intervention can be effective might be a way of escaping from the deadlock of producing contradictory evidence. N. Davis (1996), for example, followed a similar approach and concluded in a study on the cost-effectiveness of Integrated Services Digital Network (ISDN) in education that ISDN can be cost-effective for secondary schools and universities, *provided* that the institutions have an ethos that welcomes innovation with flexible learning and new technology.

COST-EFFECTIVENESS ANALYSIS: ARE WE THERE YET?

In the debate on costs and effects of virtual or ICT-based instruction, the central question to bear in mind is not, "Is technology effective?" but "How can ICT be used to improve learning for each individual student, preferably at a good price?" The key to promoting improved learning with technology appears to be how effectively the medium is exploited in the teaching-learning situation (Owston, 1997). Technology is too often considered and used as an extension of what is already being done in education with more established tools. We need a new frame of reference to assess the full potential of technology and the related costs it incurs.

In this chapter, the author hopes to have convinced the reader that conducting in-depth and meticulous research on the costs and effectiveness of using ICT in education is very helpful in giving shape to or shedding light on the features of this new frame of mind that is required to assess the impact of technology within the learning process. In addition, as long as we have only a limited understanding of the conceptual and methodological problems inherent in cost-effectiveness research, translating the findings into practice and policy (one of the primary objectives of CE) is difficult and even undesirable.

From the perspective of costs, this chapter has pointed out a dual complexity. The first aspect concerns the identification of all types of costs incurred by the implementation of ICT, and the second pertains to valuing the inputs entailed in the correct way. Both aspects of the cost analysis become increasingly difficult to deal with the more one endeavors to obtain quantifiable data. Therefore, it seems plausible for the research community to consider whether it is really necessary to account for hard-to-define and hard-to-measure costs (e.g., hidden and unexpected costs). The question of the extent to which their exclusion impedes a valid CE is legitimate. There is no one correct answer to this problem; the decision taken by the researcher/decision maker about whether to include hard-to-compute and largely intangible costs is by necessity primarily pragmatic in the short term.

This author agrees, however, with Moonen (1990) that taking as complete a perspective as possible (including estimates and subjective values of intangible costs) and being less exact/minute is the most rewarding avenue for establishing a valid framework for assessing costs of educational technology in the long run. From a conceptual perspective, this author advocates a comprehensive approach that leaves scope to account for the inclusion of new cost components produced by unpredictable and unexpected educational changes triggered by technology.

The latter proposition introduces this basic contention from the perspective of effectiveness of ICT-based instruction. Based upon the analysis of the state of the art of assessing effects of educational technology, proving effectiveness is to a considerable degree impeded by the occurrence of intangible and new benefits of using ICT, for the measurement of which presently existing evaluation methods are inadequate.

Researchers should devote a great deal more attention to identifying new effects of ICT at the level of input, throughput, and output of the educational process. An appropriate evaluation of the effectiveness of ICT also involves revealing/unearthing patterns of interaction among input, throughput, and output variables that produce optimal learning outcomes. This approach holds the promise of identifying the right conditions for ICT to be effective and of finding causalities between a technology investment embedded in a particular educational setting and specific learning/attitudinal/psychological (and undetermined) outcomes.

In addition, current research activities should give priority to addressing the development of new assessment methods and instruments appropriate to the new learning outcomes encouraged by the use of ICT in education. Such efforts will not only bring benefits through increasing our competency in assessing the effectiveness of using technology, but they are also essential to guide educators in their practical implementation of ICT in such a way that its full impact can be realized. Indeed, effectiveness improvement can be thwarted by an evaluation approach that is co-linear with existing practices and ignores factors affecting technology implementation (Merrill, 1995).

In conclusion, rather than engaging in difficult but inadequate CE analyses, this discipline would at present benefit from in-depth investigation of a series of conceptual and measurement problems that have yet to be solved both from the perspective of costs and of effectiveness. It is only when these challenges have been tackled that the final step in conducting CE can be reliably taken: the linkage of costs to effects, a step that is essential for CE to prove its utility as a powerful decision-making tool.

REFERENCES

Barker, R., & Franklin, G. (1996). *It's not a toy: Using Pocket Book computers in the National Literacy Association Docklands Learning Acceleration Project.* London: National Literacy Association Docklands Learning Acceleration Project.

Bates, A. W. (1995). *Technology, open learning and distance education.* London: Routledge Kegan Paul.

Cambre, M. A. (1991). The state of the art in instructional television. In G. J. Anglin (Ed.), *Instructional technology: Past, present and future.* Englewood, CO: Libraries Unlimited.

Carnoy, M. (Ed.). (1995). *International encyclopedia of economics of education* (2nd ed.). Oxford: Pergamon Press.

Claeys, C. R., Lowyck, J., & Van der Perre, G. (1997a). Innovating education through the use of new technologies: Reflections from the field. *Educational Media International, 34*(3), 144–153.

Claeys, C. R., Lowyck, J., & Van der Perre, G. (1997b). Reflections from the field on ICT and new roles for teachers: Conditions for success. *Educational Media International, 34*(4), 199–204.

Clark, R. E. (1997). *Reconsidering research on learning from media* [Online]. Available: http://www.educom.edu/program/nlii/articles/clark.html. (Accessed July 31, 1997).

Collis, B. (1994). An analysis of conferencing as technology for distributed training. In R. J. Seidel & P. R. Chatelier (Eds.), *Learning without boundaries: Technology to support distance/distributed learning* (pp. 7–25). New York: Plenum Press.

Commission on National Investment in Higher Education, Council for Aid to Education. (1997). *Breaking the social contract: The fiscal crisis in higher education* [Online]. Available: http://www.rand.org/publications/CAE/CAE100/. (Accessed March 16, 1999).

Cox, B. (1997). Evolving a distributed learning community. In Z. Berge & M. Collins (Eds.), *The online K12 classroom* [Online]. Cresskill, NJ: Hampton Press. Available: http://www.virtualschool.edu/cox/OnlineClassroom.html. (Accessed March 18, 1999).

Davis, E. L. (1997). *The future of education* [Online]. Available: http://www.wco.com/mktentry/edfutur.html. (Accessed July 31, 1997).

Davis, N. (1996). *Cost-benefit analysis of Integrated Services Digital Network in education and training* (Working Paper). Exeter, England: University of Exeter, School of Education.

Educom Review Staff. (1996). Why technology? *Educom Review* [Online], *31*(3), 11 pages. Available: http://www.educause.edu/pub/er/review/reviewArticles/31324.html. (Accessed March 16, 1999).

European Round Table of Industrialists. (1997). *Investing in knowledge: The integration of technology in European education.* Brussels, Belgium: Author.

Glennan, T. K., & Melmed, A. (1996). *Fostering the use of educational technology: Elements of a national strategy* (RAND Report MR-682-OSTP). Washington, DC: RAND.

Herman, J. (1994). Evaluating the effects of technology in school reform. In B. Means (Ed.), *Technology and education reform: The reality behind the promise* (pp. 133–168). San Francisco: Jossey-Bass.

Hiltz, S. R., & Turoff, M. (1978). *The network nation: Human communication via computer.* London: Addison-Wesley.

Jennings, C. (1995, June). Organisational and management issues in telematic-based distance education. *Open Learning, 10,* 29–35.

Keltner, B., & Ross, R. (1996). *The cost of school-based educational technology programs.* Washington, DC: RAND's Critical Technologies Institute.

Kotlas, C. (1998). *Assessment of multimedia technology in education: bibliography* [Online]. Available: http://www.unc.edu/cit/guides/irg-11.html. (Accessed March 18, 1999).

Kulik, J. (1994). Meta-analytic studies of findings on computer-based instruction. In E. L. Baker & H. F. O'Neil, Jr. (Eds.), *Technology assessment in education and training* (pp. 9–33). Hillsdale, NJ: Lawrence Erlbaum.

Kulik, J. (1995). Effectiveness of educational technology. In A. Melmed (Ed.), *The costs and effectiveness of educational technology: Proceedings of a workshop.* Santa Monica, CA: RAND's Critical Technologies Institute.

Lever-Duffy, J. (1993, November). *Multi-access education: A model for instructional delivery in the Information Age.* Paper presented at the Annual Conference of the League for Innovation in the Community College, Nashville, TN.

Levin, H. M. (1983). *Cost-effectiveness: A primer: Vol. 4. New perspectives in evaluation.* Beverly Hills, CA: Sage.

Levin, H. M. (1995). Cost-effectiveness analysis. In M. Carnoy (Ed.), *International encyclopedia of economics of education* (2nd ed., pp. 381–386). Oxford: Pergamon Press.

Means, B., & Olson, K. (1994). The link between technology and authentic learning. *Educational Leadership, 51*(7), 15–18.

Means, B., & Olson, K. (1995). *Technology's role in education reform: Findings from a national study of innovating schools.* Menlo Park, CA: SRI.

Merrill, D. (1995). Evaluating technology effectiveness. In A. Melmed (Ed.), *The costs and effectiveness of educational technology: Proceedings of a workshop.* Santa Monica, CA: RAND's Critical Technologies Institute.

Mikropolous, T. A., Kossivaki, P., Katsikis, A. & Savranides, C. (1994). Computers in preschool education: An interactive environment. *Journal of Computing in Childhood Education, 5*(3–4), 339–351.

Moonen, J. (1990). *Costs, effectiveness and expectations: Concepts and issues with respect to educational technology* (Report Submitted to the Educational Center of British Columbia). Twente, The Netherlands: Faculty of Education, University of Twente.

Moonen, J. (1996). *The efficiency of telelearning.* Paper presented at the Online Educa Korea Conference, Seoul, South Korea.

Owston, R. D. (1997). The World Wide Web: A technology to enhance teaching and learning. *Educational Researcher, 26*(2), 27–33.

Peck, K., & Dorricott, D. (1994). Why use technology? *Educational Leadership, 51*(7), 11–14.

Pournelle, J. (1994, July). An educational trip. *Byte, 19*(7), 197–210.

Rothstein, R. I., & McKnight, L. (1995). *Technology and cost models of connecting K–12 schools to the National Information Infrastructure.* Cambridge, MA: MIT Research Program on Communications Policy.

Rumble, G. (1992). *The management of distance learning systems.* Paris: United Nations Educational, Scientific and Cultural Organization.

Russell, T. L. (1997). *The "no significant difference" phenomenon* [Online]. Available: http://teleeducation.nb.ca/nosignificantdifference/. (Accessed March 16, 1999).

Sikorsky, M. F., Niemic, R. P., & Walberg, H. J. (1989). The bottom line for education and training. *Performance Improvement Quarterly, 2*(4), 42–50.

Software Publishers Association. (1996). *Report on the effectiveness of technology in schools, '95–'96: Executive summary* [Online]. New York: Interactive Educational Systems Design. Available: http://www.spa.org/project/edu_pub/summary.htm. (Accessed March 16, 1999).

Starr, P. (1996, July–August). Computing our way to educational reform. *The American Prospect,* No. 27, 50–59.

Task Force "Educational Software and Multimedia." (1996). *Report of the Task Force "Educational Software and Multimedia."* Brussels, Belgium: European Commission.

Tella, S. (1995). *Virtual school in a networking learning environment.* Helsinki, Finland: University of Helsinki/OLE Publications.

Tsang, M. C. (1995). Cost analysis in education. In M. Carnoy (Ed.), *International encyclopedia of economics of education* (2nd ed., pp. 386–392). Oxford: Pergamon Press.

Twigg, C. A. (1994). The need for a national learning infrastructure. *Educom Review* [Online], 29(5), 3 pages. Available: http://www.educause.edu/pub/er/review/reviewArticles/29516.html. (Accessed March 16, 1999).

U.S. Department of Education, Office of Educational Research and Improvement. (1994). *Technology and education reform* [Online]. Washington, DC: SRI International. Available: http://www.ed.gov/pubs/EdReformStudies/EdTech/. (Accessed March 18, 1999).

Watson, P. G. (1972). *Using the computer in education: A briefing for schools.* Paris: United Nations Educational, Scientific and Cultural Organization.

CHAPTER 3

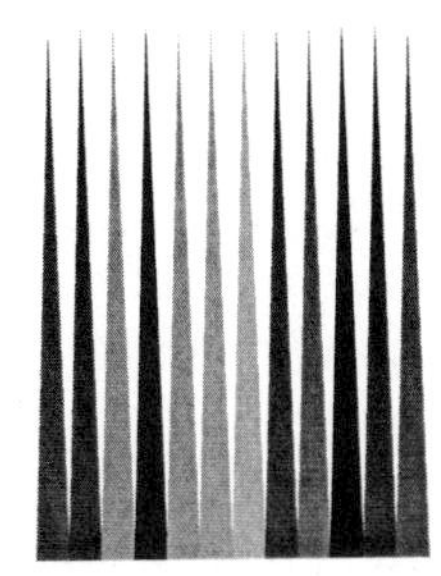

Educational Vision, Theory, and Technology for Virtual Learning in K–12

Perils, Possibilities, and Pedagogical Decisions

Elizabeth Wellburn
Canada

SETTING THE CONTEXT

Virtual instruction has the potential to create significant change in our familiar educational system. The availability of virtual learning environments will have an impact on how individual learners determine the courses, types of educational interactions, and schedules that will best meet their needs. It will also affect the operation of schools. This chapter and this book describe some of the many new "virtual learning" options that will soon be widely available. Throughout these pages are discussions of how these options might best unfold and of the issues and problems in education that can be addressed through innovative technologies.

Technological advancement is one of the reasons educational systems around the world are facing serious decision making. The expressed public dissatisfaction with schools is another. A Canadian professor of education, Kieran Egan (in press), describes a climate in which international comparisons of educational outcomes are continuously being made, based on "progressive" views that are now outdated. These views and comparisons, misguided as they might be, fuel an ongoing attempt to find scapegoats for alleged educational failures. Rather than continuing with the fruitless exercise of assigning blame to teachers, administrators, politicians, and others for schools that haven't lived up to what is probably an ill-defined set of expectations, Egan suggests that a different perspective is necessary: "We have a confusion at the root of the system; running faster with improved style will not help us if we are going in the wrong direction. . . . If we want to improve our schools, it is with the abstract and awkward realm of ideas that we must first deal."

Egan's statement is included in this introductory section to set the stage for a thoughtful look at the future. As educators, we must ensure that embracing the powerful innovations that will help us deliver learning experiences does not hide the fact that the content of some of those experiences might be inappropriate or inadequate in the context of our current social reality. Exciting as the new technologies often are, it is important to be prepared for all the consequences of their adoption and to face the "realm of ideas" that is their foundation.

QUESTIONS IN EDUCATION

In an era of great educational need and uncertainty about the future, educators everywhere are looking for answers. Can public education survive? Will it be able to meet the increasing variety of needs and wants of a rapidly changing society? Can it do so in an era when budgets are stretched to their limit? The technology surrounding us seems to have the ability to provide at least some of those answers, with virtual education options currently playing a key role for a variety of reasons, not the least of which is economic pressure, a topic that will be discussed in more detail later in this chapter and is also discussed in other chapters of this book.

It is important to realize that any educational innovation can lead to more pitfalls than benefits unless those involved in implementing it have a grasp of the complete picture and act accordingly. Progress in one dimension might have unanticipated negative consequences in another. As virtual instruction becomes more widespread, those responsible for its planning and implementation must not lose sight of the importance of the wide range of functions that education serves in society. It is certain that there will be no "easy" answers, just as it is also certain that educators and learners can expect to see change at many levels.

In this chapter, virtual instruction and related concepts are described. There are also discussions of the current status of the educational system, how virtual instruction should be incorporated into the system to best serve the needs of the community, the ways in which virtual instruction might address some pertinent educational problems, implications of educational theory for educational technology in a virtual setting, and ways in which educators can use new technologies to provide effective environments in which students can create knowledge. Although many of the ideas presented here apply to learning at all levels, the focus of the chapter is on the K–12 learner.

WHAT IS VIRTUAL INSTRUCTION?

In the introductory chapter to this book, virtual instruction has been defined as that which makes use of telematics (computer-mediated communications, or CMC), takes place either synchronously or asynchronously at a distance, and which involves interaction between students and instructors. This is a broad definition that includes concepts that have been incorporated into a wide range of educational opportunities at all levels. In the literature, implementations incorporating most or all of these concepts have been referred to as distance education, distance teaching, distance learning, interactive distance learning, distributed learning, distributed training, open learning, online courses, the virtual classroom, and so forth. At present, the terminology is somewhat confusing because the amount of technology used and the level of interaction (student to instructor and student to student) vary widely across different instances of the above. By the definition used in this book, virtual instruction always includes a high level of communication and interaction.

Exciting possibilities related to virtual instruction include an expansion of the range of courses and types of educational interactions available to learners. Students who live away from urban centers can now have access, through technology, to the same lessons, learning materials, and human expertise as those students who are in metropolitan areas. Both rural and urban students will be able to choose when and how they learn. The virtual environment allows for flexible, individualized scheduling, the customization of courses, access to a vast set of learning resources, and opportunities for collaboration with subject experts and with other learners, all accessible from any location.

One thing is clear: As formal learning is becoming increasingly independent of time, location, or both, the local "school" no longer has a monopoly on the provision of education. School administrators and other educators might wonder how the role of schools will be affected by course offerings that originate outside of their jurisdiction. Teachers, learners, and parents need to know what to expect. Finally, the adoption of wide-scale learning that takes place outside of the traditional school walls also implies change at a social level, a fact that needs to be taken into consideration by those who are involved in educational planning and implementation.

EDUCATIONAL EXPECTATIONS AND TECHNOLOGY

Numerous trends in K–12 education at present involve a complex mix of factors that are sometimes in apparent contradiction with each other. The big picture is not easy to view. There is a requirement for students to attain higher level skills and lifelong learning abilities to meet the demands of today's job market. There is uncertainty about the future requirements of the job market and a related concern about how educational institutions can turn out effective candidates for the jobs that will be available. While there are both a demand for an increase in the number of high-end computers available for student use and a desire for greater student access to the Internet, there is also a range of concerns regarding technology use, including issues related to safety on the information highway. Teachers are expected to update their computer skills on a regular basis but often have little support to do so.

Several trends show a lack of confidence in the public school system. Charter schools* are becoming a popular option in many places, and there is an increase in parents who take their children out of the public school system altogether, opting for home schooling or private schools. In some instances, the decision to leave the public school system is based on a concern for the child's physical safety.** Budgets are declining for all public educational institutions, and a range of sometimes controversial partnership and fund-raising solutions is being considered in many jurisdictions. These are just a few of the pressures that the educational system is facing.

From the education "consumer's" point of view, life is getting potentially much richer but also more complicated. In the relatively recent past, there were few options. Most of the parents who are currently facing an increasing array of educational choices for their own children probably came from families

---

*Dobbin (n.d.) states that charter schools are "one of the principal weapons that opponents of public education use to both undermine confidence in the public education system and to begin the actual erosion of that system." Not everyone would share this extremely negative view of the impact of charter schools. It is, however, fair to say that the agenda of many who would turn to the charter school option is not in alignment with the goal of equitable learning experiences for all students.

**Whether this concern is genuine or not is of course dependent on the jurisdiction. My personal experience includes a discussion with a young adolescent who was well aware of the publicity surrounding violence in the schools and was fearful even in a school and district where the incidence of violence is extremely low. It is beyond the scope of this chapter to discuss learning environments in which the incidence of violence is not low, but it is appalling that any part of our system has created and maintained a culture where some children cannot be safe with each other in school.

where it was a simple fact of life that each child would march through a series of preordained activities in the nearest brick building. Now, in a trend that seems sure to continue, there are many possibilities, a sort of smorgasbord of educational experiences that can be selected or rejected to meet individual needs. Technology is most certainly a major factor in creating this variety of options.

ISSUES OF SELECTION IN THE VIRTUAL ENVIRONMENT

Theoretically, students can select their virtual education from anywhere, and for this reason, there is motivation for developers to market their product aggressively. The world is their audience. A critical question relates to how the selection is made by (and for) the learners who will ultimately use these products.

It is possible, and in some cases even quite likely, that the decision makers (parents, teachers, school administrators, governments, or the learners themselves) will find it difficult to assess all the options. They may not have the time, information, or skills to make the best decisions. As more and more commercialized learning packages become readily available, it could turn out that the glossiest promotion of virtual instruction will attract the largest audience. To draw an analogy, the Western world's experience with the marketing of fast food has shown us that brand recognition and market share are not related to the nutritional value of the food provided. If this trend occurs with the packaging of education, the resulting situation could be bad for individual learners and even worse for society as a whole. In a complete "free market" scenario for education, the gap between the educational "haves" and the "have-nots" might become increasingly wider, as well-advertised, relatively inexpensive, but educationally empty course offerings become the standard fare for all but the few who have the resources to pick something better.

Conversely, if those who make the decisions *do* have the resources to pick appropriately, the increase in options available might eventually ensure access to high-quality, "nutritious," customized learning experiences for all students. A high level of awareness regarding a variety of educational issues is required as part of the filtering mechanism. The educational selection process should involve input from people who have the expertise to understand the needs of each learner; would be available to explain the advantages and disadvantages of the variety of offerings; would ensure that all students are involved in a complete curriculum of quality and relevance; and would take into account the broad community issues, such as social equity, cultural identity, and so forth. It is necessary to consider a new role, that of assisting learners as they make their selections from the "smorgasbord," mentoring them as they progress through their course work, and evaluating the results on an ongoing basis. Because the decisions require a high level of expertise and have social consequences on a long-term basis, the facilitative roles should be taken on by informed individuals at local institutions, such as schools, school districts, and ministries of education.

In fact, this process may have already begun, as students and teachers make greater use of the interactive power of computers. There is an increasing overlap between the types of learning experiences that can happen successfully both in and out of the traditional classroom (Wellburn, 1996). Distance education experiences may soon be seen as a common part of school, as students find out about and even engage in virtual instruction through facilities available to them via their local school. Other boundaries are changing as well, as "new technologies are being used to considerable effect in the K–12 system to meet the needs of students in smaller centers, to blur the boundaries between the secondary and post-secondary sectors, and to provide improved school-to-work transitions" (Distributed Learning Task Force, 1997, p. 38).

There are conflicting pressures on students, who may prefer to learn in groups but appreciate the convenience of the flexible schedule that distance education can provide. Simonson (1997) discusses this and notes that for distance education to become a successful part of mainstream education, equivalent learning experiences must be provided to all.

Further work is required to provide the necessary structure and guidelines for educational decision making in the new environment. Funding, staffing, and other issues need to be resolved. There is a need for a working set of tools to help those who take on the ongoing responsibilities associated with the new opportunities. Even when teachers or administrators (rather than parents or learners) make educational decisions related to the innovations that surround us, they face a very complex and daunting task. Increasing the implementation of technology and expanding virtual learning opportunities must be done in a way that is both educationally effective (a term that is not easily defined against our background of rapidly changing expectations) and acceptable to human and social values.

Menzies cautions us about the motivation of those who would commercialize education and describes how in this mindset "education is increasingly transformed into educational packages, a commodity to be consumed—and it is less and less a holistic experience in real life, grounded in real communities" (1994, p. 12). The economic metaphor in education can be seen as a process that leads to atomized decision making, appearing to provide equal opportunities, while actually reducing the ability of collective action to improve the quality of education for all (Whitty, 1997).

On a more positive note, Menzies (1994) suggests that it is possible to resist the commercial model by creating a community-centered model of education that focuses on public interest. She sees information technologies as useful tools in the process and concludes that clear-eyed analysis and imagination are the most important ingredients of such a model.

TECHNOLOGY AND CHANGE IN EDUCATION

The prospect of teaching and learning in a virtual environment is relatively new to most participants in the educational system. Within K–12, those educators who have been effectively integrating technology into the traditional curriculum in the traditional school setting are still a minority. It should not come as a surprise that people in the field are often unclear about what is meant by the many terms used to describe various implementations of interactive distance education. Just the same, a growing number of educators and students see tremendous potential in concepts related to virtual instruction, and they are eager to explore their new options. A significant part of the change they can expect to see, already evident in many of the successful virtual learning experiences, will be in their personal roles as instructors and learners.

The introduction of computer technology into traditional K–12 educational settings over the past 10 to 15 years has generated a range of responses, from anxiety, apprehension, and cautious optimism, to the unbounded enthusiasm of teachers who have seen their students unexpectedly blossom and who have found a rebirth of relevance in their own jobs because of something that only a virtual environment could offer. The emotions and attitudes of the participants are a very important factor here, partly because it is still (and may always be) a difficult task to quantify objectively the impact of technology in education, on either the learning dimension or the cost-effectiveness dimension. In fact, Roblyer (1996) notes that educational technology research has recently made a shift from a machine-centered focus on the impact of technology to a more human-centered concern about the ways in which technology helps teachers change what they do.

Of course, "educational technology" is not a single entity, and this adds to the problem of evaluating either its impact or its role in facilitating change. During the latter part of the twentieth century, we have been inundated with a steady current of new and varied technologies designed to enhance teaching, and together with these, a variety of methodologies attempting to deal with all of these options, while still maintaining the focus on learning (Cornell, 1996, p. 53). Adding the wealth of options that are available via virtual environments increases the complexity of a situation that is already extremely challenging.

Equitable access to the technology required to take advantage of the many options for changing educational approaches is another issue that must be considered. Steps must be taken to provide access to technology for lower income learners to prevent the creation of two groups of "knowers" and "know-nots," a situation in which a large portion of society would be relegated to low-tech, low-paying jobs (Distributed Learning Task Force, 1997, p. 9).

An educational vision (see Apple, 1991; Bates, 1995; Wellburn, 1991; and many others) incorporating a commitment to the issues of equity in society and a conscious understanding of how learning takes place (which will be described in more detail in the "educational theory" section of this chapter) can form a platform that supports effective educational decision making and provides guidelines to assist with the selection, implementation, and evaluation of virtual and traditional learning experiences.

VIRTUAL INSTRUCTION AND THE K–12 EDUCATIONAL SYSTEM

Some problems in education are widely voiced and highly visible. It is very common to read or hear that schools are out-of-date and unaccountable, the education system has an unacceptable dropout rate, students are uninterested and find little relevance in what they do at school, graduates lack basic literacy skills and are unprepared to meet the demands of the workplace, and so forth. To make matters worse, in current educational discussions, a recurring theme is the impact of economic pressures and declining budgets. Schools want, need, and are expected to offer more but are compelled to do so with less money. The literature is full of examples (see Cornell, 1996; Cox, 1997; Educom Review Staff, 1996; Menzies, 1994).

Nidds and McGerald (1996) describe the general assault on the public school system by the print media and state, "Is it any wonder that conscientious educators often feel depressed, frustrated, angry, or defensive?" (p. 61). For many, computers were initially seen as a panacea for at least some of the problems listed above. In recent years, schools have been increasingly judged by the degree of technology that they make available to students. The ratio of students per computer has been, and continues to be, a common yardstick when comparisons are made between schools or school districts. Often such ratios are discussed without any reference to how students actually use the machines.

Unfortunately, even though an enormous portion of scarce financial resources (not to mention time and effort) has gone toward it, there is a growing dissatisfaction with the results of the implementation of computer technology in schools. "If one would try to find an area today that is ill-conceived, expensive, and misappropriated, it would probably not be far from the school's computers" (Gilman, 1996, p. 61). The backlash against educational technology is even more apparent in popular publications such as the *Atlantic Monthly*, in articles with inflammatory titles such as "The Computer Delusion" (Oppenheimer, 1997).

This chapter has already described how virtual instruction and related technologies have the potential to provide flexible and relevant educational experiences for learners. Why has the technology used to date not been more consistent in realizing that potential, thus coming closer to meeting the needs of the educational system?

Hodas (1995) and others explain this failure in relation to the fact that the greatest acceptance of technology has tended to be in those areas where the technology reinforces preexistent ways of doing things. "Technologies are variously embraced and resisted in the effort to perpetuate this system and maintain the organizational status quo. . . . [Educational technologies] are the uses of machines in support of highly normative, value-laden institutional and social systems" (Hodas, 1995).

In a similar but more targeted explanation, Gilman (1996) states, "Most teachers teach the way they were taught and will continue to do so" (p. 61). Those teachers who do not teach the way they were taught probably teach the way they were taught to teach, which might also be inappropriate for the current environment.

In describing the mismatch between what schools were designed to do and what students need in the world that now exists around them, Hodas uses the term *misalignment* and suggests that schools are not failing but actually performing exactly as they have been intended, based on what was considered important to previous generations. It is argued in a later section of this chapter that the "knowledge transmission" model of education (familiar to the parents, grandparents, and great-grandparents of today's students) is a large factor in the perpetuation of the status quo. If so, change must be facilitated by a move to a perspective of learning based on a different theoretical premise. The premise must be one that can be facilitated by technology, and the technology must be consciously designed to work within that premise.

The virtual learning environment has the potential to move beyond the status quo and could provide education that is engaging and relevant to a wider audience. Powers (1997) and many others suggest that virtual instruction is more than a way to reach the students who were previously inaccessible because of their remote geographical location. Virtual instruction reaches students everywhere, including urban areas, providing a set of new and innovative types of learning experiences with a focus on flexibility.

There is also some evidence that ultimately this enhanced service could be provided at a reduced cost. For example, Romiszowski (1993) notes that items necessary for virtual instruction, such as telecommunications, are falling in price while the costs related to traditional education, including classroom space, staffing, and transportation, are rising. Mason (1994) states that "it is no coincidence that the use of telecommunications media in education and training is growing at the same time as education and training budgets are decreasing" (p. 19). The issue of cost-effectiveness in education has never been simple, however, and it is possible, as Owston (1997) warns, that an assessment of current virtual learning situations may not include the hidden costs of the many additional hours of development and implementation time that are willingly given to make the innovation work. This issue is further discussed by Christel Claeys in Chapter 2.

At this point, we must ask if the benefits provided by technology are worth the additional challenges to the educational system. Previous discussions in this chapter suggested that educational change of any sort is difficult to implement and that many decisions regarding technology in education have been based, by necessity, on a "gut feeling" or perhaps on a trial-and-error basis.

Educational evaluation may never become an exact science, and although there are many reasons for wanting to measure the effectiveness of educational innovations on the basis of test scores or other objective criteria, the type of learning that technology best enhances is difficult to quantify (see Johnson, 1996). It is important to note that, in spite of being difficult to quantify, this learning relates to values that most interested parties would agree need to be interwoven throughout the K–12 curriculum (and beyond). Riel (1994) has stated that technology helps students "develop a broad, deep, and creative understanding of community, culture, economics and international politics, past and present, and acquire the social skills to work across differences and distances" (p. 452). From personal experience with students involved in telecommunications projects, it is easy to understand Riel's enthusiasm relating to the increased effort that students put into work that is intended for a real audience. When online contacts with students in other communities are made, one also sees students coming away with a greater degree of awareness of the reality of life in different locations. Many case studies in the educational journals confirm this.

> Technology is merely an enabler. However, what it enables is nothing less than human individuals, organizations and cultures, newly empowered to understand and misunderstand each other across time and space boundaries that have separated us since antiquity. The implications are too vast to be predicted, controlled or designed. Established institutions must either evolve to compete in this new global climate or be displaced by emergent new institutions who can (Cox, 1997).

The Future with Virtual Learning

It would be an unlikely and unappealing outcome if the world of virtual learning caused a complete disappearance of the classroom as it is currently known in K–12. Nor should paper and books disappear from education, be it local or at a distance. The preferable option is to use the components from each situation in a combination that works well to accomplish individual needs. Students in very remote communities might indeed experience most of their learning through distance education, using technology when it is appropriate. Students in major centers might turn to virtual learning to accommodate scheduling conflicts within their school. Teachers might include virtual experiences within the classroom, because they can accomplish objectives for all learners that cannot be accomplished in any other way (sharing data about how plants grow in different climates, communicating with children who are living in a war zone, reading a variety of perspectives on daily world events in online newspapers from around the globe) or because the virtual environment provides a good match for the learning styles of some of their students.

In the future, historians may look back to the final years of the twentieth century and provide explanations for the economic and other pressures that are currently facing virtually all social institutions, including education. They might conclude that technology itself (or our tendency to accept it uncritically) was a factor leading to the budget cuts, increased work load, and loss of public approval that has brought many institutions to the crisis point. Perhaps paradoxically, the system has spent considerable effort looking to technology as a solution to its problems, and there is every indication that it will continue to do so. In education, however, if the needs of the learner are considered within a complete view of the educational picture, it is possible that the virtual environment will, in fact, provide us with the understandings that are required to overcome our self-created obstacles.

"Technology is only one component of a social system that can never be understood outside the larger context of the culture in which it is used. Technology almost always serves the power structure. When it does not, it is often considered revolutionary" (Ohler, 1995, p. 177). It seems that there is more than one power structure involved in an institution as complex as education. Taxpayers, governments, teachers, parents, the corporate world, and the students themselves have expectations of the educational system. Perhaps, because of technology, we are on the verge of an educational revolution. It will be interesting to find out which power structure is disrupted.

One can hope that humanistic sentiments, such as those expressed by Dyson (1997), will win the day. She describes the role of education in fostering equality and calls it "just about the most important job a community can do" (p. 35). She adds that virtual learning will be an important factor and views the Internet as a tool that can foster a decentralized environment. She concludes that this is something that needs to be paid for by society as a whole, because it benefits society as a whole.

To achieve the social benefits that technology and a virtual educational environment have the potential to bring, we must remember that "efficiency is not the straightforward, value-free quantity that those who most embrace it suppose it to be" (Hodas, 1995), and, in education, it is important never to lose sight of the many educational goals and the underlying philosophies that permeate the system.

EDUCATIONAL THEORY AND TECHNOLOGY

A variety of theories of learning can be incorporated into virtual instruction, just as they can be incorporated into most other technology-based educational approaches. An often forgotten fact is that when any new medium or technology is brought into the educational picture, there is a responsibility on the part of those introducing it to understand its underlying educational theory, understand how learner/teacher roles are defined by that theory, and ensure that the theory is not in contradiction with the overarching goals or vision of the educational experience that is intended.

In a discussion of current learning theory, it is important first to define two very different approaches to education, although, as Roblyer (1996, pp. 12–13) has pointed out, a person would have to have been living on another planet not to be aware of the conflicts over methodologies that have taken place between those who support teacher-centered classrooms and those who prefer a more learner-centered approach. The two viewpoints have deeply contrasting philosophical foundations.

The objectivist (also known as behaviorist, instructivist, rational, or directed learning) viewpoint assumes that the role of the teacher or instructor (note that a "teacher" may be a set of instructionally designed "programmed learning" materials or even a "teaching machine") is to transfer or transmit knowledge to a student, who is a more or less passive recipient.* In this model, the content of "what is to be learned" is considered to be a stable entity that can be organized into a structure involving a series of steps or subcomponents that are often followed in sequence. The teacher or instructional designer directs the process of transmitting the sequence of structured content. The traditional "correspondence course" model of distance education was often largely based on this approach, as were (and are) many classroom experiences, including lectures, worksheets, drill and practice software, and so forth.

In contrast, the constructivist approach incorporates the notion that learners build a knowledge base through personal experience. Knowledge is not viewed as something to be poured into an empty vessel. Constructivists maintain an emphasis on learning by problem solving and apprenticeship in real-world contexts (Brown, Collins, & Duguid, 1989).** The process is learner centered; students are encouraged to collaborate with

---

*Note that in some directed learning/instructional views, including that of Anderson, Reder, and Simon (n.d.), knowledge transmission is considered to be most effective when students are actively engaged. In describing situated learning and constructivism, these authors maintain that the recommendations of these paradigms have little foundation in cognitive psychology, but they agree with the constructivists that learning must be an active process, that "learning requires a change in the learner, which can only be brought about by what the learner does." The teacher's role is to "cause" students to take part in activities that they would not undertake on their own. The teacher may guide the student in tasks that promote skill acquisition through examples, practice, and/or interaction among students and teacher.

**The 1989 Brown, Collins, & Duguid paper is one of the foundations of a strong constructivist tradition. They argue that "learning and cognition are fundamentally situated," and that there is no separation between "knowing and doing" (p. 32). Activities within a contextual framework are what produce learning. In spite of this, the primary concern of most schools seems to be the dissemination of decontextualized information and concepts, without regard to the vital roles of context and activity.

each other; the teacher does not have all the answers; and the actual learning that takes place may not match any particular set of predefined outcomes. As technologies become available that allow virtual learning to include interaction and group collaboration, the constructivist environment is becoming more and more of a reality for learning experiences that take place at a distance.

In a time when lifelong learning skills are required to ensure that we keep up with the rapid pace of change, constructivism seems to be an appropriate educational consideration. It is the theory that comes closest to the goal of allowing students to "learn how to learn." Current thought in educational theory is largely constructivist (although there is still debate). In much of the very recent literature (Egan, 1997; Hannafin, Hill, & Land, 1997; Peel & McCary, 1997), there is a fairly strong agreement that the society of the future will require individuals who can engage in critical thinking and knowledge-creation activities, assess and evaluate information for themselves (as opposed to having it already prepackaged and transmitted via a textbook or lecture), and work collaboratively, all concepts that are in alignment with a constructivist viewpoint.

The fact that this book has selected the term *virtual instruction* does not imply a viewpoint that excludes the knowledge construction potential of virtual educational environments. Both objectivist and constructivist theory can be embedded in virtual instruction as it is envisioned here. In situations where there is not a clear vision of the type of learning environment desired, it is possible to make bad choices at both the design and implementation stages. Unfortunately, educators have often operated without articulating their philosophy at a conscious level. As mentioned earlier, they tend to teach as they were taught or perhaps as they were taught to teach. This can lead to confusing results when dealing with innovations, especially when the technology involved can be somewhat intimidating in and of itself (see Kerr, 1991, 1994).

Much of the current literature is extremely positive about the potential relationship between technology and education. Research indicates that interactive, self-directed learning and higher order thinking can be fostered by technology, but the selection of that technology and the manner in which it is used is critical to realizing the potential benefits. Technology is not a solution unto itself. Without a clear understanding of the reason *why* it is being incorporated into the mix, technology becomes just another add-on. As Apple (1991) and others have noted, educational technology often focuses on the "how to" and sometimes never gets beyond the technical issues.

Hodas (1995) describes how technologists have focused on the transfer of information to students and explains that this tendency is related to the fact that information transfer is one of the few processes in schools that can be measured. He also mentions that the use of technology can be threatening to the self-perception of teachers if it causes them to lose their sense of control in any way. Because the constructivist learning environment implies that the teacher is no longer the central authority, the combination of constructivism and technology requires a dramatic change in traditional teaching. Hodas also acknowledges progress, saying that "educational technologists increasingly are people whose values are more child-centered than those of their predecessors. This is reflected in the software they create, the uses they imagine for technology, and their ideas about exploration and collaboration." In other words, educational technology may be making important moves toward constructivism.

Carnine (1993) and others have considered how aspects of both constructivism and objectivism might be appropriate depending on the context of the learning situation. In situations where there is a discrete body of information to be learned (the first-aid training that might be part of a physical education program is an example that comes to mind, along with fact-laden subcomponents of many other subject areas), the strategies of directed learning theory might well provide an effective learning environment.

That the results of different theoretical approaches will vary, based on the situation, seems to be a fairly obvious statement, but the constructivist/objectivist dichotomy is pervasive and has led to many heated philosophical arguments about the nature of education. The fact that these issues (and the ideas that could lead to their reconciliation) seem to be largely ignored in practice has perhaps always been the source of problems in education, but now, in an era when there is a huge range of choices, it is probably more important than ever to put conscious effort into utilizing the theories that have been developed.

Egan (in press) states that the 100-year-old "progressive arguments about the development of life, of civilization, and of individual improvement . . . have resulted in systematic and pervasive mistakes about children's thinking, learning, and development." The degree to which educators are unaware of how children actually think (assuming, for instance, that a "correct" answer on a test demonstrates an understanding of the subject at hand) and the contradictory nature of many educational practices indicate that radical change should be on the educational agenda.

Transcending the objectivist/constructivist dichotomy, Egan (1997) points out that the goals of education in our culture include (1) shaping the young to the current norms and conventions of adult society, (2) teaching them the knowledge that will ensure that their thinking conforms with what is real and true about the world, and (3) encouraging the development of each student's individual potential. He argues that although those three objectives are mutually incompatible, they are so familiar to us that we have become comfortable with the discomforts they cause. This leads to confusing and thwarted learning experiences for students.

Virtual instruction must ensure that it does not perpetuate what is already wrong with the system. To paraphrase Egan's (in press) statement (quoted in the introduction to this chapter), running with greater speed and style is not an improvement unless it takes us to the right place.

It is important to help learners become critical thinkers who can assess information and who will continue to learn throughout their lives. A constructivist perspective is a necessary component of the educational experiences that will lead students to a meaningful use of the vast amount of information that is now available to them through technologies, including the virtual environment. Those who are responsible for designing and selecting virtual instruction must be able to understand what constructivism is and what it can accomplish.

Virtual Pedagogy

Constructivist virtual educational experiences imply a decentralized and flexible model, where traditional roles and social dynamics no longer apply. Technology is an important part of these experiences but should not be a central focus. The learning needs of the student must be the foundation of any successful educational program, virtual or otherwise.

What pedagogical approaches work in the new virtual territory? The term "pedagogy" has often been used in relation to teacher-centered or didactic forms of instruction, but it can also be used to describe the much wider variety of ways in which student learning can be facilitated, even in a virtual, constructivistic environment. Exemplary pedagogy here may involve having students negotiate the subject matter or research projects that they embark upon, rather than imposing such choices on students based on the requirements of a static (and possibly not very relevant) curriculum. It may involve organizing activities, encouraging discussions, or suggesting the use of learning resources that are related to some goal of the negotiated curriculum. Good pedagogy can accommodate interests that are unique to a specific learner or group of learners. It may involve the flexible use of media, and if so, it most certainly must ensure that young (or older) learners have the skills to make effective use of the media selected.

As the role of the teacher must change if constructivism and virtual learning are to be accommodated, so must the role of the learner. Learner responsibility becomes more important in virtual educational situations because there are fewer constraints on time and place (Locatis & Weisberg, 1997). On a similar train of thought, Harasim, Hiltz, Teles, and Turoff (1995) stress the importance of student motivation as a factor for successful CMC for learning. It should not come as a surprise that in any learning environment, students learn best when they are motivated (for example, by personally relevant activities), but when a teacher is not physically present, there is a new set of challenges. A high level of motivation and personal responsibility are fairly typical of the adult learners who have been the pioneers of virtual learning. (They are not a captive audience and have chosen to pursue an extension of their education.) Learner responsibility and high levels of motivation are not always the case for younger learners, which raises the issue of the importance of instructor/ learner and learner/learner interaction as virtual education moves farther down the K–12 age group.

Kearsley (1997) has noted that interaction among participants is the most important element of successful online education. Sherry (1995) and many others in the field who view effective distance education as being highly interactive echo him. Virtual instruction is not intended to be a form of learning that takes place completely independently and in isolation. The telecommunications component of virtual instruction is geared toward allowing people to be in contact with each other's ideas, and isolation does not have to be an issue. Quality of discourse, however, is more problematic, because not all online interactions are created equal. An important role for teachers, mentors, and/or instructional designers is to ensure that quality interactions are maximized and less relevant ones are minimized. Anyone who has participated in an online chat session, or even an academic teleconference, will be aware of the fact that good filtering techniques are required. All of the information received must be evaluated, and often much of it should be discarded. The techniques for effective filtering can pose a challenge.

Owston (1997) and others note that the World Wide Web appeals to the way students like to learn, although there are many cautions in the literature implying that the environment requires a new way of dealing with vast amounts of information. Online information sources, such as the Internet, often lead learners to information that is controversial, contradictory, or worse (see Linn, 1996). How these forms of communication are used is a factor in what Ferdi Serim (in an interview conducted by Prior in 1997) describes as the "gap between the people who use technology as just another form of TV and those who grasp that this can actually change and enrich their lives. . . . The more powerful technology becomes, the worse the gap becomes."

Hannafin, Hill, and Land (1997) suggest that "the World Wide Web requires thought, action and reflection to transform generic free-standing information into personally-relevant knowledge. . . . Access alone does little to promote understanding" (p. 97). They note that, unlike those of past generations, today's children must not only understand the enormous quantity of accumulated knowledge but also be guided to develop learning strategies for a lifetime of learning, and those in leadership roles bear the responsibility to support and encourage the changes needed.

Certainly the constructivist viewpoint, with its implications of open-ended education, does *not* imply a "free-for-all" with respect to the pedagogy of virtual learning. Perhaps more than ever, there is a need for vision and policy to provide appropriate services to learners. Findley and Findley (1997) state that "we must be sure that we have curriculum-driven technology rather than technology-driven curriculum. We must know what goals we want to accomplish and then seek the technology to best deliver those goals" (p. 119).

The goals ideally included in the policymakers' agenda would address the individual learning needs and interests of students and ways of dealing with change, while ensuring that communities, social dynamics, and cultural identities are not disrupted (Hozaki, 1996). Policymakers must also plan how to provide educators with the tools and techniques that will be required to implement these changes.

Another way of stating the goals of virtual education from the constructivist viewpoint is through a set of questions (Locatis & Weisberg, 1997, p. 103):

1. Can we create integrative environments that foster cooperation and harmony rather than competition and violence?

2. Can we create virtual spaces that are attractive to students?

3. Will these spaces enable students to thrive?

4. Can we maintain intellectual discourse in the face of the mass of readily available information and the constant flow of stimuli that divert attention in this world of instant gratification?

As yet, we cannot turn to the Internet for the answers to these questions, because much still remains to be discovered about its effectiveness in education.

Locatis and Weisberg (1997) may be correct in suggesting that too little is known. Perhaps the replicable formula does not yet exist. But there have been successful pilot implementations of virtual instruction to date, such as British Columbia's New Directions in Distance Learning project (NDDL), in which a variety of technologies, including the Internet, have been used in a range of secondary (grades 11 and 12) courses (Open Learning Agency, 1995). Benefits described in this project include flexible scheduling and enhanced course offerings, including the availability of courses that would have been impossible to schedule otherwise, due to small local class sizes. Students were able to graduate without leaving their remote communities, and busing was minimized. Course completion rates were above 75 percent. Mentoring was an important part of the NDDL project, and participants agree that the mentoring role has been critical to its success.

In another of many relatively small-scale examples of success in implementing a virtual learning environment, Latchem (1995) describes educational technology use by Alaskan Natives and Native Canadians in Northern Alberta. These communities have used videoconferencing to achieve local control of education and to overcome social and geographic barriers and limited resources.

Virtual education, especially in K–12, is truly the work of the most dedicated pioneers. Their strategies need to be articulated for educators across the board.

CONCLUSION

As the information technologies that accommodate virtual learning become more widely available, aspects of education ranging from the arrangement of timetables to the design of school buildings are likely to undergo radical changes. The roles of teachers and learners are changing and can be informed by an understanding of learning theory. The implications of institutional change and the changing roles of individuals within those institutions are often neglected, and in the current climate of a rapidly changing society, there is a real danger of unanticipated negative consequences on a large scale. There is a need for policy at a level that addresses the big educational picture and anticipates the consequences of change across the broad spectrum of educational goals. The focus must be on strategies that best meet the needs of learners within their social context (see Pacey & Penney, 1995).

Learning theory suggests that a constructivist approach addresses many of the challenges that the current, information-rich technological environments pose for learners. To succeed in a constructivist virtual environment, the learner must be self-directed and must acquire the skills to become independent of the instructor, who is no longer the main source of information. Although "the digital world will profoundly change how people learn, how they work, and what they produce, . . . at the same time it won't change human nature nor the need to give children a moral as well as intellectual education" (Dyson, 1997, p. 35). The human values of society must be maintained, and issues of equity in education are more important than ever.

"One has to hope that there will be voices who demand of education that it should help people to understand something of whence our lives come and whither they go" (Egan, 1997, p. 181). In the face of new technologies and economic pressure, it is all too possible for the human perspective to become lost.

Neil Postman has suggested that, "public education does not serve a public. It creates a public" (1995, pp. 17–18). It is possible to revise this thought and say that education, regardless of its source, creates a public. What kind of public do we choose to create? In formulating and implementing our educational vision, which includes the benefits that can be provided by virtual instruction, we must ensure that the entire educational structure, including development processes; funding strategies; selection criteria; and roles of teachers, learners, parents, governments, and others, is working in a way that is conducive to the creation of the social harmony and equity that we desire.

REFERENCES

Anderson, J., Reder, L., & Simon, H. (n.d.). *Applications and misapplications of cognitive psychology to mathematics education* [Online]. Available: http://act.psy.cmu.edu/ personal/ja/ misapplied.html. (Accessed March 16, 1999).

Apple, M. (1991). The new technology: Is it part of the solution or part of the problem in education? *Computers in the Schools, 8*(1–3), 59–81.

Bates, A. W. (1995). Creating the future: Developing vision in open and distance learning. In F. Lockwood (Ed.), *Open and distance learning today* (pp. 42–51). London: Routledge Kegan Paul.

Brown, J. S., Collins, A., & Duguid, P. (1989). Situated cognition and the culture of learning. *Educational Researcher, 18*(1), 32–42.

Carnine, D. (1993). Effective teaching for higher cognitive functioning. *Educational Technology, 33*(10), 29–33.

Cornell, R. (1996). Editorial: Creativity and technology . . . hardly a non sequitur in the 90s! *Educational Media International, 33*(2), 53–54.

Cox, B. (1997). Evolving a distributed learning community. In Z. Berge & M. Collins (Eds.), *The online K12 classroom* [Online]. Cresskill, NJ: Hampton Press. Available: http:// www.virtualschool.edu/cox/ OnlineClassroom.html. (Accessed March 18, 1999).

Distributed Learning Task Force. (1997). *Access and choice: The future of distributed learning in British Columbia.* Victoria, British Columbia, Canada: Center for Curriculum, Transfer and Technology.

Dobbin, M. (n.d.). *Charting a course to social division: The charter school threat to public education in Canada* [Online]. Available: http:// www.osstf.on.ca/www/issues/charter/charter.html. (Accessed March 16, 1999).

Dyson, E. (1997). Education and jobs in the digital world: The human connection. *Communications of the ACM, 41*(2), 35–36.

Educom Review Staff. (1996). Slicing the learning pie: Stan Davis interview. *Educom Review* [Online], *31*(5), 4 pages. Available: http://educause.edu/pub/er/review/reviewArticles/31532.html. (Accessed March 16, 1999).

Egan, K. (1997). *The educated mind: How cognitive tools shape our understanding*. Chicago: The University of Chicago Press.

Egan, K. (in press). *Getting it wrong from the beginning: The mismatch between school and children's minds* [Draft; Online]. Available: http://www.educ.sfu.ca/people/faculty/kegan/Wrongintro.html. (Accessed March 16, 1999).

Findley, B., & Findley, D. (1997). Strategies for effective distance education. *Contemporary Education, 68*(2), 118–120.

Gilman, D. (1996). We screw up everything, but we compensate with quality. *Contemporary Education, 67*(2), 60–61.

Hannafin, M., Hill, J., & Land, S. (1997). Student-centered learning and interactive multimedia: Status, issues and implication. *Contemporary Education, 68*(2), 94–99.

Harasim, L., Hiltz, S., Teles, L., & Turoff, M. (1995). *Learning networks: A field guide to teaching and learning online.* Cambridge, MA: MIT Press.

Hodas, S. (1995). *Technology refusal and the organizational culture of schools, 2.0* [Online]. Available: http://www.seas.upenn.edu/~cpage/techref.html. (Accessed September 8, 1997).

Hozaki, N. (1996). What needs to be considered about creativity and media use in a group-oriented society? *Educational Media International, 33*(2), 61-63.

Johnson, D. (1996). Evaluating the impact of technology: The less simple answer. *From Now On: A Monthly Electronic Commentary on Educational Technology Issues* [Online], *5*(5). Available: http://www.pacificrim.net/~mckenzie/jan96/reply.html. (Accessed September 9, 1997).

Kearsley, G. (1997). *A guide to online education* [Online]. Available: http://gwis.circ.gwu.edu/~etl/online.html. (Accessed March 17, 1999).

Kerr, S. (1991). Lever and fulcrum: Educational technology in teachers' thought and practice. *Teachers College Record, 93*(1), 114–136.

Kerr, S. (1994). *Toward a sociology of educational technology* [Online]. Available: http://weber.u.washington.edu/~stkerr/ethb94.htm. (Accessed September 9, 1997).

Latchem, C. (1995). See what I mean? Where compressed digital videoconferencing works. In F. Lockwood (Ed.), *Open and distance learning today* (pp. 98–107). London: Routledge Kegan Paul.

Linn, M. (1996). Key to the information highway. *Communications of the ACM, 39*(4), 34–35.

Locatis, C., & Weisberg, M. (1997). Distributed learning and the Internet. *Contemporary Education, 68*(2), 100–103.

Mason, R. (1994). *Using communications media in open and flexible learning.* London: Kogan Page.

Menzies, H. (1994). Learning communities and the information highway. *Journal of Distance Education, IX*(1), 1–16.

Nidds, J., & McGerald, J. (1996). Corporate America looks critically at public education: How should we respond. *Contemporary Education, 67*(2), 62–64.

Ohler, J. (1995). What K-12 teachers want to know about telecommunications in education. In Z. L. Berge & M. P. Collins (Eds.), *Computer mediated communication and the online classroom* (pp. 175–189). Cresskill, NJ: Hampton Press.

Open Learning Agency. (1995). *New directions in distance learning, 1994–95: Phase 2 review.* Burnaby, British Columbia: Author.

Oppenheimer, T. (1997, July). The computer delusion. *The Atlantic Monthly, 280*(1), 45–62.

Owston, R. (1997). The World Wide Web: A technology to enhance teaching and learning? *Educational Researcher, 26*(2), 27–33.

Pacey, L. M., & Penney, W. P. (1995). Thinking strategically: Reshaping the face of distance education and open learning. In J. M. Roberts & E. M. Keough (Eds.), *Why the information highway? Lessons from open & distance learning* (pp. 15–39). Toronto: Trifolium Books.

Peel, J., & McCary, C. (1997, May). Visioning the "little red schoolhouse" for the 21st century. *Phi Delta Kappan,* 698–705.

Postman, N. (1995). *The end of education: Redefining the value of school.* New York: Alfred A. Knopf.

Powers, S. (1997). Three little words: Interactive, distance and learning. *Contemporary Education, 68*(2), 92–93.

Prior, L. (1997). *Not how, but why: Ferdi Serim on the Internet in the classroom* [Online]. Available: http://www.4teachers.org/keynotes/serim/. (Accessed March 17, 1999).

Riel, M. (1994). Educational change in a technology-rich environment. *Journal of Research on Computing in Education, 26*(4), 452–474.

Roblyer, M. (1996, October). The constructivist/objectivist debate: Implications for instructional technology research. *Learning and Leading With Technology, 24*(2), 12–16.

Romiszowski, A. (1993). *Telecommunications and distance education.* Syracuse, NY: ERIC Clearinghouse on Information Resources. (ERIC Digest No. ED 358 841).

Sherry, L. (1995). Issues in distance learning. *International Journal of Distance Education* [Online], *1*(4), 337–365. Available: http://www.cudenver.edu/~lsherry/pubs/issues.html. (Accessed March 18, 1999).

Simonson, M. (1997). Distance education: Does anyone really want to learn at a distance. *Contemporary Education, 68*(2), 104–107.

Wellburn, E. (1991). *Information, telecommunications and learning: A review of the research literature* (Occasional Paper). Sidney, British Columbia, Canada: Education Technology Centre of British Columbia.

Wellburn, E. (1996). *The status of technology in the education system: A literature review* [Online]. Available: http://www.etc.bc.ca/lists/nuggets/EdTech_report.html. (Accessed September 8, 1997).

Whitty, G. (1997). Creating quasi-markets in education. *Review of Research in Education, 22,* 3–47.

CHAPTER 4

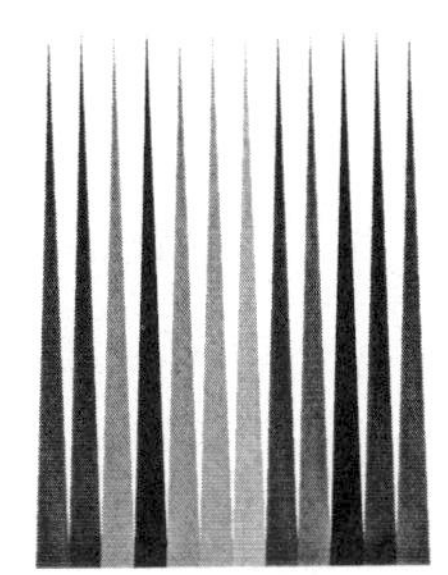

Learners and Learning in Information and Communication Technologies (ICT) Environments

Constructing an Instrument

Joost Lowyck and Jan Elen
European Union

INTRODUCTION

Distance education is currently in a state of rapid evolution (Collis, 1993). The value of distance education, as compared to traditional methods, has been the delivery of courses to students who are geographically dispersed. The basic instrument for this course delivery has been printed materials, delivered back and forth between learners and tutors, using ordinary postal services. These fundamentals are now changed by the introduction of state-of-the-art information and communication technologies (ICT) into the learning environment (Cennamo, Savenye, & Smith, 1991). Educators, eager to provide instruction in a more efficient way, have brought these new technologies into the distance education environment, adding a new dimension to it: "open" learning.

Open learning aims at meeting the needs of adults to (1) take responsibility in choosing what, how, and at what pace to learn; (2) have access to individually tailored study paths through modular structures in the curriculum; (3) choose studies that are constantly reconciled with the demands of the labor market; (4) receive support for independent study; and (5) be freed from both preconditions for formal entry and participation requirements (Caspersen, 1993).

These characteristics of open education place the learner and learning at the center of the education experience. This evolution toward open learning and a focus on the learner are supported by both the development of new learner-centered instructional methods and an increasing knowledge base about how to design materials that support learning (Lowyck, Elen, Proost, & Buena, 1995).

Telematics (telecommunications and informatics) and, more specifically, the aim to create telematic learning environments (TLEs), form the latest development in open and distance learning (ODL). Specific to these TLEs is a variety of technologies used as delivery systems, such as audio conferencing, videoconferencing, CD-ROM, interactive video, and so forth. As in most learning environments, the use of a mix of delivery systems is the rule rather than the exception (Norman, 1990).

By linking TLEs with ODL, challenging possibilities for raising the quality of ODL arise. Most strikingly, there is an increase of communication facilities among students, tutors, and peers. With the introduction of teleconferencing systems, distance education found a way to overcome one of its inherent handicaps, namely the absence of face-to-face contact. Face-to-face interaction, although at a distance, has become a real possibility, even if in a "virtual setting" (Fetterman, 1995; Gaede, 1995; Hernàndez-Dominguez, 1995).

These evolutionary changes in ODL and, more specifically, the trend toward learner-centered education, have placed learners and their interactions with the different components of TLEs at the top of the research agenda in educational technology. Little is known about how students/learners interact with TLEs. Although an extensive research base can be found on how students learn with written materials and even with computers, the study of learners in telematic environments has barely begun. A first contribution toward both explorative and hypothesis-testing research relates to the construction of theoretically sound and empirically valid research instruments. In this chapter, the construction of such an instrument is discussed.

First, the "mediating perspective" is introduced as the theoretical background of the research instruments. Moreover, an overview is presented of student variables that mediate the possible effects of TLEs. The different steps toward an empirically valid instrument are presented in the next sections. The resulting instrument with four scales is delivered in the concluding section.

THEORETICAL BACKGROUND

The Mediating Perspective

Multimedia and telecommunications provide new opportunities and challenges for the educational community. However, an increased availability of multimedia and telecommunications will not automatically result in educational innovation. Only when the mediating role of learners is acknowledged and fully taken into account while designing TLEs can educational innovation occur. This assertion is central to the mediating perspective.

The underlying assumption of the mediating paradigm, rooted in cognitive psychology, is that the activities of the learners are the main determinant of learning outcomes. The impact of environmental elements (such as technological devices, characteristics of multimedia, and instructional methods) is mediated by a series of learner characteristics (see Figure 4.1). Learning environments do not have a direct impact on learning outcomes. A variety of student variables mediates between the TLE and the learning output or effect. Students' interpretations of these environmental cues mediate the effects of interventions. The interpretation, rather than the intervention itself, triggers the learner to engage in particular learning activities. Within this tradition, it has been shown that instructional interventions are suboptimally used by students either because they are neglected or are used in a manner different from the intended one (see, e.g., Willems, 1987). Multiple studies (e.g., Winne & Marx, 1982, 1983) have shown instructional interventions to be effective only if the learner is "calibrated," making appropriate (often as intended by the instructional designer) use of them (Butler & Winne, 1994). The use of instructional interventions seems predicated by the student's perception of the task and the engagement of adequate (emotional and motivational) control strategies and perceptions about the value of the instructional interventions.

Fig. 4.1. Mediating perspective.

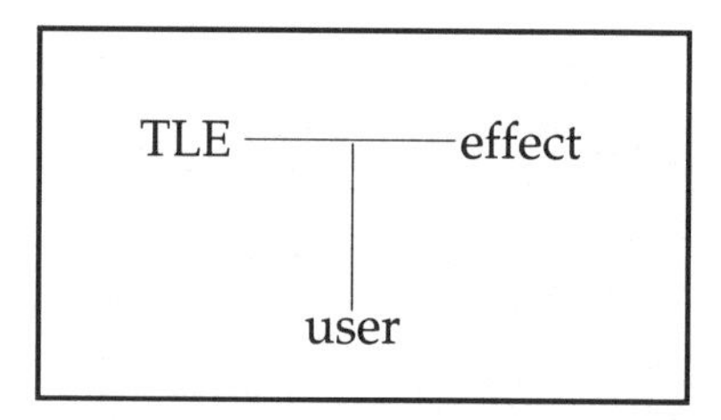

In a similar vein, it has been shown that students attribute values to external cues. Only if a positive value is attributed is the cue actually considered and hence capable of being effective. (For an elaborated example on feedback, see Butler & Winne, 1994.) In André's (1979) theory, the following prediction, which illustrates the cognitive mediational paradigm more precisely, is made regarding the effects of questions and adjunct aids in instructional texts: "Questions and other adjunct aids will have maximum effect when the subject perceives his task to be one of getting through the instructional materials with a minimum of effort. Under such conditions, questions influence the subject by changing what he perceives to be the minimum task" (p. 288).

Overview of Mediating Variables

A variety of mediating variables have been proposed. One of the most important variables is prior knowledge. It directly influences the ability of learners to acquire knowledge and also affects how learners deal with components of a learning environment (Dochy, 1992). It has been repeatedly demonstrated that different levels of domain-related prior knowledge allow the use of different learning activities.

Figure 4.2 provides an overview of student variables that, in addition to prior knowledge, may affect the interaction of students with TLEs. The concentric model shows the strength of the relationship of each student parameter with the mediating variable.

Fig. 4.2. Important parameters in students' interactions with TLEs.

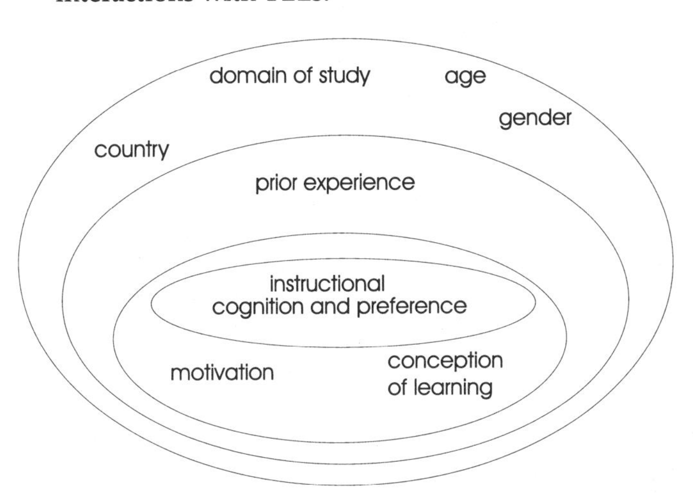

Gender, age, domain of study, and country are most distant from the center. These variables are found to influence instructional cognition and preference via other variables, such as prior experience. A number of studies show a more positive perception of males over females toward the use of computers in education (Busch, 1995; Shashaani, 1994). Not gender itself but other gender-related factors are responsible for these differences (see Proost, Elen, & Lowyck, 1997). Advocates of socialization theory associate gender differences in attitudes and involvement with computers to sociocultural factors. In their view, socialization of sex-typed behavior at home and school through parental and school educators' expectations and encouragement creates sex-differential beliefs and behavior (Eccles, 1987; Jacobs, 1991; Serbin, Zelkowitz, Doyle, Gold, & Wheaton, 1990). Other studies emphasize learning experience as a major factor in the establishment of sex-differential involvement (Chen, 1986; Gressard & Loyd, 1987; Lever, Sherrod, & Bransford, 1989; Loyd & Gressard, 1984). Males have outnumbered females in fields such as engineering, computer and information science, mathematics, and the physical sciences, whereas the percentage of women in areas such as education, home economy, language, and psychology exceeded that of men (Shashaani, 1994). Based on this perspective, women's lower participation and interest in computing are related to their lack of experience and activity in this field. Analogous assertions can be made for age. According to Clark and Salomon (1986), age influences attitudes toward computers through such other factors as motivation, experience, anxiety, perceptions, and need for cooperation.

The linking of TLEs to open and distance education brings with it the challenge of multicultural education. Students can now be brought into real, face-to-face contact, even if still at a distance, with others from all over the world. Scott, Cole, and Engel (1992) report some interesting aspects of computer use in multicultural settings and document the complexity of the cultural dimension of telematic networks for different cultural groups.

Motivation and conception of learning, together with "instructional metacognition," have a more direct impact on how learners act in TLEs. Motivation is perceived as the willingness to invest mental effort due to personal interest and is closely related to and dependent on the perceived competence of the person for the task at hand. Motivation can have two main orientations: One may pursue an area of study because of personal interest in the subject (intrinsic orientation) or to reach external goals (extrinsic orientation). Motivation affects the extent to which the learner will be willing to invest the mental effort necessary to realize learning results (Lowyck & Elen, 1994). In a concrete learning situation, involvement in learning is related to perceived task demands (level of difficulty) and perceived self-efficacy (personal judgment about one's own skillfulness or perceived competence; Sugrue, 1994). It is not the so-called objective difficulty nor the externally defined attractiveness of a learning task that define motivation, but rather the student's interpretation of the level of difficulty or attractiveness compared with the student's assessment of his or her own skills related to the task requirements (Salomon, 1981).

Conceptions of instruction have a strong relationship to students' conceptions of learning, which are ideas and notions regarding what learning is about and what a proper definition of learning could be. They form one aspect of "mental models" students have of learning (Vermunt, 1992) and can range from a "reproductive" conception to a "productive" conception. In a reproductive conception of learning, knowledge is regarded as a good that can be acquired. A productive conception stresses that the individual constructs knowledge. Students' conceptions of learning influence their perception and interpretation of the learning environment (Vermunt, 1992).

Studying beliefs, conceptions, mental models, and perceptions of individuals that are directly related to learning in an instructional setting is a growing area of research (for an overview, see Schunk & Meece, 1992). Attention is paid to a variety of perceptions that are regarded to be important: epistemological beliefs (Schommer, 1994), conceptions about the relationship between knowledge and beliefs (Alexander & Dochy, 1995), task perceptions/orientations toward learning (Dweck, 1986; Marshall, 1993), emotional and motivational control strategies (Corno, 1993), functionality of technological devices (Waldrip & Treagust, 1995), cultural background (Waldrip & Giddings, 1995), and conceptions related to subject matter (Vosniadou & Brewer, 1987). Generally, these studies reveal the number of variables related to self-regulation and learning in instructional settings. In this chapter, an additional variable is proposed—instructional metacognition—whose relationship and unique contributions to our understanding are still to be investigated.

Instructional metacognition can be described as "a student's instructional cognition and preference." The term "metacognition" is used to highlight the specific nature of this variable. The variable relates to the conceptions and preferences of learners about the relationship between their own learning and environmental variables. To understand the effects of this variable on the activities of students in a learning environment, it is important to look at this mediating variable in terms of instructional cognitions and student preferences.

Instructional cognition refers to the knowledge and perception a student has of the learning environment, in this case the TLE. This is not content-related, but rather metacognitive, knowledge about learning and the learner, the task and the learning environment (see Lowyck & Elen, 1994).

A student's instructional preferences are the affective and emotional values people attach to different components of the learning environment. The object of these preferences is not content-related elements but rather parameters of the learning environment such as the technology itself, the learner control provided, and social contacts made possible in a virtual setting. Understanding these preferences might provide insight into possible positive orientations toward TLEs.

CONSTRUCTING A QUESTIONNAIRE FOR RESEARCH ON STUDENTS' LEARNING IN TLEs

As indicated, a first step toward systematic research on students' learning in TLEs is the construction of theoretically sound and empirically valid research instruments. To study the impact of instructional metacognition, it was decided to develop a targeted questionnaire. According to Rosier (1990), four broad categories of instruments can be distinguished within survey studies, depending on the concrete nature of data to be gathered: (1) background characteristics, (2) knowledge, (3) attitudes, and (4) behavior. The substantial part of the questionnaire, consisting of gathering data on a student's instructional cognition and preference, relates primarily to attitude studies. (Lowyck et al., 1995 state that attitudes and opinions can be measured by the degree to which respondents agree or disagree with statements about attitudinal objects.) A well-known instrument in this perspective is the Likert scale, in which the respondent has response options for statements. Sixty-four items were extracted from the literature, with each item having five Likert-type response options, ranging from "totally disagree" to "totally agree." The instrument was field tested and revised prior to its administration.

Formulation of the Questions

As already indicated, instructional metacognition is a multidimensional construct. The questionnaire tries to cover the different dimensions. Because TLEs form an integration of existing technological devices in one environment, it is hypothesized that conceptions of discrete components of the environment will determine the conception of the whole configuration. The computer often plays a central role in the environment, so many questions address the computer.

Instructional cognition

The dimensions covered by the conception of the learning environment are level of difficulty, interaction in TLEs, presentation of information, and the economic aspect. In addition, students' perceptions of requirements of information modalities for learning, as well as their perceptions of requirements of traditional tools for learning, are measured.

Because TLEs form a complex configuration of different technological components, information is offered in different modalities: Audio information is complemented with visual or pictorial information. It is hypothesized that, in such an environment, people who are positively disposed toward each information modality will also favor a combination of these information modalities, as is the case in a TLE. Other questions ask for the perceived potential of the new technologies to promote learning, providing some indication of students' perceptions of what the technologies can do for education.

Instructional preference

The dimensions covered by instructional preference are learner control, social contacts, educational format, and delivery device. Learner control can be given on the curriculum level and the level of the specific course. For the latter, control can be given over the content, the volume, the sequence, the presentation, the pace, and the time of study. One question measures preference for external control. Other questions are formulated on the level of the curriculum ranging from no learner control to complete learner control.

Different items measure the preference of students for social contact. Some pertain to preference for social contact in general, although they often refer to social contact with "people from all over the world." Social contacts can fulfill several functions. According to Webb (1982), explaining to a partner seems to help students generate relations between new and existing information, resulting in deep processing of lesson content. People might also expect to get support from others via the network. Lowyck et al. (1995) contend that generating and receiving help is positively correlated with learning outcomes. Asking for help is not. A third function that can be fulfilled by the network is to work together on a problem-solving task or a simulation game.

An important aspect of the technologies used in TLEs is their potential for communication, at a distance and in the absence of face-to-face contact. Several dimensions of TLEs can be distinguished, referring to general communication aspects, such as information modality, time dependency or independence and immediacy, and number of participants (see Lowyck et al., 1995).

The absence of direct face-to-face contact in the TLE is stressed by asking the respondents to keep in mind "a learning situation where all interactions with the tutor and with other students are via technologies, that is, no face-to-face contact." The questions pertain to the different communication dimensions of the TLE. Different technologies offer information in different modalities. A broad distinction can be made among verbal, para-verbal, and nonverbal information. For example, with an audio conferencing system, verbal and para-verbal information can be transmitted. Videoconferencing also allows nonverbal information to be exchanged.

Further, communication in a TLE can be synchronous or asynchronous. Synchronous is a synonym of real-time (Hoadley, Berman, & Hsi, 1995). Asynchronous is time-independent (see Lowyck et al., 1995). A dimension closely related is "immediacy," referring to the delay between sending a message and receiving feedback. Questions are formulated around this immediacy.

Another dimension of the communication in the TLE is the number of participants involved. Riel and Levin (1990) propose the following descriptors for categorizing telematics:

1. One-to-one dialogues, in which the communication process occurs between two participants only;

2. One-to-many broadcasts, where one sender distributes messages to many receivers;

3. Many-to-many group interactions.

A last category of questions about interaction in the absence of face-to-face contact refers to the perceived need for some kind of support or additional information in the TLE.

Preferences for educational format and delivery devices might also provide some insight into a possible positive perception of TLEs. Several educational formats are questioned. For delivery devices, a distinction is drawn between traditional methods and technologies. It is hypothesized that people who have a strong preference for traditional methods or traditional educational formats such as the classroom will not welcome new technologies in education.

Figure 4.3 (pp. 76–79) presents an overview of the questions discussed so far.

These questions concern the mediating variable, "a student's instructional cognition and preference." As mentioned previously, other student parameters are found to have important relationships with this mediating variable. The following sections discuss how the questions were formulated around the student parameters of experience, motivation, and conception of learning.

(Text continues on page 80.)

Fig. 4.3. Overview of the questions.

Instructional cognition

Level of difficulty

It takes a lot of energy to learn to use a computer.

Learning with telematics is very labor-intensive.

Learning with telematics requires a high level of educational competence.

Technologies are very difficult to use.

Interaction in TLEs

In telematic environments, there is no good access to the tutor.

In telematic environments, small-group learning can become disorganized since there is no group leader or coordinator.

There is an important lack of "natural" interaction in telematic environments since there is almost no face-to-face contact.

Presentation of information

The information presented by technologies is not of good quality.

Recent technologies allow a quick exchange of information.

Economic aspect

Learning with technologies is very expensive.

Information modality

Audio information is necessary in order for me to learn.

Pictorial information is necessary in order for me to learn.

Audiovisual information is necessary in order for me to learn.

Delivery systems

Necessity for traditional systems

Written or printed text is necessary in order for me to learn.
My own notes are necessary in order for me to learn.
A handbook is necessary in order for me to learn.

Potential of technologies

I think audiocassettes can improve my learning.
I think a computer can improve my learning.
I think a CD-ROM can improve my learning.

Instructional preference

Learner control

Level of the specific course

Within a specific course, I prefer to choose the specific topics to study.
Within a specific course, I prefer to control the amount of information I want to study.
Within a specific course, I prefer to define the sequence in which to study the information.
Within a specific course, I prefer to choose the mode of display of the information: pictures, sound, text, and so forth.
I prefer to control the pace of a lesson.
Within a specific course, I prefer to choose when I want to study.
No learner control: I like courses with well-structured study material.

Curriculum level

No learner control: I like to follow a prescribed program of study.
Some learner control: I like to select part of my courses myself.

Fig. 4.3.—Continued

Complete learner control: I like to select all of my courses myself.

Social contacts

General

I like to learn in teams or small groups. / I like to learn on my own.

I am willing to cooperate with other students in a learning situation.

I like to work with a computer in small groups. / I like to work on my own with a computer.

I would like to get feedback about my work from people all over the world.

I would like to ask questions of people from all over the world.

I would like to work together on a problem-solving task with people from different countries.

I would like to engage in simulation games with people from all over the world.

Information modality

I like to have contact with the tutor and other students via telephone in order to exchange verbal information.

I like to have contact with the tutor and other students via computer in order to exchange text-based messages.

I like to have contact with the tutor and other students via videoconferencing in order to exchange text, voice, and pictures.

Time (in)dependency/immediacy

If I have a question, I like to get an immediate answer.

I like to save up my questions until a certain moment when I can ask them all at once.

Number of participants
I like to have the possibility of simultaneous interaction with the tutor and all the other students.
I like to interact with one person at a time.

Support or additional information
I like to have an introductory session to meet all the people involved before starting with the educational program.
I like to have seminars where I can meet the other students on a regular basis.
I like to have a short session to get acquainted with the technology before starting with the educational program.

Educational format
I like a classroom setting.
I like a lecture format.
I like theory-oriented courses.
I like practice-oriented courses.
I like to write papers.

Delivery tools
Technologies
I would like to study with a computer, even if this is very complex. / If studying with a computer turns out to be too complex, I would like to have the opportunity to return to traditional education methods.
Studying only with audiocassettes is acceptable to me.
Studying only with videocassettes is acceptable to me.
Studying only with a computer is acceptable to me.

Traditional methods
I prefer staying with traditional education methods.
Studying only with lectures is acceptable to me.
Studying only with printed materials is acceptable to me.

Experience

Experience is measured toward telematics in general, telematics for educational purposes, and distance education. To get a clear picture of the experience, a distinction is made between "a lot of experience with telematics," "some experience with telematics," and "no experience at all." The technologies, here referred to as telematics because they are integrated in the TLE, are telephone conferencing, computer conferencing, videoconferencing, interactive video, computer, CD-ROM, and the Internet. Hypertext and multimedia are also included, but cannot be considered as technologies but rather as recent developments in informatics and software.

Motivation

As already mentioned, motivation is conceptualized as the willingness to invest mental effort due to personal interest and is closely related to and dependent on the perceived competence of the person for the task at hand. A distinction is made among motivation to study in general, motivation to study with traditional methods, and motivation to study with a computer. Within these categories, a distinction can often be made between dimensions of motivation.

Motivation can also have two main orientations: One can study because of personal interest in the subject (intrinsic orientation) or to reach external goals (extrinsic orientation). Figure 4.4 provides an overview of the questions measuring motivation.

Conceptions of learning

Conceptions of learning are students' ideas about what good learning is. These conceptions may range from reproductive to productive (Vermunt, 1992). In the questionnaire, learning as reproduction of knowledge is stated as, "For me, learning is trying to remember the course content presented to me." Learning as an active and productive process is stated as, "For me, learning is to consult additional information sources in case

Fig. 4.4. Overview of the questions measuring motivation.

Motivation in general

Mental effort

I always finish a task I've started, even if it becomes very difficult. / If a task becomes too difficult, I am likely to drop it.

I invest a lot of energy in my studies. / I prefer easy courses that don't require much effort.

Interest

I like to study.

Perceived competence

Studying requires a lot of energy for me. / I learn new things easily.

Motivation to study with traditional methods

Mental effort

I am prepared to invest a lot of energy in studying with traditional education methods.

Motivation to study with a computer

Mental effort

I am prepared to invest a lot of energy in learning to use a computer.

Interest

I am interested in using a computer to learn or to study.

Orientation

Intrinsic motivation

The only reason I study is for pure interest in the subject.

I chose to study in a higher education institution for the challenge of it, to see if I could succeed (test oriented).

Extrinsic motivation

I study to prepare myself for a good job or to improve my current professional functioning (job oriented).

The most important reason to study is to earn a certificate or diploma (certificate oriented).

of comprehension problems" and "I feel I've really learned something only when I can use the learned information to solve practical problems."

Sample

The selection of the sample was based on several criteria. The questionnaire was sent out to students age 18 and above, studying in either a European traditional institution or a distance education setting. All respondents were assumed to have sufficient knowledge of English to understand and answer the questions.

Several channels were used for the distribution of the questionnaire. The main channels were professors and teachers at traditional universities in different countries, student organizations with representatives in most of the European countries, study centers, and organizers of distance education (e.g., EuroPACE 2000, Consorzio Nettuno).

The overall response rate to the questionnaire was 34 percent. Although this percentage was not very high (due to different factors), this was not regarded to be a crucial problem because the absolute number of respondents was 1,368.

The most important hindrance to obtaining a high response rate was the fact that we were depending on intermediate channels for the distribution of the questionnaire. It was not possible to distribute the questionnaires directly because the study was aimed at students in different countries all over Europe.

In Table 4.1 the sample of respondents is described in terms of region, gender, age, and domain of study. Countries are grouped together on the basis of geography: Western Europe (Belgium, the Netherlands, Austria, Germany, Switzerland, France), British Isles (United Kingdom, Ireland), Southern Europe (Italy, Spain, Portugal), Eastern Europe (Czech Republic, Poland, Slovakia), and the Scandinavian countries (Finland, Norway, Denmark).

Table 4.1
Distribution of Respondents Based on Region, Gender, Age, and Domain of Study

Region	N	%
Western Europe	881	64.5
British Isles	51	3.7
Southern Europe	342	25.0
Eastern Europe	34	2.5
Scandinavian countries	58	4.2
Gender		
Male	945	69.4
Female	416	30.6
Age		
<25	294	21.5
25<=age<29	377	27.6
29<=age<35	358	26.2
>35	339	24.8
Domain of study		
Science & Technology	835	61.4
Humanities	526	38.6

This table shows that Western Europe is the most strongly represented. This is not surprising because most respondents were Belgian students. These students could most easily be reached through professors at the University of Leuven and the Flemish coordinating office of study centers. Within Southern Europe, Spain especially is strongly represented.

Males are more strongly represented in the questionnaire responses than females. Almost 70 percent of the respondents were males. This result might relate to the high representation of students in science and technology (more males than females) compared to students in the humanities. This last bias is probably attributable to the fact that the channels addressed for the distribution of the questionnaire were mostly in the field of science and technology and also because of reference to the courses given in the European Open University Network

(EOUN) project (environmental sciences, elementary statistics, and the "Chaos programmes").

The data show that the population was young, which is to be expected because they were all students.

Table 4.2 shows the distribution of students based on experience with the use of a computer. The data show that most people have at least some experience with the computer and that the majority of respondents (71.1 percent) use a computer at home. Results of a student survey of the British Open University show that in their population the overall access to a computer at home is 81 percent, which is 10 percent higher.

Table 4.2
Distribution of Students Based on Experience with and Use of a Computer at Home

	N	%
Experience with the use of a computer		
No experience at all	90	6.6
Some experience	631	46.4
A lot of experience	638	46.9
Use of a computer at home		
No	393	28.9
Yes	967	71.1

Computers seem to be more commonly used than telematics. Table 4.3 shows that most people do not have experience with possible components of TLEs. Among those components with which people do have experience, the most popular are CD-ROM, the Internet, and multimedia, respectively. The Internet seems to be the most deeply penetrated in the field of education. In the survey of the British Open University, 18 percent of the students have access to the Internet, while in our population 38 percent have experience with the Internet. This might be an overestimation.

Table 4.3
Distribution of Students Based on Experience with Components of TLE

Experience with TLEs (in education)	N	%
Telephone conferencing	197 (88)	14.8 (6.6)
Computer conferencing	138 (65)	10.4 (4.9)
Videoconferencing	97 (48)	7.3 (3.6)
Interactive video	80 (43)	6.0 (3.2)
CD-ROM	521 (234)	39.2 (17.6)
Hypermedia	216 (102)	16.3 (7.5)
Multimedia	316 (159)	23.8 (11.9)
The Internet	508 (284)	38.1 (21.0)

Table 4.4 shows that although telematics are not so commonly used, most of the respondents are aware of telematics, and if they have not worked with them themselves, they may have seen other people working with them. One exception is "hypermedia." Less than 50 percent of the respondents had heard

Table 4.4
Number and Percentage of Students Who Have Heard of TLE Components

Knowledge of TLEs	N	%
Telephone conferencing	1096	82.4
Computer conferencing	1047	78.8
Videoconferencing	1084	81.4
Interactive video	1058	79.8
CD-ROM	1254	94.3
Hypermedia	631	47.6
Multimedia	1141	86.0
The Internet	1247	93.5

of it. CD-ROM and the Internet, on the other hand, were known by almost all the respondents.

FACTOR ANALYSIS

A factor analysis is carried out as a basis for the construction of scales. To measure the mediating variable, we wanted to construct scales with a high reliability. The factor analysis can also be used as a basis for comparison with the underlying structure of the questionnaire originally derived from the literature. Some results are given later in this section. First factor analysis and how it is done are described. A comparison is made with principal component analysis. Then the results of the factor analysis are presented and discussed.

Factor analysis consists of a number of statistical techniques used to simplify complex sets of data (Kline, 1994). It is a type of latent variable analysis. Factor analysis was only carried out on the items in the questionnaire regarding "instructional cognition and preference." The factor analysis simplifies a matrix of correlations between the responses on the items so that they can be explained in terms of few underlying factors. Interpretations of factors are based on the loadings of the items on the factors. It is usual to regard factor loadings as high if they are greater than 0.6 (the positive or negative sign being irrelevant) and moderately high if they are above 0.3 (Kline, 1994). Other loadings can be ignored.

Distinction Between Components and Factors

The terms "components" and "factors" are often used as if they were interchangeable. In fact, there is a real distinction. Components are derived directly from the correlation matrix, whereas common factors of factor analysis are hypothetical because they are estimated from the data (Kline, 1994). Statistically this means that, for the latter, instead of unity in the diagonals, some other estimate of commonality is inserted. This also means that, while in the first case all the variance in a matrix is explained, in the latter it is not. The fact that not all the variance is explained theoretically is an advantage because it is unlikely that factors ever could explain all the variance in a matrix and because the latter method accounts for errors in the measurement.

Principal component analysis is almost identical to factor analysis, except that instead of 1s in the diagonal of the correlation matrix, the commonalities are estimated. There are different ways to estimate the commonalities, affecting the number of factors that are extracted. The method used in this study for estimating the commonalities is called the squared multiple correlation (Kline, 1994). The squared multiple correlation is obtained by computing the multiple correlations between each variable and other variables in the matrix. The squares of these are placed in the matrix.

Extracting Statistically Significant Factors

The major aim of the factor analysis was to construct scales, measuring "a student's instructional cognition and preference" with a high reliability estimate. The question asked was "What is an acceptable number of factors to retain so that we can construct meaningful scales on the basis of it?"

We based the analysis on two complementary methods to decide upon the number of factors to retain: the mineigen = 1 criterion, and looking at the scree plot of eigenvalues. The mineigen = 1 criterion is based on the eigenvalues of the factors. The eigenvalue of a factor is the total amount of variance explained by the factor. The larger this value, the more variance is explained by the factor. The mineigen = 1 criterion demands that the eigenvalue of the factor be at least 1 to belong to the solution. The maximum eigenvalue is equal to the number of items included in the analysis. The mineigen = 1 criterion delivered eight factors. The scree showed that the solutions 4, 7, and 15 might be valid ones. The best interpretable solution was chosen, in this case the solution with four factors.

Interpretation of Factors

Interpretation of factors is based on the factor loadings of the items. Before the factors can be interpreted, they have to be rotated first. Different methods can be employed. We used the orthogonal rotation. The resulting factor structure consists of the correlations of the original variables with the rotated factors. The factor structure loadings of a rotated factor analysis are the equivalent of the factor loadings in the unrotated factor matrix. The factor structure after orthogonal rotation for this analysis is presented in Appendix 1. The proportion of variance explained by each of the factors can be retrieved from Table 4.5.

Table 4.5
Proportion of Variance Explained by Four Rotated Factors

Factor 1	5.88
Factor 2	4.32
Factor 3	3.16
Factor 4	3.07

The total proportion of variance explained by this factor structure is (5.884 + 4.321 + 3.159 + 3.066) / 64 (number of items in the analysis) or 26 percent, which is limited. Because the aim of the factor analysis was to form the basis for the scale construction, we did not consider this to be a crucial problem. More attention should be paid to it if the factor analysis is intended to give a good idea of the basic structure of the questionnaire.

The interpretation of the factors is based on the items loading on them. Some items, however, do not load on any of the factors. We give our interpretation of each of the factors and speculate about why some items were not included in the factor analysis below. Only loadings of at least .30 are considered.

The items loading on the first factor all refer to preference for social contacts, whether face-to-face or virtual (via networking). The items also show that students, who are eager to have social contact with other students, would also like to have this social contact when it is delivered via the computer, the telephone, or videoconferencing. Some items, although they were expected to, did not load significantly on the scale. These items are, "I like to interact with one person at a time," "If I have a question, I like to get an immediate answer," "I like to save up my questions until a certain moment when I can ask them all at once," and "I like to have a short session to get acquainted with the technology before starting with the educational program." Most of these statements pertain to the communication dimensions of TLEs: time dependency or independence and the number of participants. They probably do not load on this factor because they do not measure preference for social contact per se but rather address the kind of social contact one would like, independent of whether one likes to have social contact at all. The statement, "I like to have a short session to get acquainted with the technology before starting with the educational program" measures more for anxiety about new technologies than for preference for social contact. The item, "I like to write papers," loads positively on this factor. This probably means that in the perception and experience of students, writing a paper is a group activity or an activity that is directed toward others.

The items loading on the second factor refer to perception of technologies and preference for traditional methods. The items about perception of technologies are all formulated negatively. However, not all negatively formulated items about perception of technologies are included, and not all items about preference for traditional methods load on this factor. The statement, "Learning with technologies is very expensive," does not load significantly on any factor. The reason for this might be that the cost of the technology is not decisive for the perception one holds of technologies in education. Concerning the preference for traditional methods, the following statements do not load significantly on the factor: "Studying only with printed materials is acceptable to me," "Studying only with lectures is acceptable to me," and "I like a lecture format." We speculate that this means that the other items all include some aspect about preference for social contact in the learning situation, whereas these items do not. If this speculation is true, this also points out that lectures are considered one-way and noninteractive by students or that lecturing is perceived as "asocial." This idea is supported by the items about interaction. Respondents who agree with the items loading high on this factor have a negative perception of the interaction in TLEs and partly for this reason might prefer to stay with traditional methods. Also, support for this idea can be found in the fact that the item, "I like to work on my own with a computer," loads negatively, while the item, "I like to work with a computer in small groups," does not load at all. The computer and the fact that no social contact is present cause students to hold a negative perception of the situation.

The items loading on the third factor refer to a preference for audiovisual and pictorial information and for technologies that deliver information in this mode, such as audiocassettes, videocassettes, and CD-ROM or the computer.

The items loading on the fourth factor refer to learner control, both at the level of the curriculum and at the level of the course. There are some unexpected results in this factor. First, the item, "I like to follow a prescribed program of study," does not belong to the solution. Probably students understand this item as a preference for a well-organized program of study, which has no relation with preference for learner control. Second, the statement, "I like courses with well-structured study material," loads positively instead of negatively. This means that preference for well-structured study material goes with preference for learner control and not with preference for external control. Third, the item, "A handbook is necessary in order for me to learn," loads positively. This might relate to the fact that the distance education environment has long been print based and is perceived as allowing a lot of learner control.

Some of the remaining items are, "I like theory-oriented courses," "I like practice-oriented courses," and "My own notes are necessary in order for me to learn." The first two items pertain to the kind of educational format that is preferred, without any reference to whether it is traditional or technology based. This might be the reason why these items do not load significantly on any factor. The same might be true for the last item, "My own notes are necessary in order for me to learn." Also, this item does not refer to a traditional method or a technology-based education system.

CONCLUSION

In this chapter, we have addressed how ICT can contribute to the optimization of education. The emphasis is on the transformation of information environments into (technological) learning environments. A basic component in raising the quality of open environments is putting the learner at the center. Indeed, because there is no direct relationship between the environment and learning outcomes, the "mediating" paradigm has been chosen as the focus of our research. This perspective has been documented by a vast amount of research on students' parameters when functioning in more complex learning environments.

The mediating parameter used in this study has been labeled as "instructional metacognition." This term refers to a set of conceptions and preferences of learners considering the relationship between the learning environment and their learning activities, processes, and outcomes. However, since the concept of instructional metacognition is relatively new in the field of educational technology and instructional design, there is an urgent need for a strong instrumentation of that construct. Consequently, in this chapter the development of an instrument, that is, a questionnaire, is reported. Through the quest for a valid and reliable instrument, the underlying model of instructional metacognition is largely elaborated to construct the instrument in a methodologically well-controlled manner.

Using factor analysis, we constructed scales that were used to investigate the impact of instructional metacognition. This means that the construction of scales results in the appropriate research instrument. For the purpose of constructing reliable scales, some items that were included in the factor analysis were left out. These deleted items had such a low correlation with the other items that they severely lowered the reliability of the scales. Items that loaded negatively on the factors were converted in such a way that a five (totally agree) becomes a one (totally disagree) and vice versa.

On the basis of this and the previous steps (the factor analysis itself), the total number of items was reduced from 64 to 49. Items loading on more than one factor are brought into one scale, based on the highest loading.

The first scale measured preference for social contacts in the absence of face-to-face contact and if realized by means of technologies. The item, "I like to work with a computer in small groups," although it loads on the first and the third factor, is categorized under this scale because it has the highest loading on the first factor. This means that in the item, students place more emphasis on the work in small groups than on the work with the computer. And as already mentioned, people scoring high on this scale also like to have the social contact when realized via the technology or when in combination with learning with technologies. The item, "I like to write papers," is left out of the scale because it lowers the reliability of the scale. Writing papers probably is not a significant indication of social contact with others.

The second scale measured negative perception of computer-based technologies and preference for traditional methods. Respondents who score high on this scale have a negative perception of TLEs (computer, telecommunications environments, and technologies), and they do not prefer to study with TLEs or to invest a lot of effort in studying with a computer. The items, "I think a CD-ROM can improve my learning" and "A handbook is necessary in order for me to learn," load on this factor and on another one. Both, however, load higher on the other factor, being Factor 3 for the first and Factor 4 for the latter.

Scale 3 measured a positive perception of and preference for audiovisual-based technologies, such as audiocassettes and videocassettes. Also, the CD-ROM is perceived as a medium delivering audio, pictorial, and visual information, more than as a computer-based technology.

Scale 4 measured the preference for learner control. Although the item, "A handbook is necessary in order for me to learn," loaded higher on Factor 4 than on Factor 2, it lowered the reliability of this scale and was therefore left out. Probably a handbook is not perceived as a medium that allows a lot of learner control. Also, the item, "I like courses with well-structured study material," is left out because of its low correlation with the other items in the scale. This is not surprising because the other items about learner control do not really relate to the structuredness of the instructional material.

Table 4.6, page 90, shows the results that are given for the scales, regarding the number of items they contain, the mean, the

Table 4.6
Basic Results for Each Scale

Scale	Description	Number of Items	N	Means	Standard Deviation	Cronbach α
1	preference for social contacts	16	1102	3.603	0.574	0.855
2	negative perception of computer-based technologies in education / preference for traditional methods	17	815	2.774	0.464	0.763
3	positive perception of and preference for audiovisual-based technologies in education	8	1194	2.881	0.601	0.719
4	preference for learner control	8	1115	3.820	0.540	0.784

standard deviation, and the reliability of the scale. Although the results are based on different numbers of respondents, the means are comparable among the scales. This table provides a sufficient basis to assert that a valid instrument has been constructed for measuring metacognition.

In future research, the validated instrument can be used both to enlarge the study to other groups of students and to gain data that contribute to the empirical validation of instructional metacognition as a central parameter in the design and development of TLEs.

REFERENCES

Alexander, P. A., & Dochy, F. J. R. C. (1995). Conceptions of knowledge and beliefs: A comparison across varying cultural and educational communities. *American Educational Research Journal, 32*(2), 413–442.

André, T. (1979). Does answering higher-level questions while reading facilitate productive learning? *Review of Educational Research, 49*(2), 280–318.

Busch, T. (1995). Gender differences in self-efficacy and attitudes toward computers. *Journal of Educational Computing Research, 12*(2), 147–158.

Butler, D. L., & Winne, P. H. (1994). *Feedback and self-regulated learning: A theoretical synthesis.* Vancouver/Burnaby: University of British Columbia/Simon Fraser University.

Caspersen, S. (1993). Challenges for future development of higher education in Europe. In C. de Vocht & P. Henderikx (Eds.), *Conference reader* (Proceedings of Flexible Responses in Higher Education, Brussels, Belgium; pp. 21–27). Brussels, Belgium: Studiecentrum Open Hoger Onderwijs (StOHO).

Cennamo, K. S., Savenye, W. C., & Smith, P. L. (1991). Mental effort and video-based learning: The relationship of preconceptions and the effects of interactive and covert practice. *Educational Technology Research and Development, 39*(1), 5–16.

Chen, M. (1986). Gender and computers: The beneficial effects of experience on attitudes. *Journal of Educational Computing Research, 2*(3), 265–282.

Clark, R. E., & Salomon, G. (1986). Media in teaching. In M. C. Wittrock (Ed.), *Handbook of research on teaching: A project of the American Educational Research Association* (3rd ed., pp. 464–478). New York: Macmillan Publishing.

Collis, B. A. (1993). Evaluating instructional applications of telecommunications in distance education. *Educational and Training Technology International, 30*(3), 266–274.

Corno, L. (1993). The best-laid plans: Modern conceptions of volition and educational research. *Educational Researcher, 22*(2), 14–22.

Dochy, F. J. R. C. (1992). *Assessment of prior knowledge as a determinant for future learning.* Heerlen, The Netherlands: Centre for Educational Technology and Innovation, Open University of the Netherlands.

Dweck, C. S. (1986). Motivational processes affecting learning. *American Psychologist, 41* (10), 1040–1048.

Eccles, J. S. (1987). Gender roles and women's achievement-related decisions. *Psychology of Women Quarterly, 11,* 135–172.

Fetterman, D. (1995). *Ethnography in the virtual classroom.* Stanford, CA: California Institute of Integral Studies and Stanford University.

Gaede, O. F. (1995). Internet information tools developed by the Florida Schoolyear 2000 Initiative. In H. Maurer (Ed.), *Educational multimedia and hypermedia, 1995* (Proceedings of ED-MEDIA 95: World Conference on Educational Multimedia and Hypermedia, Graz, Austria; pp. 235–240). Charlottesville, VA: Association for the Advancement of Computing in Education (AACE).

Gressard, C. P., & Loyd, B. H. (1987). An investigation of the effects of math anxiety and sex on computer attitudes. *School Science and Mathematics, 87*(2), 125–135.

Hernàndez-Dominguez, A. (1995). An adapted virtual class based on two approaches: CSCW and intelligent tutoring system. In H. Maurer (Ed.), *Educational multimedia and hypermedia, 1995* (Proceedings of ED-MEDIA 95: World Conference on Educational Multimedia and Hypermedia, Graz, Austria; pp. 324–329). Charlottesville, VA: Association for the Advancement of Computing in Education (AACE).

Hoadley, C. M., Berman, B. P., & Hsi, S. (1995). Networked multimedia for communication and collaboration. Paper presented at the annual meeting of the American Educational Research Association, San Francisco, CA.

Jacobs, J. E. (1991). Influence of gender stereotypes on parent and child mathematics attitudes. *Journal of Educational Psychology, 83*(4), 518–527.

Kline, P. (1994). *An easy guide to factor analysis.* London: Routledge Kegan Paul.

Lever, S., Sherrod, K. B., & Bransford, J. 1989. The effects of Logo instruction on elementary students' attitudes toward computers and school. *Computers in the School, 6,* 45–65.

Lowyck, J., & Elen, J. (1994). *Students' instructional metacognition in learning environments (SIMILE).* Leuven, Belgium: Centre for Instructional Psychology and Technology.

Lowyck, J., Elen, J., Proost, K., & Buena, G. (1995). *Telematics in open and distance learning: Research methodology handbook.* Leuven, Belgium: Catholic University of Leuven, Centre for Instructional Psychology and Technology.

Loyd, B. H., & Gressard, C. (1984). The effects of sex, age and computer experience on computer attitudes. *AEDS Journal, 18,* 67–77.

Marshall, H. H. (1993). *Children's understanding of academic tasks: Work, play or learning.* San Francisco/Berkeley: San Francisco State University/University of California.

Norman, K. L. (1990). The electronic teaching theater: Interactive hypermedia and mental models of the classroom. *Current Psychology: Research and Reviews, 9*(2), 141–161.

Proost, K., Elen, J., & Lowyck, J. (1997). Effects of gender on perceptions of and preferences for telematic learning environments. *Journal of Research on Computing in Education, 29*(4), 370–384.

Riel, M. M., & Levin, J. A. (1990). Building electronic communities: Success and failure in computer networking. *Instructional Science, 19*(2), 145–169.

Rosier, M. J. (1990). Survey research methods. In J. P. Keeves (Ed.), *Educational research, methodology, and measurement: An international handbook* (pp. 107–113). Oxford: Pergamon Press.

Salomon, G. (1981). *Communication and education, social and psychological interactions.* Beverly Hills, CA: Sage Publications.

Schommer, M. (1994). *Beliefs about knowledge and learning: An outline of the talk.* Wichita, KS: Wichita State University.

Schunk, D. H., & Meece, J. L. (Eds.). (1992). *Student perceptions in the classroom.* Hillsdale, NJ: Lawrence Erlbaum Associates.

Scott, T., Cole, M., & Engel, M. (1992). Computers and education: A cultural constructivist perspective. *Review of Research in Education, 20,* 191–251.

Serbin, P., Zelkowitz, A., Doyle, D., Gold, D., & Wheaton, B. (1990). The socialization of sex-differentiated skills and academic performance: A mediational model. *Sex Roles, 23*(11/12), 613–627.

Shashaani, L. (1994). Gender differences in computer experience and its influence on computer attitudes. *Journal of Computing Research, 11*(4), 347–367.

Sugrue, B. (1994). A theory-based framework for assessing domain-specific problem solving ability. (Paper presented at the annual meeting of the American Educational Research Association, New Orleans, LA). Los Angeles, CA: CRESST, University of California.

Vermunt, J. D. H. M. (1992). Leerstijlen en sturen van leerprocessen in het hoger onderwijs: Naar procesgerichte instructie in zelfstandig denken [Learning styles and the guiding of learning processes in higher education: Toward process-oriented instruction in independent thinking]. (Doctoral dissertation, Katholieke Universiteit Brabant). Amsterdam: Swets & Zeitlinger.

Vosniadou, S., & Brewer, W. F. (1987). Theories of knowledge restructuring in development. *Review of Educational Research, 57*(1), 5167.

Waldrip, B. G., & Giddings, G. J. (1995). *Multicultural learning environments: Influence of culture on learning environments.* Perth: Curtin University.

Waldrip, B. G., & Treagust, D. F. (1995). *Students' perceptions of video-conferencing between two university campuses.* Perth: Curtin University.

Webb, N. M. (1982). Student interaction and learning in small groups. *Review of Educational Research, 52*(3), 421–445.

Willems, J. M. H. M. (1987). *Studietaken als instructiemiddel [Assignments as instructional tools].* Nijmegen, The Netherlands: K. U. Nijmegen, I. O. W. O.

Winne, P. H., & Marx, R. (1982). Students' and teachers' views of thinking processes for classroom learning. *The Elementary School Journal, 82*(5), 493–518.

Winne, P. H., & Marx, R. (1983). *Final report: Vol. 1. Students' cognitive processes while learning from teaching.* Burnaby, British Columbia: Simon Fraser University.

APPENDIX 1

Table 4.7
Loadings on Rotated Factors

	FACTOR 1	FACTOR 2	FACTOR 3	FACTOR 4
NETWORK1	0.70376	-0.11152	0.00263	0.14784
NETWORK3	0.67233	-0.24376	0.04766	0.06345
NETWORK5	0.65207	-0.22186	0.03859	0.03978
NETWORK2	0.62271	-0.11201	-0.02861	0.06719
INTERAC7	0.62199	0.10159	0.22923	-0.04105
INTERA12	0.61033	0.27773	0.10838	-0.04007
NETWORK4	0.57000	-0.13764	-0.00636	0.14229
INTERAC5	0.55932	-0.13401	0.05543	0.15402
INTERAC6	0.52555	0.09749	0.24674	0.02235
LBEHSAST	0.52260	-0.01547	-0.03786	0.00924
PREFTEAM	0.49318	0.10909	0.19553	-0.10585
INTERA11	0.47974	0.26362	0.07789	-0.02221
NETWORK6	0.45617	-0.28993	0.20803	0.11109
MOTCINT4	0.38683	0.09634	0.35209	-0.05191
INTERAC4	0.35718	0.23329	0.17012	0.11730
PREFPAPE	0.31509	-0.10207	-0.01856	0.04797
INTERA13	0.29004	0.23828	0.06778	0.06366
INTERAC9	0.21093	0.15516	0.04786	0.11174
PREFLECT	0.20706	0.09233	-0.04836	0.06241
ACCONLY1	-0.26530	0.17161	-0.26105	0.18097

Table 4.7—Continued

	FACTOR 1	FACTOR 2	FACTOR 3	FACTOR 4
PREFOWN	-0.31148	-0.06841	-0.19564	0.30379
MOTCINT2	-0.06224	0.56517	-0.09248	-0.08627
MOTCDIFF	-0.08179	0.55444	0.10369	0.04959
MOTDITE3	-0.10961	0.48976	0.09762	0.05022
INTERAC3	0.11157	0.47511	-0.15395	-0.08084
MOTDITE1	-0.03089	0.44007	0.03374	-0.08364
PREFCLAS	0.27902	0.42481	0.04817	-0.05402
MOTDITE2	0.07404	0.41443	0.11132	0.06866
PERTECH1	-0.15700	0.39325	0.03268	-0.05527
INTERAC1	0.06190	0.37772	-0.14913	-0.06374
MOTCPER2	-0.08660	0.36047	-0.11244	0.15204
INTERAC2	-0.00439	0.32458	0.00176	-0.00245
LBEHINM2	-0.00093	0.30146	-0.19092	0.21119
INTERAC8	0.17164	0.28197	0.17913	0.16873
ACCONLY2	0.02475	0.26845	0.07538	0.03601
LBEHINM3	0.22252	0.24955	-0.00750	0.18656
PERECO	0.09641	0.23798	0.11190	0.08854
PERTECH2	0.22324	-0.30020	-0.08376	0.20920
MOTCINT3	-0.00300	-0.31720	-0.08338	0.18036
ACCIMPR3	0.27721	-0.42490	0.35683	0.12668
ACCONLY5	-0.13560	-0.44372	0.27467	0.11285
MOTCPER1	0.20727	-0.50151	0.23116	0.09406

	FACTOR 1	FACTOR 2	FACTOR 3	FACTOR 4
ACCONLY3	-0.13710	0.05364	0.58415	-0.09195
ACCIMPR1	0.15761	-0.03811	0.54615	0.05649
ACCONLY4	-0.15623	-0.01173	0.54140	-0.04320
ACCIMPR2	0.19156	-0.16654	0.52347	0.11904
LBEHINM5	0.11066	0.02753	0.50355	0.07714
LBEHINM1	0.11646	0.09715	0.42794	-0.05596
ACCIMPR4	0.13063	-0.32836	0.40882	0.15926
LBEHINM4	0.11189	0.00971	0.37931	0.10066
PREFPRES	0.09847	0.18253	0.22870	0.14171
INTERA10	0.02028	0.05398	0.16060	0.12848
PREFTHEO	0.08197	0.08717	-0.09732	-0.02905
PREFSELP	0.13667	-0.00237	-0.03481	0.60775
LC5	-0.08884	-0.14471	-0.07015	0.57000
LC1	0.17204	0.07010	0.17450	0.53937
LC6	-0.05922	-0.09432	0.11054	0.53747
PREFSELA	-0.10739	-0.05657	0.03528	0.53588
LC3	0.16060	0.03361	0.11988	0.51016
LC2	0.06609	0.07322	0.17162	0.46438
PREFSTRU	0.08387	-0.04992	-0.08430	0.33835
LBEHINM6	-0.01653	0.31048	-0.04846	0.31602
LC4	0.21599	0.02507	0.23672	0.31318
PREFPRAC	0.12600	-0.00481	0.07242	0.20902

APPENDIX 2

Table 4.8
Overview of the Scales

Scales	Codes	Items	Cronbach α
1	network1	I would like to share information and ideas with people who have the same interests	0.855
	network3	I would like to work together on a problem-solving task with people from different countries.	
	network5	I would like to ask questions of people from all over the world.	
	network2	I would like to negotiate or discuss topics with people from different backgrounds.	
	interac7	I like to have the possibility of simultaneous interaction with the tutor and all the other students.	
	interal2	I like to have seminars where I can meet the other students on a regular basis.	
	network4	I would like to get feedback about my work from people all over the world.	
	interac5	I like to have contact with the tutor and other students via computer in order to exchange text-based messages.	
	interac6	I like to have contact with the tutor and other students via videoconferencing in order to exchange text, voice, and pictures.	
	lbehsast	I am willing to cooperate with other students in a learning situation.	

Scales	Codes	Items	Cronbach α
	prefteam	I like to learn in teams or small groups	
	interal 1	I like to have an introductory session to meet all the people involved before starting with the educational program.	
	network6	I would like to engage in simulation games with people from all over the world.	
	motcint4	I like to work with a computer in small groups.	
	interac4	I like to have contact with the tutor and other students via telephone in order to exchange verbal information.	
	prefown(-)	I like to learn on my own.	
2	motcint2	I prefer staying with traditional education methods.	0.763
	motcdiff	It takes a lot of energy to learn to use a computer.	
	motdite3	Technologies are very difficult to use.	
	interac3	There is an important lack of "natural" interaction in telematic environments since there is almost no face-to-face contact.	
	motdite1	Learning with telematics is very labor-intensive.	
	prefclas	I like a classroom setting.	
	motdite2	Learning with telematics requires a high level of educational competence.	

Table 4.8—Continued

Scales	Codes	Items	Cronbach α
	pertech1	The information presented by technologies is not of good quality.	
	interac1	In telematic environments, there is no good access to the tutor.	
	motcper2	If studying with a computer turns out to be too complex, I would like to have the opportunity to return to traditional education methods.	
	interac2	In telematic environments, small-group learning can become disorganized since there is no group leader or coordinator.	
	lbehinm2	Written or printed text is necessary in order for me to learn.	
	pertech2 (-)	Recent technologies allow a quick retrieval of information.	
	motcint3 (-)	I like to work on my own with a computer.	
	accimpr3 (-)	I think a computer can improve my learning.	
	acconly5 (-)	Studying only with a computer is acceptable to me.	
	motcper1 (-)	I would like to study with a computer, even if this is very complex.	
3	acconly3	Studying only with audio-cassettes is acceptable to me.	0.719
	accimpr1	I think audiocassettes can improve my learning.	
	acconly4	Studying only with video-cassettes is acceptable to me.	

Scales	Codes	Items	Cronbach α
	accimpr2	I think videocassettes can improve my learning.	
	lbehinm5	Audiovisual information is necessary in order for me to learn.	
	lbehinm1	Audio information is necessary in order for me to learn.	
	accimpr4	I think a CD-ROM can improve my learning.	
	lbehinm4	Pictorial information is necessary in order for me to learn.	
4	prefselp	I like to select part of my courses myself.	0.784
	lc5	Within a specific course, I prefer to choose when I want to study.	
	lc1	Within a specific course, I prefer to choose the specific topics to study.	
	lc6	I prefer to control the pace of a lesson.	
	prefsela	I like to select all of my courses myself.	
	lc3	Within a specific course, I prefer to define the sequence in which to study the information.	
	lc2	Within a specific course, I prefer to control the amount of information I want to study.	
	lc4	Within a specific course, I prefer to choose the mode of display of the information: pictures, sound, text, and so forth.	

CHAPTER 5

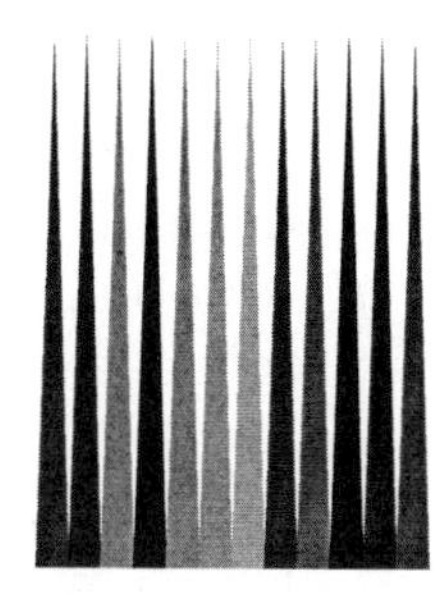

Educational Innovation and Information and Communication Technologies (ICT)

Revolution or Evolution?

Georges Van der Perre
European Union

THREE FUNDAMENTAL CHALLENGES

The Knowledge Society Creates a Need for Lifelong Learning

The rationale for lifelong learning is often presented in terms of the need for knowledge, because in the industrialized world of today knowledge has become the most important basic resource. Industrial and societal activity has become more and more knowledge based. More and more people need more and more knowledge in every phase of their lives. Our society is a knowledge society.

Moreover, we live in an ever-changing world. As a result of successive technological developments, the work environment changes continuously, as does our daily life. The wave of automation and computerization has not died yet, and the information superhighways, or information and communication technologies (ICT), are opening the virtual world of the Internet, multimedia, videoconferencing, and so forth. Teleworking, telebanking, teleshopping, telemedicine, and telelearning have become part of daily life.

Not only the direct environment of daily life but also the entire world is in continuous change. Global changes are affecting all of us. We are said to live in a "global village." In this "changing knowledge world," the ability to learn (in the broadest sense, implying the mental skills of flexibility and adaptability) is essential for the individual's functioning and well-being.

The "changing knowledge society" presents new demands for education. Probably there will be a shift from diploma-oriented education (limited to childhood and adolescence and compartmentalized into specific curricula for specific target groups) to modular, personal, needs-based lifelong learning for everybody. In this transition, ICT is expected to play an instrumental role. Exploiting the new ICT tools of the information society to respond to the new learning needs of the knowledge society is an important goal (Van der Perre, 1996).

However, is the development of society completely determined by global economic and political mechanisms to which individuals and communities can only submit or to which they must adapt? Is learning only related to this functional adaptation? Aren't people expected to build society? How about education? Doesn't education have to play an essential role in this building process?

Education in a Learning Society

Education has been defined as "the process by which a community preserves and transmits its physical and intellectual character" (Jaeger, 1946); "education ideally provides perspectives and tools for participating in society, for understanding society, and for shaping society" (Schuler, 1996).

But what if a community suffers an identity crisis, if society itself is in mutation? What if religions and ideologies—those spiritual and intellectual constructions and models that try to bring higher order into real-world chaos—are either collapsing or evolving into fundamentalism and obscurantism? What if traditional values are questioned (or even unmasked) and traditional walls are tumbling down? What if technology—ICT, as well as biotechnology—unceasingly confronts society with the dilemma of considering what is technically possible and what is ethically justified?

Society on the verge of a new millennium seems to be back to ground zero, in need of learning everything again from scratch. This is "constructive learning" in a new, very literal meaning: reconstructing our world by learning. We need to analyze carefully and critically, to evaluate and validate what has been acquired by tradition, while at the same time inventing and creating a new world and a new society. We need to find a new balance between nature and culture, between individual freedom and social responsibility.

How do children, youngsters, students, workers, and adults learn in a society that is itself in need of learning? How can the information society develop into a society of collaborative learning? How can we integrate lifelong learning by each single individual with worldwide learning by society, and how can we integrate professional-skills-oriented learning with sociocultural, life-oriented learning (Leirman, 1996, chap. 5, p. 147)? Can society rebuild itself through learning by and with youths?

Communication in the real sense of the word is the key: Only communication will allow cross-fertilization between generations and between cultures, between tradition and innovation. ICT has and will continue to have a strong impact on society. Will we be able to exploit its potential for reconstructing society through learning?

Learning: A Joy for Everybody?

Learning is supposed to be a fascinating "self-discovery" in the double sense of that term: that is, the autonomous discovery and construction of knowledge, as well as the discovery and deployment of one's own potential, skills, career, emotionality, and personality. Learning should be the fascinating discovery and construction of oneself, integrated with the fascinating discovery and construction of the world and society.

Yet learning is very often boring, threatening, or both for the privileged who have access to it, while remaining an unattainable dream for others. Can we make ICT, a dominant factor in our world today, an instrument to change this paradoxical situation? Is the "joy of learning" (European Lifelong Learning Initiative [ELLI], 1997) to become attainable for everybody? This is another fundamental—and not so new—question.

IMPLEMENTING ICT-BASED INNOVATION IN ESTABLISHED EDUCATION

The previous section outlined three broad, basic issues: the widely accepted lifelong learning paradigm, society in need of reconstructing itself through learning, and learning as an exciting process of self-discovery. The third issue includes two aspects: enhancing (or even creating) excitement, motivation, and efficiency for the privileged who have access to learning; and opening access for the have-nots. With these three basic issues in mind, let us focus on the question of ICT-based innovation in an established educational system, including the whole "educational chain" (European Round Table of Industrialists [ERT], Education Policy Group, 1995) from kindergarten to vocational training and higher education, with an extension to continuing education and adult learning.

Despite the need for drastic change that might seem apparent from considerations like those developed in the first section of this chapter and despite the huge potential for new ways of learning that appear to be offered by ICT (Dillemans, Lowyck, Van der Perre, Claeys, & Elen, 1998, Pt. I), there is one simple but hard basic rule: Handle with care! Implementing changes in education is like implementing changes in a software package or a railway schedule: Small improvements in one place can create disaster in all the rest. As explained by Elizabeth Wellburn in Chapter 3 of this book, real innovation in education first of all requires a holistic and systemic approach. She points out that it is important to realize that any educational innovation can lead to more pitfalls than benefits unless those involved have a grasp of the complete picture and act accordingly.

Keeping this basic principle in mind, one can yet adopt different philosophies and strategies for the implementation of ICT-based innovation in education. The following discussion covers the revolutionary versus the evolutionary philosophy on one hand, and the top-down versus the bottom-up strategy on the other hand (Dillemans et al., 1998, Pt. III).

The revolutionary philosophy starts from idealized models (blueprints) for the learning and education system of the future. The models are based on a rational analysis of the learning needs of society and the potential of ICT for learning in relation to these needs, as well as of the impact of ICT on society at large. The revolutionary philosophy aims at creating a new educational system through the implementation of these blueprints.

The evolutionary philosophy aims at implementing incremental changes that have an immediate added value for the existing educational system. The immediate improvements expected from these small steps are directly linked to clearly identified faults and weaknesses in the actual operation of the educational system rather than to its basic concepts and structures.

In the top-down strategy, the responsible authority on the macro level (government, national network of schools, etc.) or the intermediate level (a school, a university) designs, develops, and implements an innovation plan. The approach is not only systemic but also systematic, that is, characterized by a precise planning of the sequential phases and a clear assignment of tasks to all actors involved.

In the bottom-up strategy, the higher level (macro or intermediate) only describes a general framework, indicating sectors for potential innovation. Financial support from the higher level is given to selected projects submitted by actors in the field (Dillemans et al., 1998, Pt. III).

In principle, "philosophies" and "strategies" are mutually independent categories; for example, an evolutionary philosophy can be realized through a bottom-up, as well as a top-down strategy. But clearly, a revolutionary philosophy will require a large amount of top-down strategy, as the lower level does not have the necessary power to change the educational system in its basic concepts and structures. An evolutionary philosophy, on the other hand, seems to be naturally linked with a bottom-up strategy. Whereas the distinction between revolutionary and evolutionary philosophies seems to be a question of principle (and sometimes almost of ideology, as illustrated by ongoing public media debates, e.g., De Dijn, 1997), this is not the case for the implementation strategies: There is a continuous grey scale from bottom-up to top-down.

The next two sections focus on philosophies. For a detailed discussion of implementation strategies and scenarios, see a study recently published for the ERT (Dillemans et al., 1998, Pt. III). The following discussion first elaborates on the differences between the revolutionary and the evolutionary approaches and then proposes an "integrative revolutionary approach."

REVOLUTION VERSUS EVOLUTION: A QUESTION OF BELIEF

The term *philosophy* is not exaggerated in this context; it is almost even a question of belief. "Revolutionists" think in the long term and often in "final" terms. They have a strong belief in the system of the future, one that will involve a fundamental and irreversible change. They assume that they are able to design that future now, in the form of blueprints and scenarios, and develop comprehensive strategies to realize them. They risk being conservative and rigid in the long term when they try to fix all details of the future beforehand without openness to human factors, unforeseen responses and effects, and continuing change. Recent and less recent collapses of "new" or utopian societal models and political systems illustrate this risk.

"Evolutionists" think in the short term and in terms of continuous improvement. They do not believe that there will be such a thing as "a system of the future." Neither do they wish that such a thing will come about, because they highly value the assets of the established system, as it was built by years or centuries of careful and continuous improvement. De Dijn (1997) illustrates this vision by quoting the chief gardener of Buckingham Palace. The latter, when asked for the secret of the marvelous lawns, answered that it was very simple: First you sow the grass and then you water it on a daily basis for 500 years.

In the specific case of ICT-based innovation in education and learning, revolutionists start from an analysis of—or a belief in—the potential of ICT for "new ways" of learning, an awareness of new learning needs, and an awareness of the drastic impact of ICT upon present and future society. Evolutionists are very skeptical about this new potential, these new needs, and the impact of ICT. They warn against a "technology-driven" approach and state as a basic principle that any ICT innovation in learning should start from a clearly defined learner need and create a clear and concrete added value. The difference between the two philosophies lies not in whether they are oriented toward learner needs but in their interpretation of "clearly defined." In the language of evolutionists, "starting from a clearly defined learner need" means aiming at a precisely predictable solution for a well-defined problem or shortcoming of the established system in the context of today (not tomorrow). Typically, revolutionists will argue that hardly any invention or innovation would ever have been created if inventing had been strictly constrained to clearly formulated needs and predefined objectives. Furthermore, they will state that by introducing ICT incrementally into the established system without reengineering the system itself, one will never fully exploit its potential.

When faced with blueprints and scenarios of the future, evolutionists typically will confront the designers with this challenge: First show us good practice examples of what is already in place today, then we will evaluate and decide. This position can lead to a vicious circle, because drastic and large-scale innovation scenarios can only be implemented through policy decisions based upon consensus. Take the example of ICT-based international interuniversity joint-degree courses. They can only start if the participating universities (and even the associated governments) on a policy level have fully accredited these courses within their own programs, which implies that they have solved all questions of credit transfer and recognition.

But even the evolutionary approach, while it is meant to adapt and thus to stabilize the established system, might lead to a snowball effect and in the longer or shorter term "reengineer" the system itself through a spontaneous process of functional adaptation. For example, Internet-based student tutoring systems that were conceived to support students in a traditional lecture- and tutorial-based system in the longer term have led to a redefinition of the functions of lectures, problem-solving sessions, face-to-face tutoring, and Web-based learning (Van Petegem & Van der Perre, in press). An incremental implementation of ICT in education usually starts with the addition of a new learning application but often ends with the replacement of a traditional learning activity by the new one (Broere, 1998) and, as such, tends to reengineer the system in a bottom-up way.

PLEA FOR AN INTEGRATIVE REVOLUTIONARY APPROACH

The lifelong learning requirements that the knowledge society creates, the learning needs of society in need of reconstruction, and the need for "joyful self-discovery learning for everybody" are the three basic challenges we outlined in the first section. The "information society" offers new means for a positive response to these challenges, namely ICT. Hence, the question is how to design the educational system in such a way that it exploits optimally the new ICT tools in response to the new learning needs. This includes integrating these new tools with well-developed and proven traditional educational methods, that is, using an "integrative" approach. It is not really original and appears rather obvious, but the interesting question is whether this optimal integration will occur spontaneously or by a process of natural evolution, or whether it will require a conscious, firm, and systematic effort.

Nyiri (1997) seems to believe in a process that is largely spontaneous. According to him, throughout history education has structured itself according to functions of information and communication technologies:

> Educational institutions have at all times been formed by contemporary information technologies. The medieval university, in particular, is representative of the European manuscript culture of the 12th and 13th centuries, with its scarcity of books, and still markedly oral communication patterns. The students' university was . . . also a framework for collective learning and memorizing. . . . With the emergence of printing, and with books becoming abundant and relatively cheap by the mid-eighteenth century, individual reading supplanted collective memorizing. . . . The modern university is centered around the university library, in particular around the university library as an encyclopedic research library. . . . Now we all know that in the era of interactive, networked, multimedia communications the role of spaces, places and locations has of course greatly changed. In many respects physical presence has become unimportant. In many respects—but certainly not in all.

Nyiri's (1997) viewpoint can be questioned or amended through the observation that established education in our day is still largely characterized by oral communication patterns and passive memorization (European Round Table of Industrialists, Education Policy Group, 1995). A common joke nowadays supposes that a human being from a century ago comes back to earth. He or she feels very insecure, as everything has changed so drastically, and many things are completely new: traffic, airplanes, (cellular) telephones, television, computers, the Internet, comfort at home, the factories, music, discotheques. Only upon going back to the old school would this person feel at home again, knowing exactly where the pupils sit and the teacher stands, what the scenario is, and so forth.

Indeed, some of society's basic structures, such as the educational system and the court system, seem hardly affected by evolution in society, let alone evolution in technology. Is this because some essential keystones of society, such as education and justice, are bound (and should be) to unchanging, basic rules? Or is this the result of power mechanisms that keep these systems isolated from the evolution and needs of society? The educational and court systems occupy (and naturally protect) a power position in society, having the power to pass judgment on people and to decide on people's futures. Recent developments in the Belgian court and police systems illustrate how dangerous such a splendid isolation can be for society. These systems are undergoing major restructuring following the unfortunate outcomes and discoveries of the heinous pedophilia crimes that took place a few years ago. The example of the events in the court system in Belgium (and probably in other countries as well) should make us think very seriously and conscientiously about the educational system and its need for continuing innovation in response to society's needs.

Typical in the educational context is a statement by Virginia Ostendorf (1996). According to her, the new communication media, in combination with new learning methods, will make traditional universities obsolete in a very short time. The only barrier to be removed is the university monopoly in awarding degrees and diplomas: "universities keep the learner emprisoned by this monopoly."

Continuous evaluation, reflection, research, experimentation, and innovative implementation based upon an integrative revolutionary approach are a must and a duty for all those holding responsibility for education. Neither the adaptation to the changing needs of society nor the optimal integration of well-proven educational methods with the new ways of learning offered by ICT will come by themselves. These changes will require strong continued effort. To illustrate what this approach might lead to, following are some possible models for the educational system of the future.

WHAT IT MIGHT LOOK LIKE: BLUEPRINTS FOR THE FUTURE

A Blueprint for the School of the Future

Following is a generic blueprint that specifically applies to general secondary education preparation for higher education (ages 14 to 18; Dillemans et al., 1998, Pt. II). Mutatis mutandis, its essential components largely apply to the whole "educational chain," ranging from preschool through basic education, general secondary education and vocational training, to higher education in colleges and universities.

The school is a learning community, integrating three components in a harmonious and flexible way. The first component is a telematics- and multimedia-based "open learning center" (also open to part-time learners and adults). This component should provide learning material and access to Internet services meeting international standards.

The second component is a learning-project-based (curriculum-based) training and qualification center (including learner assessment and testing). This component should apply learning, evaluation, and testing schemes approved by national consensus and accredited by public authorities.

The third component is an organization that facilitates, supports, and coordinates the group activity of learners. This component should maximally develop self-orientation of the group and interaction with parents and the local community, as well as the international community of peer learners. It aims at the development of values, attitudes, and interpersonal skills through group activity involving not only class/teacher interaction but also group/leader (e.g., a 16+-year-old) and group/local-community (parents) interaction, especially through self-directed and self-oriented activity of the group itself. The activity is very diverse: projects, sports, discussions, participation in cultural events, artistic and creative activities, nature exploration, social exploration, survival-type challenges, and so forth.

In the school, the traditional teacher functions of content expert, tutor, and examiner might be split among the members of a team. Control of the school is located in a formal "school system" (government operated or controlled), awarding credits according to skills-based criteria and objective evaluation and testing. The schools develop in permanent interaction with the parents, the local community, the regional and international network (the latter through projects such as Web for Schools), public authorities, and industry. A balance must be sought among maintaining transparency, level, and quality of qualifications (meeting standards defined on a macro level);

self-determination by the group in interaction with the local community; and self-determination by the individual.

This schematic blueprint is only meant to inspire concrete models. Concrete elaborations of such models should take into account not only educational but also financial, management, organizational, technological, and logistical aspects. No monolithic model should be developed: There should be a variety of schools, adapted to regional needs and cultures.

The *Studiehuis* ([Learning House], 1997) project in the Netherlands is an excellent real-life example of such a concrete model. The Arthur Andersen School (Maeselle & Morton, 1990) is another interesting example, launched and supported by industry. A typical practical aspect of both models is that the time spent in the classroom is drastically reduced.

Real (and) Virtual Universities

The university's tasks and responsibilities

The schematic blueprint for the school of the future, as presented above, fully applies to higher education. However, this section does not elaborate on the specific application of this schematic blueprint to the case of the university; that is left to the imagination of the reader. This discussion focuses on the "virtual university concept," asking how far this concept will allow the universities to improve their learning service to society.

First let us try to identify the different target groups of university education in relation to the very particular demands from the knowledge society the universities as knowledge centers are facing. What was generally stated in the first section applies in particular to higher education: There will be an extension from degree-oriented education (limited in target group and time) to lifelong learning for wider target groups. The learning tasks and responsibilities of universities include the following target audiences: (1) the "regular" (graduate and undergraduate) students; (2) the graduates ("diploma with a service contract"); (3) industry and the different sectors of economic and social activity (learning on demand); (4) autonomous learners, part-time learners, alternating learners, and second-chance learners; and (5) society at large and particular societal target groups. For a discussion of the universities' tasks with respect to these target groups, see Van der Perre, Van den Branden, Van Heddegem, and De Witte (1994). Concerning the last target group, society at large, there is a need for reconstructing society by collaborative learning; universities, as centers of critical reflection and fundamental research, have the responsibility of playing a leading role in the societal debate on fundamental values; culture; and the social, ecological, economic, and political organization of the world. Research universities have—apart from learning, education, and training—a task of knowledge development and transfer, aiming at industrial development and the creation of employment for skilled people. With this checklist of responsibilities in mind, the next discussion looks at some present and future virtual university concepts.

Concepts of a virtual university

First of all, what is meant by a virtual university? There are at least two different concepts of a virtual university: the "online university" and the "distributed university." The online university is basically a Web site on the Internet. As a learner, you surf into it, get welcomed into the virtual university, get information on programs, conditions, and teachers; you can register, find courses and take part in them, consult libraries, participate in question-and-answer and problem-solving sessions, interact with peers and teachers, take tests and exams, and so forth. Such a virtual university can be run by one institution, a distance university or a regular university (such as the Colorado State University Online, for example), or jointly by several institutions (such as "Virtual-U" in Canada). It can also be run by completely new types of organizations, not at all related to established universities, as by a group of independent leading experts working in different places or by industry (the United Kingdom government initiative on a "Virtual University for Industry"). There are commercial firms building virtual universities for universities and organizations on demand.

The distributed university is a network of universities using not only the Internet (and, for example, a virtual university in the above-mentioned meaning) but also other ICT (like videoconferencing and computer conferencing) to integrate physical campuses into one common virtual campus. Universities use this joint virtual campus for some very specific learning activities, not for all activities. This is the model developed and deployed by the trans-European university network, EuroPACE 2000, together with its partners in the framework of the "Virtual University for Europe" project ([VirtUE]; Van den Branden, 1997).

The distributed virtual university

In the European context, while on the one hand each university should maintain its freedom and uniqueness, on the other hand a university is not a "stand-alone" institution but a node in and a gate to a trans-European and even a global network. The international dimension is essential for the university, because of the level of scientific expertise involved and the context in which the graduates will develop their professional careers. Three types of network functions can be distinguished (Van der Perre, 1995):

1. Virtual class and virtual campus (for "on-campus" students). A student who enrolls in a university automatically gains access to a European (global) virtual campus: to the lectures, seminars, and so forth, given at that campus (virtual classes) and to the professors, assistants, researchers, and students living at that campus (virtual campus). One concrete, existing example involves European graduate and Ph.D. programs: Students in an advanced course from five to ten universities participate in joint virtual seminars via ISDN videoconferencing and stay in permanent contact via computer conferencing (the model of EuroPACE 2000). Another example is provided by "virtual mobility" projects (various project proposals for the European Union's SOCRATES and Telematics Application Programme). Yet a third example is the use of videoconferencing to make lectures accessible at a remote campus, from a "mother" university to a remote college or from one country to another.

2. Network for open and distance learning (for "off-campus" students). Here the emphasis is on taking the learning to the learner instead of vice versa—to homes, companies, and regional study centers—for the target audiences of open university, continuing education, and postgraduate programs. Conventionally, one has the traditional "open university" model in mind; that is, taking education from one institution to many sites. The virtual university network adds a new dimension: It allows taking the learning (education, training) from many institutions to many sites.

   This dimension has been exploited recently by EuroPACE 2000 (a trans-European network of universities, companies, and training organizations). An interesting large-scale pilot is currently taking place in Flanders, where EuroPACE 2000, together with Flemish universities and industry, is running videoconferencing and Internet-based interuniversity master's-level programs for updating professional engineers in informatics and advanced telecommunications (Ketels, 1998). In a second phase, which is now in preparation, these courses will be extended to a continental scale and, for example, offered in some countries of Central and Eastern Europe. Working in a European network creates obvious economies of scale and allows the provision of access to top-level expertise.

3. Network for on-demand learning. In a trans-European network of 50 universities, research centers, companies, and training institutions such as EuroPACE 2000, top-level knowledge in all areas of science is available (especially taking into account the fact that each of the nodes has its own network of contacts). Theoretically, any demand for knowledge or learning (coming from a company, a sector, a region, etc.) can be answered from the network. The big challenge is how to establish the network organizationally, logistically, technically, and so forth, so as to enable it to fulfill this function effectively.

An integrated multimodal university

Some find the two definitions of a virtual university too conservative, because they are too much under the control of established institutions. As stated previously, according to these critics, the new communication media, in combination with new learning methods, will soon make traditional universities obsolete. Learners will shop for learning in a global virtual university offered on the Internet and through other communication media and compose their learning programs autonomously. The only barrier is the university monopoly in awarding degrees and diplomas (Ostendorf, 1996). On-demand learning will be financed by giving every student leaving secondary education an "education voucher" allowing that person to learn three or four years "à la carte." With this voucher, learners can optimally adapt their learning to their professional and human development goals, for example, by taking two years of general higher education first, starting professional activity, and spending the remaining learning credit for professional-development-focused learning (Delors, 1997).

Other commentators plead for the traditional residential university where students spend four or more years. During a crucial moment in their lives, a large group of young people come to the university after they have acquired a certain degree of autonomy (and the ability to loosen the strong ties with their family) and before they bind themselves again to a family and a job. This period of *scholé*, literally "free time," is of enormous importance not only for the individual student but also for society. At the university, students familiarize themselves with the various science-based disciplines and practices that are relevant for society and culture, and they are able to do this "from the inside." "They acquire this familiarity by the contact with those who are the masters in these disciplines and practices and devote their lives to the development of the latter" (De Dijn, 1997). Furthermore, De Dijn emphasizes the importance of an open intellectual environment; of learning to deal with different backgrounds and cultures; discussing with peers, professors, and others; and acquiring intellectual responsibility, as well as modesty.

As the reader could predict, this author pleads for a differentiated and integrated approach. We must design and develop a university of the future that improves on its traditional role and at the same time responds to new learning needs, both by making smart use of the potential of ICT. A multimodal university will combine "real university" approaches with "virtual university" developments and respond to a wide variety of learner needs. In various fora and through various studies (for example, CRE 1998), European universities nowadays exchange ideas and experiences that have to do with the ways they are restructuring themselves in view of present challenges.

CONCLUSION

This chapter began with a reflection on three basic challenges: the need for lifelong learning resulting from the knowledge society, society in need of reconstructing itself through learning, and the joy of learning by self-discovery. How can ICT-based innovations be implemented in established education to respond better to these needs? After a discussion of a revolutionary versus an evolutionary philosophy, this author pleaded for an integrative revolutionary approach. The main argument in favor of this approach is that education as a pillar of society has a duty to question itself constantly in view of the changing needs of society and the rapidly developing potential of technology. Education should constantly and actively fight the natural tendency of powerful societal institutions to become self-contained and self-sufficient.

Attempts at such an integrative revolutionary approach have been illustrated in this chapter through blueprints for the school and the (virtual) university of the future. Are these the models through which society will be able to meet the three basic challenges this chapter started with? The answer remains to be seen.

The second challenge, society in need of reconstructing itself through learning, in particular still needs a great deal of vision to be developed. I hope this chapter sets some creative people to thinking.

REFERENCES

Broere, W. (1998). Rules of thumb for evolutionary implementation: The Print/Comenius project. In R. Dillemans, J. Lowyck, G. Van der Perre, C. Claeys, & J. Elen (Eds.), *New technologies for learning: Contribution of ICT to innovation in education* (pp. 215–223). Leuven, Belgium: Leuven University Press.

CRE (Conférence des Recteurs Européens). (1998, April). *Restructuring the university: New technologies for teaching and learning—Guidance to universities on strategy* (CRE guide no.1).Geneva: Author.

De Dijn, H. (1997, July 16). De universiteit is breed [The university is broad]. *Knack Magazine*, 35–36.

Delors, J. (1997). *Learning: The treasure within—report to UNESCO of the International Commission.* Lanham, MD: Bernan Associates.

Dillemans, R., Lowyck, J., Van der Perre, G., Claeys, C., & Elen, J. (1998). *New technologies for learning: Contribution of ICT to innovation in education: Part I. Knowledge base on ICT, learning and education; Part II. What will it look like: ICT and the educational systems of the future; Part III. Implementation scenarios.* Leuven, Belgium: Leuven University Press.

European Lifelong Learning Initiative (ELLI). (1997, July). *The joy of learning: Proceedings of the ELLI Conference.* Helsinki: Author.

European Round Table of Industrialists (ERT), Education Policy Group. (1995). *Education for Europeans: Towards the learning society.* Brussels: Author.

Jaeger, W. (1946). *Paideia: The ideals of Greek culture.* Oxford: Basil Blackwell.

Ketels, M. (1998, June). Bridging companies and universities for postgraduate training: Two large scale case studies. *Proceedings of the Annual EDEN Conference, Bologna*, 62–64.

Leirman, W. (1996). *Four cultures of education.* Detroit: Michigan Ethnic Heritage Center.

Maeselle, R., & Morton, E. (1990). *A new system of education: World class and customer focused.* Chicago: Arthur Andersen.

Nyiri, J. C. (1997). Open and distance learning in an historical perspective. *European Journal of Education, 32*(4), 347–357. (Carfax Publishing Limited, PO Box 25, Abingdon, Oxfordshire OX14 3UE, United Kingdom.)

Ostendorf, V. (1996, June). The future of distance learning. Oral communication at TeleCon Europe, Rome, Italy.

Schuler, D. (1996). *New community networks, wired for change.* New York/Reading, MA: ACM Press/Addison-Wesley.

Studiehuis (Learning House) [Online]. (1997). Available: http://www.aps.nl/vo/studhuis/studhuis.htm. (Accessed March 18, 1999).

Van den Branden, J. (1997, June). A virtual university for Europe. *Proceedings of the Annual EDEN conference, Budapest,* 189–192.

Van der Perre, G. (1995). Telematics and the European University of the future. In P. Held & W. F. Kugemann (Eds.), *Telematics for education and training: Proceedings of the Telematics for Education and Training Conference* (pp. 165–168). Amsterdam: IOS Press.

Van der Perre, G. (1996, October–November). Higher education: Matching the needs of the knowledge society with the tools of the information society. Paper presented at the colloquium "People First: Living and Working in the Information Society" of the European Commission DG V, Dublin.

Van der Perre, G., Van den Branden, J., Van Heddegem, J., & De Witte, K. (1994). Continuing education and training: Response from higher education. In *Contribution to innovation in continuing education and training* (COMETT-evaluation report, DGXXII). Brussels: European Commission.

Van Petegem, W., & Van der Perre, G. (in press). Web based learning: Engineering mechanics for undergraduate students. *Proceedings of the Annual SEFI-Conference, July 1998, Helsinki.*

CHAPTER 6

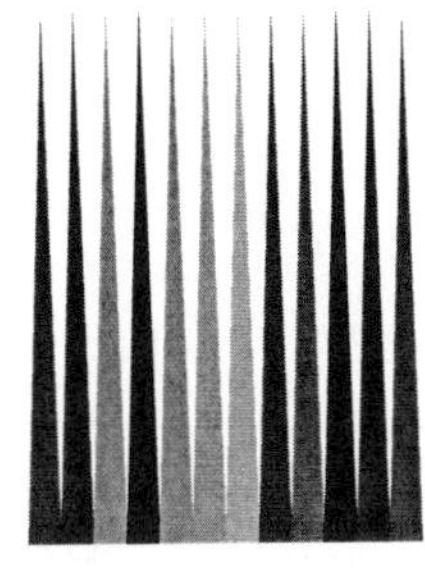

Bridging the Gap or Keeping the Distance

Videoconferencing in Education and Training

Sally Reynolds and Han Fraeters
European Union

INTRODUCTION

This chapter deals with some of the issues surrounding the effective use of videoconferencing in education and training, drawing specifically upon the experience and findings of the SAVIE (Support Action to facilitate the use of Videoconferencing In Education) initiative, a European Commission-sponsored project that is producing training and information resources to help teachers and trainers begin to use videoconferencing in a pedagogical context. This initiative began in September 1996 and produced its first outcomes, including training modules for teachers and trainers in the effective use of videoconferencing for teaching, in September 1997. Some of the guidelines and recommendations from this initiative are presented later in the chapter.

THE CONTEXT

Videoconferencing technology has taken some time finding its place in the educational and training environment in Europe, although it has been around for quite a while. As early as 1990 many of the more technically advanced universities and educational institutions were starting to experiment with videoconferencing based on 2-mbit fixed lines; telecommunications companies had begun to install these lines in response to demand from business people wishing to use videoconferencing for meetings. University College Dublin was one of these first pioneers, with its STAR project, a series of lectures delivered from studios in Dublin from 1990 to 1992 to students in the Regional Technical College in Letterkenny, Donegal, in the northwest of Ireland. Throughout Europe, universities, in particular those with distributed campuses, recognized the contribution such technology could make in helping them stretch their dwindling budgets by saving on travel and other costs. Personnel from university and college administrations, along with their colleagues in the business world, were also quick to recognize that meeting virtually could help them work more effectively and efficiently.

However, it is true that Europeans have been slower to catch on to using videoconferencing in education and training than North Americans and Australians. Many reasons can be given for this, such as a general reluctance to use other forms of technology-supported learning systems, such as those based on satellite and radio; the relatively high costs of networks in Europe; and suspicions about the effectiveness of this kind of learning.

The European Commission was quick to support some of the early initiatives; then in the Telematics Applications Programme, it specifically funded a number of pilot projects and studies that utilized videoconferencing and other types of audiovisual communications in educational and training settings. For example, the Multimedia TeleSchool project, managed by Berlitz European Projects in Frankfurt and partially funded under the Telematics for Flexible and Distance Learning Programme (1990–1994), provided telematics-supported courses in language learning and various other topics to learners at their workplaces in nine different European countries (*DELTA catalogue*, 1994). For this initiative, a variety of technologies were used for teaching courses at a distance, including interactive television, where material was distributed via satellite, and ISDN-based videoconferencing. A number of other channels were then used for interaction with remote sites.

In 1995, The European Open University Network, partially funded by Directorates XII, XIII, and XXII of the European Commission and managed by the European Association of Distance Teaching Universities in Heerlen, The Netherlands, broadcast courses in environmental awareness, basic statistics, and information technology, again using a variety of means, including interactive television with videoconferencing return, point-to-point, and multipoint videoconferencing. These courses were primarily aimed at the EADTU's network of EuroStudy Centres located throughout Europe (Patel, 1996).

There were many such projects, initiatives, and developments in Europe during the early 1990s within regional, national, and cross-border scenarios. For further examples, see Carpio and Ramos (1995).

CURRENT POSITION

Videoconferencing in Europe has now become primarily associated with the ISDN network, which has become part of the standard telecommunications service offered in most parts of Central and Western Europe. Although there are also some interesting examples of videoconferencing pilots in the educational and training world in which the signal is sent via satellite networks (promoted and encouraged by the European Space Agency, among others), it is still true to say that, in Europe at least, when people talk about videoconferencing, they usually mean videoconferencing via ISDN. There has been a massive upsurge in the number of systems available in educational and training environments in the past two years. Such is the demand that institutions that have bought single systems for experimental purposes are now increasingly finding themselves having to establish regular operational services to support videoconferencing among their staff. It is interesting to note how videoconferencing equipment, usually housed initially in the learning development department or audiovisual center, is turning up more and more as part of the normal department infrastructure, in much the same way as a language laboratory is part of a language department. Videoconferencing equipment is being used to support the teaching of a wide range of subjects in Europe in a variety of configurations, whether the systems employed are desktop, rollabouts, or portables.

CURRENT ISSUES

As with any new teaching technology, videoconferencing has its supporters and opponents. Many questions remain unanswered about its effectiveness in a pedagogical setting, despite ongoing research. For a comprehensive overview of these issues, see Fox (1995).

One of the regularly asked questions in our experience is, "How does the use of such technology change the role of the teacher?" The obvious answer is that it clearly effects a change; a keypad is different from a piece of chalk, and a television monitor is very different from a live audience. However, these changes imply only practical adaptations and alterations and do not affect the nature of the various roles a teacher assumes when delivering a class. Neither do they affect the teaching activities that can be carried out. It is simply necessary to take into account the limitations, demands, and possibilities inherent in the use of videoconferencing. Later in this chapter we return to this specific point.

Once the factors just mentioned are taken into account, videoconferencing is suited to every kind of teaching: lecturing, demonstrating, interacting, and so forth. Pedagogical objectives are set by the teacher or the governing institution, irrespective of the way the classes will be delivered. If lecturing is considered to be the most appropriate means, it can be used quite effectively over a videoconference link. While it is true to say that the effectiveness of lecturing is seriously questioned by many people in the field of technology-supported distance education, we argue that this is a debate about the validity of lecturing as a teaching methodology, rather than a debate about the feasibility of lecturing via videoconferencing.

What about the effectiveness of using videoconferencing to teach all subjects? This question should be viewed in the context of whether there is really an alternative. If a class has a choice between having a teacher in the classroom in person, as opposed to at a distance using videoconferencing, it is fair to say that the class will normally opt for the traditional model. However, it is also true to say that teachers using videoconferencing often have to be somewhat more inventive and have to plan their courses more effectively, a factor that can result in some course attendees preferring the remote option.

But what if there is no other option, or none at least that allows for real-time simultaneous audio/video? Experience shows that there are few subjects that cannot be taught by videoconferencing, although those familiar with the limitations of the technology will have realized that highly practical subjects can be quite challenging. Those wishing to teach cookery or car mechanics will need to be particularly ingenious in finding ways to overcome some of the inherent barriers associated with teaching via videoconferencing. Language teaching is a particularly contentious issue, with many people arguing that videoconferencing can have little place in courses aimed at people wishing to increase their language skills. We disagree; and indeed, taken in the overall distance learning context, there is much that the effective use of videoconferencing can do to enhance the learning experience when compared to more traditional distance learning methods. Both bandwidth and the way the equipment is set up and operated can greatly enhance the technology's contribution; again, as with all subjects, competent and experienced language teachers generally find ways to overcome the limitations of the equipment.

Another issue is whether teachers should have continuous access to and support from a technician during videoconferencing sessions. While most institutions will build this in initially, the usual experience is that after some time, teachers usually manage well, independent of such support, apart from maintenance and system breakdown support. Should teachers be expected to handle the various interfaces, manage their classrooms (local and remote), and teach, all at one and the same time? We feel that the answer to this lies in the amount of training and orientation an institution is willing to provide and, furthermore, insist upon in the first place. Teachers should control the various tools at their disposal in a classroom, for only then can they guide and manage the session in the way that they wish and according to the pedagogical guidelines they want to follow. Videoconferencing equipment is usually designed for one-person operation and is generally fairly easy to master, provided adequate time and support are given to those wishing to use it.

When it comes to the general availability of videoconferencing for teaching purposes in Europe, one of the factors that affects its eventual adoption in an institution is how that institution plans the process. A constantly recurring theme is the resistance within the teaching profession; therefore, it is worth considering some of the factors that seem to be causing this resistance in Europe today. One of the very clear factors is the lack of available training and access to experienced personnel. Teachers are expected to use the equipment without sufficient time to become familiar with it, in which case they often experience failure early on; it is then very difficult to convince them that such technology can indeed be very effective. Another factor is that very often in the budget-conscious educational environment of today, an institution will be introducing videoconferencing as a teaching method in an effort to reduce costs. Perhaps administrators wish to increase the number of students accessing a particular course or to cut down on the costs of travel and time away from work associated with tutors and trainers having to travel from one training center to another. In this case, imposing videoconferencing on teaching personnel frequently meets with failure unless adequate steps have been taken to ensure that compensation of one kind or another is provided and that decisions regarding implementation are made in cooperation with teaching staff in a carefully planned and timely fashion.

Buying the right equipment for the intended purpose is an additional factor affecting the chances of successful adaptation. In our experience, institutions frequently decide to "try out" videoconferencing by buying and installing a small desktop system suitable for one- or two-person use and then expecting it to do the job of a room-based, "rollabout" system. Again, after a succession of predictable failures, people lose their enthusiasm, and the system (and moreover the idea of videoconferencing itself) is consigned to the garbage can of great ideas that didn't work.

So just how much training do teachers or users need before they can be described as being competent? As always, this depends to a certain extent on individual expectations and skills. We feel that adequate time for familiarizing oneself with the equipment, along with appropriate guidelines, and if possible the help and support of an experienced teacher along the lines of a one- or two-day in-house course, will usually be enough to get teachers over the first couple of hurdles. They will then normally acquire sufficient confidence to start using the equipment; the rest is often up to experience as they discover what does and does not work in their own particular teaching situations. The range of publicly available options for providing training and orientation to the teaching professionals who are expected to use these systems is not very extensive, however, and is one of the reasons why the SAVIE project was initiated.

THE SAVIE INITIATIVE

The SAVIE initiative was proposed for funding to the European Commission's *Telematics Applications Programme—Education and Training* sector by the Audiovisual Department (AVD) of the Katholieke Universiteit (Catholic University) in Leuven, Belgium, with its partners from the Lifelong Learning Institute Dipoli, Helsinki University of Technology (HUT), Finland, in January 1996. The promoters of the proposal, AVD and HUT, had been active in the use of interactive television and videoconferencing in education and training for many years, including many of the earlier European Commission-supported activities within the education and training sector. Furthermore, both have also been leading institutions in the use of advanced learning technologies in their own institutional and national contexts.

In addition to their long history in video production, AVD's particular experience includes their involvement in

- the MTS project of the DELTA program, 1992–1994,
- the Humanities Project (initiated and managed by the Coimbra Group of European Universities, 1995–1997),
- the EOUN (European Open University Network) in the "Joint Call" projects during 1995,

as well as their extensive experience in both using and teaching others to use videoconferencing in an educational and learning environment. AVD has also conducted a number of online videoconferencing training sessions with remote study centers in Ireland, Switzerland, Germany, France, Spain, and Austria, where staff in these centers were trained remotely in the effective use of videoconferencing for educational purposes (Vanbuel, 1995).

HUT has been active in videoconferencing since 1989 and has used this technology in various national and international educational projects, for example, DISKO, MTS, and TELESCOPIA (Salkunen, 1996). HUT produced two different courses in 1994–1995 that were delivered by various cable television operators around Finland to 360,000–550,000 households. For this program, the HUT Center for Educational Technology (CET) developed a study guide for learners, a house-style guide for the lecturers and tutors, and a certification mechanism in conjunction with the relevant HUT departments offering the course for credit. These materials are used for different distance education purposes with videoconferencing, tutoring, and question and answer sessions. Currently, HUT CET manages a directory of various videoconferencing sites throughout the world, primarily dedicated to educational and training purposes.* This directory forms part of the Web-based information resource included in the SAVIE initiative.

*See http://www.savie.com.

The SAVIE initiative was also supported by a number of partners with an interest in the field. These included Videra Oy, the Finnish videoconferencing equipment supplier; EuroPACE 2000, the network of European universities and research institutions; IOS Press (the educational publisher); and Alcatel Bell. These partners provided vital links for the partnership to a range of key markets and resources. The initiative began in September 1996 and continued until August 1997, by which time the first two training modules had become available in French, English, and Dutch language versions.

The first training module, called the stand-alone module, consists of an easy-to-follow handbook packed with sound advice and ideas, as well as a 40-minute videotape. It represents about four hours of self-study and is aimed at people who have little or no experience in using videoconferencing in a teaching and learning environment. The handbook describes issues that teachers need to take into consideration when they start to use videoconferencing; it offers advice on how to plan individual lessons and on how to lead, steer, and manage a videoconferencing session; and it gives plenty of good advice about practical matters, such as setting up the conference room, preparation of audiovisual support materials, and general use of equipment. The accompanying lively videotape includes a wealth of examples and illustrates many of the points made in the handbook.

The second module, the teletutored module, includes a handbook, a 25-minute video, and participation in two 90-minute hands-on training sessions via videoconferencing. This module is aimed at small groups (approximately eight participants) of newcomers to videoconferencing, particularly those who lack in-house expertise. An experienced tutor, who tailors each session to suit the group's needs, leads these two hands-on videoconferencing training sessions. This training module represents about eight hours of instruction/self-study.

Both are introductory courses, supported by an extensive information resource on the World Wide Web.* This Web site provides information about teaching and learning in the videoconferencing environment, links to other sites, and the

*See http://www.savie.com.

opportunity to register institutions using videoconferencing for educational and training purposes in the videoconferencing directory, which provides a service to those interested in making contacts and linking with other institutions through this medium.

Additional language versions have been planned and are still under negotiation. The tutoring network is managed by the AVD, who work with the support and cooperation of a number of educational and training institutions in Europe. These institutions provide tutors who are trained and available, which allows people who have decided to use the teletutored version of the training course to choose from a list of possible tutors in various European countries and with a variety of teaching backgrounds. The tutoring network has been designed with maximum flexibility in mind; participants taking the teletutored version of the training course can decide on a tutor with a similar background and who speaks their language. In addition, they can also decide together on a time suitable for the participants.

The first beta versions of these training packages have already been tested with over 70 typical users in Belgium, the United Kingdom, the Netherlands, France, and Finland, and the response has been positive. It seems that teachers and trainers are becoming aware of the need to acquire familiarity with the technology before they start using it themselves and that a flexible training program designed and run by experienced users who are first and foremost teachers themselves can help them to achieve that goal. It is important that the approach remain flexible, and from the outset it must allow for a great deal of hands-on experience in using the technology.

WHY THE SUPPORT OF THE EUROPEAN COMMISSION?

The European Commission supported the SAVIE initiative primarily because of the glaring need for such training in Europe. While pockets of expertise certainly exist in various European countries, thus far there has been no Europe-wide initiative that takes into account the diversity and complexity of the European training and educational environment. Training packages do exist, which originate usually in North America or Australia; however, these often do not "translate" well, relating as they do specifically to non-European situations.

European institutions are now investing in equipment, and recent figures certainly show a dramatic increase in the number of videoconferencing systems being purchased in Europe; but little or no thought is being given, or budget being allocated, to the training of the users of these systems, with many people depending on the manufacturers' manuals for ideas and suggestions (Fraeters, Reynolds, & Vanbuel, 1997). While these certainly help, they are a poor substitute for the support of an experienced tutor and appropriate, attractive course materials specifically designed with the teacher in mind.

JUST ANOTHER TEACHING TOOL: THE SAVIE APPROACH

Undoubtedly, when teachers are first confronted with the possibility of using videoconferencing equipment, they have been made familiar with the advantages such equipment brings. This is most likely to have been by the person who decided to invest in the equipment and who has decided that she or he—the teacher, not the buyer—wishes in the near future to be a living example of the instructor of the future. Unlike the "ordinary" teacher of the past, this type of teacher will not tend to lecture or discuss but will provide knowledge and trigger interaction. The distance learning teacher will finally be able to look over the shoulder of each student in the process of performing tasks.

The limitations of the technology, however, are rarely mentioned at that critical time when the teaching staff, often quite reluctant to exchange their familiar classroom for the new distance learning classroom, have to be persuaded to do so. This is, in fact, the point at which training should begin. Many properties inherent in videoconferencing technology do create terrific opportunities, but others contain unexpected limitations. A newcomer to any unfamiliar teaching tool, be it the overhead projector, the language laboratory, or videoconferencing equipment, has to learn what works and what doesn't. Otherwise, that person's class will fail.

Generally speaking, there is nothing for the neophyte to worry about. In the first place, from a technological point of view, it is not any more difficult to use a videoconferencing facility than it is to operate the average videorecorder with programming functions. Second, delivering a class over a videoconference link does not require any change in teaching habits. The only important—and concrete—issue is how to adapt classes to this medium. How should a lecture or discussion be adapted in such a way that what was intended to be communicated is not lost somewhere on the rough journey between "here" and "there?"

BEGINNING AT THE BEGINNING: THE TECHNOLOGY

What a teacher needs to know about videoconferencing technology can be summarized in a few lines. Knowing less than this would not be sufficient, while knowing more is for those who are really interested. Such additional knowledge contributes toward better understanding of the complexities of the tool, but it is not necessary to teaching more effectively. The only purpose of explaining how technology works is to make teachers realize what the limitations of this technology are.

Videoconferencing Technology: Six Things a Teacher Should Know

1. Videoconferencing is two-way audio and video over a telephone line.

2. Ordinary telephone lines do not suffice because they do not have enough capacity; therefore, digital lines are used.

3. Even then, moving images contain too much information to be sent over such a digital telephone line (one second equals approximately 5,000 pages of text).

4. That is why audio and video signals are compressed.

5. But compression means that a substantial part of the audiovisual information is sacrificed.

6. This operation causes two main inconveniences: Compression takes time, and image as well as sound quality suffer to some extent.

Poor image quality and delays are the inconveniences encountered when working with videoconferencing over ISDN. Movements appear jerky, clothing with complex patterns (e.g., blue-red checked shirts) becomes fuzzy, and whatever is said takes around half a second to reach its destination. A teacher should be aware of these factors and at the same time remember that what the far end sees of him or her appears in most cases on a rather small rectangular television screen.

Removing the symptoms appears to be the first and most obvious way to deal with these inconveniences. If movements appear jerky, the teacher should try not to move too much. If blue-red checked shirts appear fuzzy, the teacher shouldn't wear them. And if there's a delay on the line, the teacher should speak continuously until finished with what she or he wanted to say.

There is more to it than that. Having to sit quietly for two hours, peering intently at a monitor with bad picture quality, is a tiring business; talking for two hours in front of a camera while using a keypad, wondering if the message is getting across in the way it is intended, is at least as tiring. Moreover, first-time users often experience the medium as "cold," and it can get colder if the members of the audience, not used to seeing themselves on a television screen, become shy and inhibited. Dealing with this kind of inconvenience is a somewhat more difficult task, because it will have to be anticipated when preparing the lesson. Variation is the key word: Dividing up the lesson program, including an icebreaker, building in breaks, delegating activities, and so forth become crucial.

Another key word is *visualization*. Unfortunately, because of compression, much subtle body language is thrown away. A frown or a twitching corner of the mouth may not reach the other end, which makes it harder for the audience to understand what is being said. Compensating for this loss of body language, simultaneously paraphrasing and visualizing the message, can help a great deal.

ACQUIRING CONFIDENCE: THE EQUIPMENT

Rare are the teachers who are willing to teach without having any prior experience with the system. Acquiring this experience entails learning how to set up the equipment, becoming able to evaluate the classroom, and, above all, familiarizing oneself with the operator interface. Every interface, be it menu-driven (as is the case for all desktop systems and a minority of the rollabout systems) or in the shape of a keypad, can be divided into four main sections, according to the four types of typical operations regularly performed:

- establishing the link (see items 1 and 9 in the list below)
- controlling the various video sources (see items 2–4 in the list below)
- controlling audio (see items 5 and 6 below)
- controlling the camera (see items 7 and 8 below).

Identifying these sections is the first step, while the second is practicing the particular functions needed to deliver a class.

Nine Operations a Teacher Should Master

1. Dial the telephone number of the other site.

2. Select the source you want your images to come from (main camera, document camera, video player, etc.).

3. Preview the image of the selected source for yourself, without sending the image to the other site.

4. Send the image of the selected source.

5. Control the volume.

6. Mute the microphone.

7. Make shots.

8. Store the most frequently used shots in memory.

9. Break off the connection.

Special attention should be paid to the camera controls. To make a transparent shot—that is, a shot that does not draw attention to itself—a basic knowledge of film language is required. To store functional camera presets, a basic understanding of the distance learning classroom is needed.

THE KEY TO SUCCESS: PLANNING

As already mentioned, teaching by videoconferencing does not require a change in one's teaching habits. However, for most people it does require a drastic alteration in preparation habits.

Drastic Change Demands Profound and Sincere Motivation

"Drastic change" basically consists of regaining the habit, probably lost a long time ago, of going step by step through the different stages in the preparation process of a class. Experience shows that relying too much on an intuitive method of preparing lessons causes newcomers to the technology to either simply "deliver content," thus neglecting the need for variation and visualization, or to forget about the content, while "directing" activities.

1. While a teaching session is being conducted, the equipment has to be operated, the learners have to be kept involved, and all the audiovisual support material has to be transmitted at the right moment. There will probably be little time left to improvise the content on the spot.

2. Because system administrators tend to be strict people, good timing is very important. Timing issues should be agreed upon while preparing a lesson.

3. Variation and visualization strategies have to be included in the plan.

4. Inevitably, extensive practical organization comes with the territory of teaching by videoconferencing. A planning guide, neatly set out on paper, will give sufficient notice of the arrangements to be made.

The Seven Stages of Planning on Paper

1. Split up content into subgoals.

2. Assign appropriate time to subgoals.

3. Match activities with subgoals and timing.

4. Match (visual) support material with activities.

5. Evaluate the lesson plan: View the film of your lesson in your mind's eye.

6. Finalize timing.

7. Foresee a contingency plan, in case of technical failure.

After planning on paper, the organizational wheels have to be put into operation. Support material has to be designed according to specific guidelines, and agreements have to be made with the system administrators at both ends.

THE FOUR ROLES: PRESENTATION TECHNIQUES

The first video lesson is often daunting and will probably be viewed as the worst from the newcomer's point of view. Becoming familiar with the camera, chairing discussions by way of a television screen, and getting shy learners to talk freely are skills some people will master more quickly than others, but they can only become second nature through practice, which a teacher simply cannot have before the first session.

Success depends to a great extent on the attitude of the teachers—being relaxed, not trying to do more than the medium can handle, accepting the slowness of the medium—and on the extent to which they are aware of the different roles the audience expects them to fulfill. The terminology is borrowed from television, which gives us the opportunity to state that this should be the only similarity between the two media.

The Four Roles a Teacher Should Assume

1. Commentator: Behave as a football commentator. Always announce what the audience is already seeing.

2. Presenter: Behave as the anchorperson of the news. Speak clearly, and be the binding agent.

3. Moderator: Make the learners participate, chair discussions, or assign chairpersons, and treat all sites equally.

4. Director: Stick to the presets as much as possible, and direct as little as possible.

Using videoconferencing for the first time to teach can be daunting for any teacher; the remoteness, the gadgets, the general feeling of not being in control can contribute to nervousness. From the learners' point of view, the whole business of staring at a screen for a long period of time can be exhausting and, frankly, off-putting. But on the positive side, the possibilities opened up by this technology in terms of access and flexibility are very exciting, assisting teachers in finding ways to adapt their teaching styles so that they can take account of the limitations while emphasizing the wonderful potential of videoconferencing. This is fundamentally what lies behind the SAVIE approach.

Additional SAVIE training modules are planned and under early development, including a training course in the effective management of multipoint videoconferences and another specifically dealing with desktop videoconferencing.

FUTURE TRENDS

Videoconferencing as a way of teaching and learning is here to stay. The technology and supporting infrastructure, networks, and so forth will certainly improve and change some of the ways we use this technology. In the meantime, it is difficult to imagine how, once we have gotten used to the possibility of overcoming distance in this way, we would willingly go back to face-to-face as the only teaching option. Factors influencing the increased availability of videoconferencing are the technology itself, the increasing experience being gathered among members of the teaching profession, and the continuous drive to find ways to make learning more available to the community as a whole.

Furthermore, there has been rapid expansion in the acceptability of various standards relating to videoconferencing; more and more truly collaborative learning and working is being made possible by the increased availability of desktop videoconferencing that adheres to common standards like T120 (a speed class of information transfer). The desktop videoconferencing capability is now becoming standard in many computers, making videoconferencing an everyday activity for many people in their normal working lives. In addition, standards relating to the use of videoconferencing over the Internet, intranet, and Ethernet are contributing greatly to its increased availability. Indeed, better processing means that bandwidth limitations are less difficult to deal with as the quality of video and audio improves. As the equipment improves, so too do the support services and associated equipment, such as multipoint bridges, which allow the source to communicate with more than one remote site. Once somewhat archaic in its operation, new developments in bridging have meant that far more sophisticated and reliable scenarios can be realized successfully, again making videoconferencing a more attractive option. Prices, too, are dropping, both with regard to the hardware itself and indeed, in relative terms, for the networks over which videoconferencing can take place.

For the teaching world, videoconferencing represents a real challenge, but also a real opportunity: an opportunity to reach new learners, adapt teaching to take advantage of remote expertise and resources, and stretch the learning experience in ways hitherto impossible. For the educator, videoconferencing represents a way to break through the barriers to remote students, see and hear the somewhat isolated learner, and link groups of learners who otherwise would have little opportunity to meet and learn from one another. Placed in the hands of committed, enthusiastic, and imaginative teachers who can wield it with care and wisdom, videoconferencing can be a mighty tool.

REFERENCES

Carpio, J., & Ramos, E. (1995). UNED-EVCN: Educational Videoconferencing Network. In P. Held & W. F. Kugemann (Eds.), *Telematics for education and training: Proceedings of the Telematics for Education and Training Conference.* Amsterdam: IOS Press.

DELTA catalogue: Telematics for flexible and distance learning. (1994). Brussels/ Luxembourg: CORDIS, European Commission.

Fox, S. (1995). *Issues in the use of video conferencing for teaching: Summary* (EOUN Project DL1003). Heerlen, The Netherlands: EADTU.

Fraeters, H., Reynolds, S., & Vanbuel, M. (1997). *Learning about videoconferencing.* Leuven, Belgium: Leuven University Press.

Patel, D. (1996, September). *The European Open University Project: Summary.* Session conducted at the Online Educa Asia International Conference on Technology in Distance Learning, Singapore.

Salkunen, K. (1996, November). *Helsinki University of Technology and the Telematics Application Programme of the European Commission.* Session conducted at the Telecon Conference, Anaheim, CA.

Vanbuel, M. (1995). *Delta demo* (ESC project CCT672). Leuven, Belgium: Audiovisual Dienst K.U.Leuven/EADTU-ESC.

CHAPTER 7

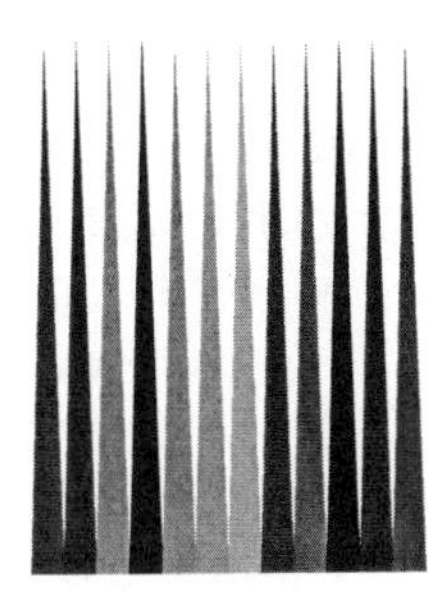

Computer-Facilitated Communications in Transition

Graeme Hart and Jon Mason
Australia

INTRODUCTION

The introduction of computer-facilitated communications (CFC) in many forms is occurring at a rapid rate in higher education and in the workplace in general. From simple electronic mail (e-mail) to more elegant Web-forum communications, the way humans communicate with each other has continued to evolve along with technical developments. As has always been the case with technological innovation, new opportunities, as well as new problems, arise in times of rapid change in CFC. This is particularly true in an educational context.

This chapter draws on experiences in the use of a range of CFC approaches with students and academic and administrative staff within an Australian higher education setting where there has been a commitment to "mainstreaming the digital revolution." In appraising the impact of this revolution on a traditional research-based Australian university, we have identified a number of real-world obstacles that became evident in early promotion and implementation of "flexible delivery" programs. We argue that emerging technologies relevant to education are potentially as alienating and intimidating as they are enabling. Specific challenges relate to existing organizational culture and work practices; market hype and unrealistic expectations; the magnitude of forces demanding change in higher education; the increased need for professional development; and problems associated with the technologies themselves, such as shortening life cycles and lack of maturity. However, we also point out that in making progress in this field, new frameworks for collaboration, drawing on diverse but convergent interests, are key foundations for moving forward.

ORGANIZATIONAL CULTURE AND WORK PRACTICES

In its commitment to internationalization, continued excellence in campus-based research, and the transformation of teaching and learning through utilization of the tools of the digital revolution, the University of Melbourne in Australia has embarked on a fundamentally new strategic orientation. Such a path is a common theme for many universities both within Australia and globally. However, unlike a number of other Australian universities, the response at Melbourne has only recently been framed in terms of flexible delivery because such terminology has generally been associated with the implication of distance education, and Melbourne is an institution that values campus life.

The transition currently underway at Melbourne reveals a number of entrenched work practices, some of which are anathema to flexibility. "Time zone inertia," the practice of preferring to "wait and see" just a little bit longer before accepting the challenge of the digital revolution, presents its own challenge. Of course, many hardworking academics may be offended by such a description, but the reality of at least a "time zone clash," with the shortening life cycles of new technologies, is very true: The traditional and luxurious time frames within which academics are used to operating are having to shrink, largely because of the impact of the relentless and rapid evolution of information and communication technologies (ICT).

One promising feature of the new technologies is the potential for extending opportunities for collaboration, particularly through distributed computing systems and groupware, where groupware is understood to describe software tools designed to facilitate group application sharing and workplace collaboration. This has enormous significance for organizational structure as the "teaming" potential of groupware extends well beyond the natural (or geographically located) workgroup. Of course, despite the fact that academics have been collaborating for hundreds of years, usually in small partnerships, the existence of groupware solutions doesn't necessarily break down the barriers that often stymie adoption of new ideas. One of the great contradictions within traditional university culture has been that excellence in research has translated into the means for acquiring or holding a teaching position. Parallel with this contradiction is the lack of explicit guidance on collaborative research, and as Bond and Thompson (1996) have observed, "There is an increasing need for researchers in universities to learn how to collaborate in order to survive as academics" (p. v).

FORCES OF CHANGE IN HIGHER EDUCATION

While the forces of change in higher education have often been economic in nature, the characteristic feature of our time is that these forces are now a complex mix of economic, cultural, and technological factors that can be both constraining and enabling.

The influences of the growth in "just-in-time" vocational training and the contraction of public funding for universities add to the pressure for effective and appropriate responses to the opportunities of the digital revolution (Dolence & Norris, 1995). Strategic planning and managerial imperatives are now just as important as the core business of research, teaching, and learning. In a way, one outcome is that mainstream academe is becoming withdrawn, an ironic situation considering the vanguard role that universities have played for nearly two decades in the development of the Internet!

CFC alone, as one component in the mix of enabling technologies now available to education, presents mainstream higher education with an opportunity and a challenge to rethink and re-articulate the nature and rigor of its core function (Mason & Hart, 1997). For, as Tiffin and Rajasingham (1995, pp. 39–40) have argued in their book, *In Search of the Virtual Class,* the basis of much of what can be called education emerges from communication processes concerned with the storing, disseminating, and processing of knowledge and whose purpose is to assist learners to become problem solvers. For this, we need communication networks that combine the four related factors of learning, teaching, knowledge, and problem.

Information is of little value in the Information Age if it cannot be communicated or understood efficiently and effectively, and without the tools that can navigate and mine this information, the net effect is information overload. Experts in the field of computer-mediated communication (CMC), such as Berge and Collins (1995), largely concur with this. We have adopted the term CFC to provide a finer focus on the potential for effective communications.

CFC: ALLEVIATOR OR ALIENATOR?

With CFC, the deeply connected link between information and communication is increasingly evident. The most basic form of CFC, e-mail, is having the most significant impact on education. While e-mail has been around for nearly three decades, it is really only during the 1990s that it became a ubiquitous feature of the workplace, in the way that the word processor and the fax machine emerged in the 1980s. E-mail is the primary means for participating in CFC. It is still predominantly restricted to text, which has advantages. In advocating the educational value of e-mail, Harasim, Hiltz, Teles, and Turoff (1995) have said, "Text-based interactions focus on the meaning of the message rather than the physical cues such as race, gender, age, physical appearance, or dress of the sender, thereby reducing some of the discriminatory cues of face-to-face communication" (p. 32). The easy access to learning communities around the world, enabling students in various places to meet on an equal footing (if only for the purpose sometimes of discussing their differences), is an immensely rich resource for education.

At the University of Melbourne, CFC had its beginnings in the early 1980s, a time when there were also a small number of enthusiasts at universities throughout Australia. Notable among these was Robert Elz, who was the first Australian to connect via a modem to ArpaNet.

Since then, things have changed dramatically, but probably the big changes began in 1989 with the framing and implementation of the university's first information technology (IT) strategic plan. A key feature of this plan was to provide networked desktop computing services to all academic and most general staff at the university. Although e-mail was soon provided as a service, a number of alternative platforms proliferated. While many staff used e-mail in a rudimentary manner, the network functioned more for file serving and print services. Computing services for students were viewed, at this stage, more in terms of laboratory facilities that provided standard word processing and spreadsheet software, with some departments supporting dedicated specialist multimedia laboratories.

Computer communications, in terms of e-mail accounts, first came to postgraduates in 1994–1995 and from 1997 were made available to all students. It is clear that IT services were delivered initially to the staff and students of the university more as information technology than as communications technology. IT as a communications enabler (and, moreover, an important tool for research and general educational purposes) has been recognized later by policy makers and educators.

So why CFC? During the early 1990s the description "flexible delivery" crept into mainstream higher education discourse largely as a result of the promising potential of the first wave of multimedia computing. CFC had already been used for a number of years before this by some of the distance education universities such as Deakin, but the "user friendliness" of early systems left much to be desired. The user-friendly desktop computer, first made popular by Apple's Macintosh and then later by Microsoft's Windows operating system, quickly became very powerful at manipulating data not explicitly alphanumeric, data that could retain graphic, video, or audio qualities. With this came hypertext and hypermedia and notions of "flexible learning" (Maurer, 1992; Snyder, 1996, pp. 4–5). But what really started to give impetus to notions of flexible delivery was the popularization of the Internet with the World Wide Web (WWW). In some ways, this notion of flexible delivery is questionable because the hype and marketing of Web-based courses is really more about flexible access. Thus, at the University of Melbourne, as at many universities, there is a new wave rolling through the campus concerned with the enabling potential of CFC and virtual learning environments (Hart & Mason, 1996b).

CFC can be used in synchronous ("real-time") and asynchronous modes, although the latter has been most prominent in educational settings, mainly through e-mail and electronic discussion lists. Significantly, both general and academic staff have used such lists, and their use has become absorbed into the campus culture. For example, at Melbourne, campus-wide lists exist for the purposes of distributing information about library acquisitions and news (ERClist), discussing and sharing technical knowledge (FLITE), and discussing academic issues associated with online education (Online-Ed). Recently, the asynchronous option has been extended with the introduction of Web-based conferencing tools such as AltaVista Forum. This latter type of environment is being tested by the faculties of arts, education, and science as a flexible extension to the learning experience of students and is used by groups of academics for the sharing of resources and ideas (The University of Melbourne, 1996). Such products are a refinement on earlier groupware tools and are the key, according to a recent Forrester report, to effective collaborative computing (Brown, Dolberg, & Johnson, 1996).

CFC as Alleviator

CFC has many positive attributes, which help support its implementation in the educational setting. For any student with basic "digital literacy," it is easy to use the software tools usually associated with CFC. The advantage of online distributed computer systems is that, with well-designed navigational cues, information linked to a course is not difficult to locate and retrieve. For students who may occasionally miss a tutorial or lecture, online versions provide a flexible and convenient solution. In fact, some would argue that working with texts in an online environment provides an optimum situation for the academic treatment and synthesis of ideas. Such texts will typically range from formal dissertations and journal articles to informal discussion from a LISTSERV or bibliographic search results. This fluid nature of the function and structure of text in the digital domain adds an important dimension to research. Clearly, notions of "literacy" will change forever as a result. In a sense, CFC is not just an alleviator but a challenge to academic endeavor.

By utilizing threaded discussions and document sharing, CFC provides both teachers and students with a communications environment rich with opportunity for reflection, a view supported by Berge and Collins (1995, p. 22). They assert that, unlike the linear flow of a traditional classroom discussion, a CFC environment allows students to continue a discussion for several days, alternating participating and lurking in the background to reflect and read, until they feel comfortable enough with their opinions to add to the discussion.

The effective and efficient distribution of information to groups and collaboration are also easily achieved through CFC, although collaboration is somewhat more difficult to realize in practice. The massive growth of groupware solutions and intranets over the last few years clearly indicates this trend, and it has been estimated by the Computer Technology Research Corporation that over 50 percent of all Web servers currently have an intranet function (Szuprowicz, 1996).

Because of its enabling character, CFC is also used for many purposes besides the conventional academic agenda. Hunt (1995, p. 94) points out that this form of communication is often used for "authentically social purposes," where the motivation may also be just to "inform or persuade a known audience." While some staff may be reluctant to use CFC, this does not apply to the majority of students who readily embrace this technology. Use of LISTSERVs and the "First Class" CFC software with students in the faculty of education was received very positively by the students (Mason & Hart, 1997).

However, CFC is not suitable for everyone and certainly does not act as a universal panacea for the deficiencies of the "traditional classroom." Furthermore, many staff have difficulty in accepting the legitimacy of CFC. Many suffer from time zone inertia, preferring to wait and see just a little bit longer before accepting the very real challenge that the digital revolution presents.

CFC as Alienator

While there is tremendous potential for collaboration with CFC, this is nonetheless difficult to realize, often because of entrenched "private" and "turf-protectionist" work practices. In the corporate context, a "slow-track" adoption of collaborative tools has been prevalent largely because working in teams, let alone online teams, is a hurdle in itself (Brown et al., 1996).

In a recent Department of Employment, Education, Training and Youth Affairs (DEETYA) report, Taylor, Lopez, and Quadrelli (1996, p. xii) demonstrated well the extreme attitudes of "technological utopianism" and "widespread skepticism" that currently exist on university campuses. In generally defending academic attitudes and practice with regard to embracing technology, they argue that embracing technology is actually a daunting task because, for academics to adapt and be able to take advantage of the new technologies to enhance teaching, they must learn to use them in ways that are pedagogically appropriate, and at the same time, develop teaching practices that foster learning. According to these authors, while both tasks are difficult, the latter is the most challenging.

Coltman and Romm (1997) also point to formidable barriers in establishing CFC tools in an organization but identify these more in terms of social network theory, organizational culture, and change. They propose a research model that can measure effective implementation of collaborative groupware solutions. They say that groupware that is explicitly designed to support changes in the interaction patterns between staff must take account of three important variables in the social networks that affect the outcome, or quality, of CFC: empowerment, performance, and satisfaction. Such a model is important because it clearly identifies that social interactions and the matching of tasks with individuals and groups are as important as booting up the forum server.

In our experience at the University of Melbourne, support for innovative pilot CFC programs has been strong at senior levels but patchy on the front line. Furthermore, many inconsistencies and anomalies exist where the technology is not really used to its full advantage. For example, some senior staff do not interact in the digital domain but prefer to have all communications printed and passed through their in-tray, preferring to opt for older organizational paradigms. This practice misses out on the experience of new "architectures" of communication, architectures that can seize the moment, unblock academic and bureaucratic inertia, give new meaning to immediacy, and give opportunity for reflection in text-based communication.

One of the very virtues of e-mail is, at the same time, one of its weaknesses. The ease of use and ready availability of e-mail can readily lead to information overload. Sending multiple copies of a document through the mail comes at a cost in terms of postage and in the time to physically handle documents, while e-mail can be forwarded to large numbers of people easily and at virtually no cost. It is not uncommon, particularly for administrative staff, to forward "snippets" from mailing lists to their own department LISTSERVs that are often of no interest or relevance to other staff.

The rapid development of CFC technology can result in it being implemented without being fully tested and debugged. There are many examples of teaching and administrative programs on the Internet in a less than fully completed state. It can be very frustrating for staff who do not have the appropriate technical skills to find that their teaching or administrative program has "gone down" and is unavailable. It is clear that with new technology comes a shift in the power base in higher education. For academics in particular, the successful and smooth running of their lectures and tutorials can very often depend on access to competent technical staff. Unlike having the ability to change a bulb in an overhead projector, an academic can be powerless if something goes wrong with equipment in a lecture hall.

Perhaps one important feature of CFC is that, as a new communications tool and as both an alleviator and alienator, writing with a computer blurs the line between thinking and writing and therefore shapes to some extent the ways in which we think (Snyder, 1996). This is clearly a fertile area for research.

TECHNOLOGY: SHELF LIFE AND FUNCTION

Technology is its own worst enemy. Its intrinsic impetus for enhancement renders many iterations obsolete when, in fact, the end-user more often than not has not even learned to explore the full feature set of the earlier version. Some Microsoft products are a good example of this, but Microsoft is certainly not alone in packaging feature-laden software. While the "shelf life" of professional knowledge is subject to contracting "use-by" dates, the technology that has factored into bringing about this situation is likewise a victim of this same imperative.

For many academics and students, the technology is still not transparent enough, however. Even though the technology is capable of delivering major productivity gains, transparency needs to be manifest just as it is for mainstream telephony; after all, who gives a second thought to holding onto a piece of plastic, talking into it, and sustaining a conversation? If telephony had been developed after the popular adoption of the Web, one wonders whether such "conversations" into plastic handsets would have been construed as "virtual" interactions.

The significant shift in core function of computer technology during the latter half of the 1990s in higher education, and perhaps even more broadly throughout the whole education and training sector, has been from being predominantly geared as a support service and productivity tool toward being a key driver with a tremendous potential for transforming teaching and learning. Clearly, this is recognized at the highest levels of university management as well as by national and state governments worldwide.

What is the net effect of this shift? Certainly, technological overload compounds the ever-expanding mass of information available and is experienced by many in this way. The problem is not just the ongoing rapid development in software and hardware capabilities, either. There are such a large number of challenges, solutions, and options, from operating systems (both desktop and network) to bandwidth considerations, to establishing simple universal e-mail access for students and staff, to integrating administrative and academic information systems. Then there are infrastructure challenges such as appropriate facilities and services, software "plug-ins," version compatibilities and proprietary enhancements, along with security and privacy issues, and the "other IP," intellectual property. There are new standards such as Platform for Internet Content Selection (PICS) and its revisions, and videoconferencing, video-on-demand, groupware, and cable-based edutainment, not to mention maintaining discourse about all the trends with "buzzword compliance." How do "mainstream" academics committed to their own particular fields, let alone the administrators managing diminishing budgets, come to grips with all of this?

CUSTOMIZABLE MULTIMEDIA INTEGRATED LEARNING ENVIRONMENTS

Since the popularization of the Web in the mid-1990s, educators have seen the possibilities of putting material online with HTML. The use of common gateway interface (CGI) scripts has provided added control over user feedback and interaction. With the added flexibility of Java applets, this approach still works well for small-scale Web teaching. However, one of the problems of standard Web sites and associated scripts is the increasing difficulty of management of resources once the number of individual files begins to increase. The traditional method of management of large sets of data has for many years been through the use of a database, but until recently traditional databases have been unable to communicate with HTML Web pages.

The advent of tremendously powerful "mainstream" structured query language (SQL) databases, being able to communicate with HTML pages as viewed by standard Web browsers such as Netscape and Internet Explorer, is being accompanied by the development of a range of "middleware" applications to facilitate the process. This has the advantage of allowing the client to access information through a platform-independent browser and giving administrators and authors the power of fully fledged relational database management of very large resources.

As an example, the first-year chemistry course at the University of Melbourne utilizes over 8,000 individual files such as digital images and Shockwave objects, all of which need to be managed both in terms of the "physical" serving up to a Web browser and the associated issues of copyright and latest versions. In addition, a large resource may well be the number of actual students in a course. Given trends in flexible delivery where students are encouraged to enroll online, increasing numbers of students will need to be accommodated in this way. The University of Melbourne, with only 30,000 students and a small, although rapidly increasing, number of courses offered online, handles approximately 400,000 HTTP connections, 30,000 FTP downloads, and over 10 million proxy requests per week. Large institutions with tens of thousands of students will have a mammoth job to provide access to hundreds of subjects via the Web. Clearly the only solution from an organizational perspective will be to utilize a database-driven approach.

A number of solutions currently are under development utilizing a database-driven approach. One such authoring and management tool for online learning currently under development by Melbourne Information Technologies Australia, part of the University of Melbourne's commercial arm, is a middleware application called CREATOR (see Figure 7.1).

Fig. 7.1. Relationship between user and resources.

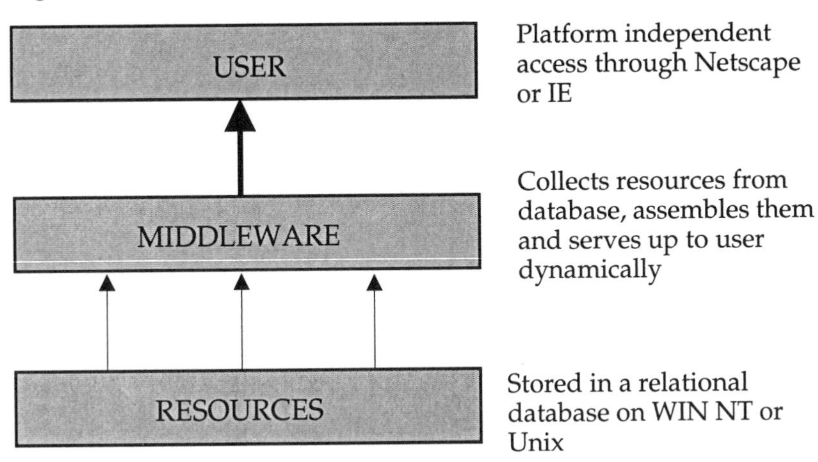

CREATOR is the name given to Customizable Multimedia Integrated Learning Environment software, written in Java and designed to provide both an authoring environment and an integrated platform for education and communication via the Internet within the one location. This includes facilities such as video/audio conferencing, newsgroups, and chat sessions, as well as managing/tracking student performance without the need for any knowledge of programming or scripting languages.

Resources such as text, images, videos, sound, Shockwave objects, quizzes, and so on, are stored in an SQL database located on a server under Windows NT. The resources can be stored in virtually any SQL database. CREATOR uses Active Server Page technology to collect individual resources from the database, assemble them in a preset sequence, and serve them up dynamically to users. This process is quite transparent to the user but has the great advantages for administrators, authors, and teachers of database management.

CREATOR provides five integrated online modules: Library, Learn, Discussion, Searching, and Administration, with which users can create their own online learning applications. Text, images, animations, video, audio, and other media objects are stored in a database for management and retrieval, allowing objects to be shared among many developers.

The Administration module, as shown in Figure 7.2, allows teachers and course administrators to manage student enrollment and assessment, and in general track student performance in an online environment. The Library module allows authors to collaborate in the creation of what are, in effect, online books. These are intended as reference material for students and may range from course outlines to lecture notes, or could be actual "books" created through the collaborative efforts of a number of academics located around the world. The module is a metaphor for a traditional on-campus library where students would go for background research/reading prior to, or perhaps following, lectures or tutorials.

Fig. 7.2. The administration module in CREATOR.

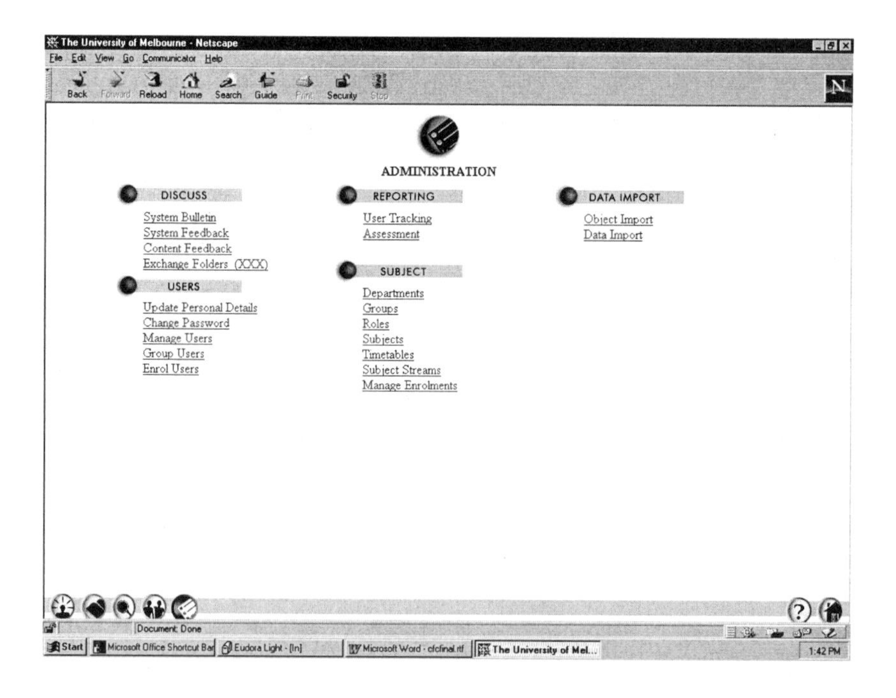

The Learn module is expressly intended to gain some form of response from students, and in this section, a learning outcome of some type is the goal. In its simplest form, students may be required to do some reading, watch a video, view an image, or search the library prior to giving a response to a quiz, newsgroup, or chat session. An example of a typical Learn module is shown in Figure 7.3.

Fig. 7.3. The learn module in CREATOR.

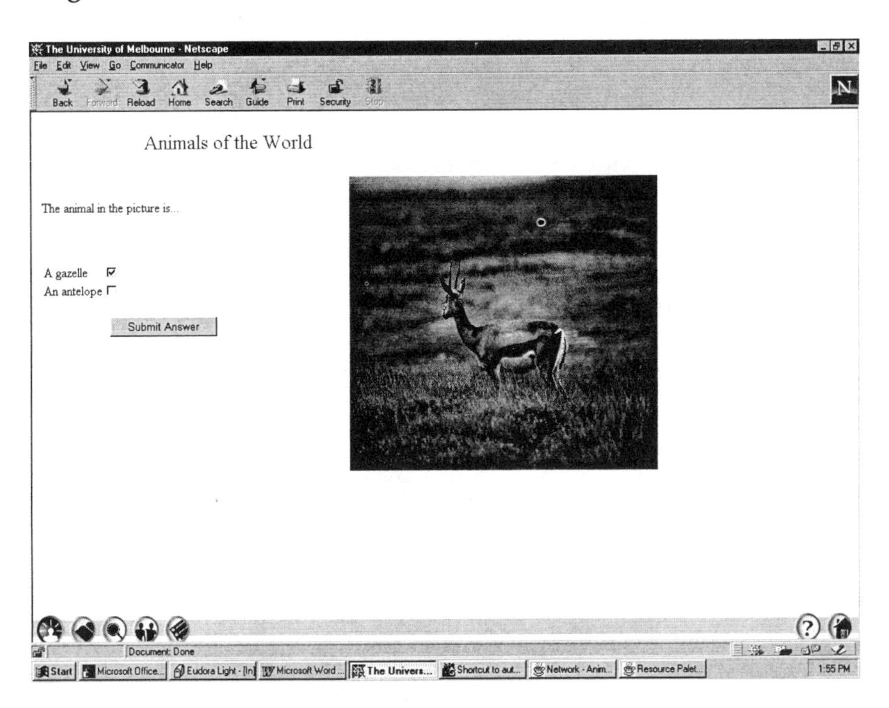

Responses from the student to the quiz are sent to the database, checked and corrected, and feedback is given to the student. Students can get more detailed feedback on why they were correct or incorrect. Every keystroke is trapped and stored in the database, as is individual student performance, including time on task, along with question performance statistics. In effect, this type of information system includes a great deal of "inbuilt" functionality that educators would otherwise have to build separately. This is typical of the push toward integrated environments in which educators can both author teaching material and deliver it online within the one environment.

Given the changing nature of the way in which academics work in an online world, integrated software such as this has the advantage of allowing online collaboration with contributors located anywhere in the world. The provision exists for individual authors to contribute chapters to a book but for that material to remain unpublished until it passes through an online editorial process. There is also provision for identifying copyright associated with individual objects in the system. An interesting account of the conversion of the University of Melbourne Veterinary Science bacteriology and mycology course into a Web-based format using CREATOR can be found in McNaught, Browning, Hart, Prescott, and Whithear (1997).

An integrated system such as this offers great empowerment for educators, because it allows them to collaboratively author and publish teaching material using inbuilt authoring tools and to use the same system to serve the material up to their students. They can also use the system to collect responses, track individual and collective student performance, and engage in asynchronous and synchronous Web-based communications. Figure 7.4 shows part of the authoring tools and a resource palette used to create a learning activity where responses are used to direct the learning activity shown in Figure 7.3.

Fig. 7.4. CREATOR authoring tools.

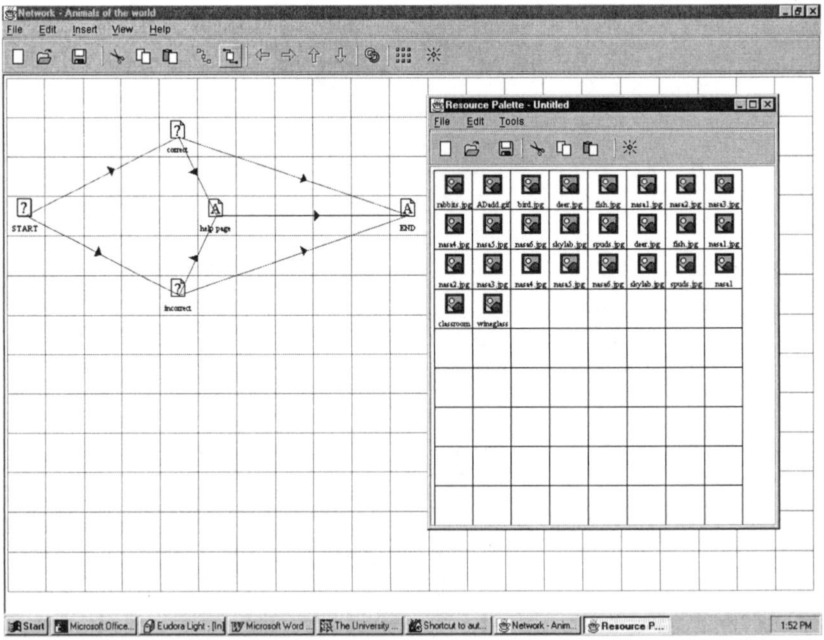

With such a scalable information system as this, the possibility exists of providing a central resource at a given university and having all teaching programs located on the one central server. This would certainly provide a solution to issues of copyright but may lead to a centralized control over teaching resources. The technology allows this, and there is no doubt that academics and administrators will engage in many spirited discussions regarding control of teaching programs.

BRINGING IT ALL TOGETHER: EDUCATION NETWORK AUSTRALIA, EdNA

EdNA is an initiative of the commonwealth, state, and territory governments together with key stakeholders from the education and training sector within Australia. It has been established to provide value-added online services to this community and as a means of optimizing the potential for communications and information technology in education and training.

Since its original conception in 1995, EdNA has undergone a number of changes. Originally, it was conceived as a physical network that emphasized infrastructure development and connectivity, particularly for the Schools and Vocational Education and Training (VET) communities (the Australian Academic and Research Network, AARNet, already well-established for universities). As Internet usage in Australia has increased over the last few years, EdNA has developed into a national framework for collaboration and cooperation among all sectors of the Australian education and training community, whose goal is to maximize the benefits of information technology and online services. A key component of this endeavor is the building of a value-added Directory Service that provides both comprehensive information about each of the sectors and a growing collection of information resources useful for educational purposes. Stakeholders have agreed on implementing metadata as a means for ensuring that resource discovery is effective and that quality of content is maintained. This is currently at an early stage of development, but much progress has already been made.

To achieve its goals, EdNA has established a number of consultative groups aimed at both facilitating the more general process of collaborative use of information technology and at establishing and developing the Directory Service.

Sectoral groups, such as the VET Advisory Group, the Schools Advisory Group, and the Higher Education Advisory Group, have been established to provide input to the development of EdNA from each sector's perspective and to exchange information and ideas about the use of ICT in education.

While this framework is also likely to lead eventually to significant cost savings by avoiding excessive duplication and overlap, this is not necessarily the main opportunity or unstated agenda. For those who wish to focus on the economic aspect, the real action may well be missed. The EdNA initiative can indeed be construed as having a strong economic appeal, particularly to government stakeholders. However, this is not the only implication. There is a decline in public funding of higher education worldwide, and governments are scrutinizing university management more closely, but with this there are also other features of a new so-called global economy. Some commentators (Castells, 1996; Kelly, 1997) prefer to talk about this in terms of a trend toward a "network economy." A tightening of public funding in higher education may be the downside, but as the networks develop, so do the opportunities and the economic rules. In this scenario, new forces of competition are unleashed, and some "nodes" on the network will naturally excel and perhaps dominate in certain fields. But the nodes are not isolated; the connections and the potential for collaboration will be a driving force for change:

> The grand irony of our times is that the era of computers is over. All the major consequences of standalone computers have already taken place. Computers have speeded up our lives a bit, and that's it. In contrast, all the most promising technologies making their debut now are chiefly due to communication between computers—that is, to connections

> rather than computations. And since communication is the basis of culture, fiddling at this level is indeed momentous. Information's critical rearrangement is the widespread, relentless act of connecting everything to everything else. We are now engaged in a grand scheme to augment, amplify, enhance, and extend the relationships between all beings and all objects. That is why the Network Economy is a big deal. (Kelly, 1997:140)

The sectoral groups and ministerial nominees, both state and commonwealth, come together in a common forum as the EdNA Reference Committee to provide advice on matters relating to the use of information technology in education and to the ministers and the Education.Au Limited Board on continuing developments in the EdNA process. Education.Au Limited is charged with implementing the functions of EdNA and is a nonprofit company owned collectively by all the Australian ministers of education and training. The Reference Committee has representatives from each state and territory school and VET system, the Catholic school system, and the independent schools sector, as well as the higher education sector, and is currently chaired by the commonwealth representative.

Thus, it is clear that EdNA has established a framework and vision for collaboration with respect to the utilization and development of online services in educational contexts within Australia. This framework maps well onto the networked architecture of the Internet, thus facilitating natural synergies that yield both opportunities (for further networking) and tangible "added value" through the Directory Service.

In terms of its overall scope EdNA is very much a unique initiative. However, there are a number of other developments around the globe that resemble aspects of the EdNA initiative. In the United Kingdom, the Department of Education and Employment in 1997 also launched a discussion paper, "Connecting the Learning Society: . . . National Grid for Learning," as part of a (narrower) consultation process that commenced in the latter part of 1997. Implementation of the National Grid began in early 1998 (see Department for Education and Employment, 1997). In North America, EDUCOM has merged with College

And University Systems Exchange (CAUSE) and released a metadata specification as a component of its Instructional Management System (IMS) Project specifically for the education community (see EDUCAUSE, n.d.).

EdNA was officially launched by the commonwealth of Australia on November 28, 1997, and more information is available on its Web site (see Education Network Australia, n.d.).

FUTURE DIRECTIONS OF CFC

A recent commonwealth government-funded evaluation, "Managing the Introduction of Technology in the Delivery and Administration of Higher Education," identified that staff development approaches will have to support "an accelerated shift from teaching to learning, delivered not by individual lecturers but by multifunctional teams" (Yetton & Associates, 1997, p. xi). Furthermore, the roles and skills of both academic and general staff are affected, with some general staff taking on "para-academic" functions. The authors of the report conclude, "The universities which get IT right will attract resources; those that get it wrong will not. There will be winners and losers." Perhaps the old saying, "publish or perish," relevant to individual academics, has a newer and broader implication, "collaborate or collapse."

That education in general and higher education in particular is changing is something of a master understatement. Prior to reforms in 1988 to the Australian education system, which removed the so-called binary system, higher education was neatly divided into the traditional research of the universities and the vocational training of the institutes and colleges. Higher education is now struggling to come to terms with the reality of having moved into a mass-market domain. Staff initially from colleges divert their time from teaching into research while staff initially from universities divert time from research into pedagogy. It may be that while academics are expected to be all things to all people, perhaps technology in the form of CFC is a way of lightening the work load as well as a means of extending the learning experiences of students. The current round of funding cuts to higher education is concurrent with the new wave of changes, probably even more significant than the removal of the binary system. It is likely that CFC will also offer a way of offsetting the contraction of university staffing.

As the vice chancellor of the University of Melbourne, Alan Gilbert, argued in his keynote speech in November 1996 at The Virtual University? Symposium, "The first step to survival is to ensure that the information superhighway runs through every great campus, and the second is to ensure that the riches it brings are in turn enriched in a real learning community" (paragraph 36).

Preparation for the challenge of "virtual education" is well underway at many institutions around the world. Competition for external funding, along with notions of quality assurance satisfying consumer demands, point to greater variety of access to teaching and learning programs for students in the very near future. The provision of course material on the Web and the option for students to complete part of a traditional series of lectures/tutorials "off campus" has met with resounding success in terms of satisfying student expectations at the university (Hart & Mason, 1996a). The approach of flexible, as opposed to distance, learning will become increasingly common in the near future.

Supporting this scenario, a "near-futures" prediction in a Forrester report about collaborative software implementation in the corporate world is likely to have similar implications in higher education: "As collaboration capabilities are woven into all aspects of corporate applications, workers who are not naturally team players will be forced to adopt new ground rules. Those that can't will be shifted off the fast track" (Brown, et al., 1996).

While many writers argue the case for embracing technology (Davidow & Malone, 1992; Rheingold, 1994), others argue against such a course (Brook & Boal, 1995) or at least raise questions about important issues such as "workplace habitat" (Acker, 1995). Universities are appealing places because they allow high-level intellectual interaction and debate. The social and informal networks can often be as important as the formal classes; committees and CFC implementers need to take account of this fact.

The march of technology is inexorable. Imagine the languid days prior to the availability of mass-produced motor vehicles or the peaceful, uninterrupted days prior to the telephone. Perhaps future generations will reflect on life before e-mail! Whatever we imagine, society never goes back on technological innovation. We shape and reshape our cities around roads to accommodate vehicles and are reshaping our communications practices with the advent of mobile phones. Technology has increased the ease with which humans can communicate with each other, both in a "real" sense of traveling physically and in a "virtual," or remote, sense. In a similar way, we are in the process of reshaping education in our society to take advantage of the availability of modern CFC.

As with all technological innovation, as access to CFC systems becomes less expensive, they will become more widespread; hence the next few years will be critically important to researching best practice in CFC. In reality, CFC is not just an alleviator or alienator in the educational setting, but also an opportunity and an inescapable challenge to rethink the nature and rigor of academic endeavor.

REFERENCES

Acker, S. R. (1995). *Space, collaboration, and the credible city: Academic work in the virtual university* [Online]. Available: http://cwis.usc.edu/dept/annenberg/vol1/issue1/acker/ACKTEXT.HTM. (Accessed March 17, 1999).

Berge, Z. L., & Collins, M. P. (Eds.). (1995). *Computer mediated communication and the online classroom: Vol. 1. Overview and perspectives.* Cresskill, NJ: Hampton Press.

Bond, C., & Thompson, B. (1996). *Collaborating in research* (Higher Education Research and Development Society of Australasia [HERDSA] Green Guide No. 19). Canberra, Australia: HERDSA Publications.

Brook, J., & Boal, I. (1995). *Resisting the virtual life.* San Francisco: City Lights.

Brown, E., Dolberg, S., & Johnson, J. (1996). Teams on the Internet. *Forrester Report: Software Strategies* [Online], *7*(6). Available: http://www.forrester.com/ER/Research/Report/Excerpt/0,1338,3603, FF.html. (Accessed March 17, 1999).

Castells, M. (1996). *The information age: Vol. 1. The rise of the network society*. Oxford: Blackwell.

Coltman, T., & Romm, C. T. (1997). Factors affecting the quality of organizational computer mediated communication: A social network perspective. In *Creative collaboration in virtual communities '97* [Online]. 34 paragraphs. Available: http://www.arch.usyd.edu.au/kcdc/conferences/VC97/. (Accessed March 17, 1999).

Davidow, W. H., & Malone, M. S. (1992). *The virtual corporation: Structuring and revitalizing the corporation for the 21st century*. New York: Harper Business.

Department for Education and Employment. (1997). *Connecting the learning society: The Government's consultation paper on the National Grid for Learning* [Online]. Available: http://www.open.gov.uk/dfee/grid/index.htm. (Accessed June 1, 1998).

Dolence, M., & Norris, D. (1995). *Transforming higher education: A vision for learning in the 21st century*. Ann Arbor, MI: Society for College and University Planning.

Education Network Australia. (n.d.). *Education Network Australia: A Directory Service for the education community* [Online]. Available: http://www.edna.edu.au/EdNA/. (Accessed March 18, 1999).

EDUCAUSE. (n.d.). *IMS (Instructional Management Systems)* [Online]. Available: http://www.imsproject.org/. (Accessed March 18, 1999).

Gilbert, A. D. (1996). The virtual and the real in the idea of a university [Keynote speech]. In *The virtual university? symposium* [Online]. 36 paragraphs. Available: http://www.edfac.unimelb.edu.au/virtu/vc.htm. (Accessed March 18, 1999).

Harasim, L., Hiltz, S., Teles, L., & Turoff, M. (1995). *Learning networks: A field guide to teaching and learning online*. Cambridge, MA: MIT Press.

Hart, G., & Mason, J. (1996a). Toward a model Website at the University of Melbourne: Pedagogy and pragmatics. In *Universities of the twenty first century: Education in a borderless world* [Colloquium proceedings]. Australia: IDP Education Australia.

Hart, G., & Mason, J. (Eds.). (1996b). *The virtual university? symposium: Symposium proceedings & case studies.* Parkville, Australia: The University of Melbourne.

Hunt, R. (1995). Collaborative investigation online: Eighteenth century literature moves to the computer lab. In Z. L. Berge & M. P. Collins (Eds.), *Computer mediated communication and the online classroom: Vol. 1. Overview and perspectives* (pp. 93–110). Cresskill, NJ: Hampton Press.

Kelly, K. (1997, September). The new rules of the new economy. *Wired, 5*(9), 140–144, 186–197. "The New Rules of the New Economy" by Kevin Kelly Wired 5.09 © 1998 The Conde Nast Publications, Inc. All rights reserved. Used with permission.

Mason, J., & Hart, G. (1997). Effective use of asynchronous virtual learning communities. In *Creative collaboration in virtual communities '97* [Online]. 53 paragraphs. Available: http://www.arch.usyd.edu.au/kcdc/conferences/VC97/. (Accessed March 18, 1999).

Maurer, H. (1992). Why hypermedia systems are important. In *IIG report.* Proceedings of the Sixth HCI Conference, Graz, Austria.

McNaught, C., Browning, G., Hart, G., Prescott, J., & Whithear, K. (1997). Redeveloping a successful multimedia project into a flexible Web-based format. In R. Kevil, R. Oliver, & R. Phillips (Eds.), *What works and why: Conference proceedings ASCILITE'97* [Online] (pp. 424–429). Available: http://www.curtin.edu.au/conference/ASCILITE97/papers/Mcnaught/Mcnaught.html. (Accessed March 18, 1999).

Rheingold, H. (1994). *The virtual community: Finding connection in a computerized world.* London: Minerva.

Snyder, I. (1996). *Hypertext: The electronic labyrinth.* Melbourne: Melbourne University Press.

Szuprowicz, B. O. (1996). *Intranets and groupware: Effective communications for the enterprise.* Charleston, SC: Computer Technology Research Corporation.

Taylor, P. G., Lopez, L., & Quadrelli, C. (1996). *Flexibility, technology and academics' practices: Tantalising tales and muddy maps.* Canberra, Australia: Department of Employment, Education, Training and Youth Affairs (DEETYA); Evaluations and Investigations Program; Higher Education Division.

Tiffin, J., & Rajasingham, L. (1995). *In search of the virtual class: Education in an information society.* London: Routledge Kegan Paul.

The University of Melbourne. (1996). *EdFac Forum* [Online]. Available: http://forum.edfac.unimelb.edu.au/. (Accessed March 18, 1999).

Yetton, P., & Associates. (1997). *Managing the introduction of technology in the delivery and administration of higher education.* Canberra, Australia: Department of Employment, Education, Training and Youth Affairs (DEETYA); Evaluations and Investigations Program; Higher Education Division.

CHAPTER 8

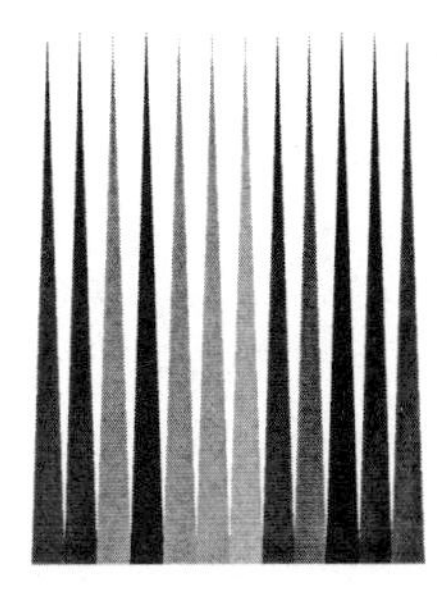

Cultural and Linguistic Diversity

Threat or Challenge for Virtual Instruction

Jef Van den Branden and José Lambert
European Union

INTRODUCTION

Today's society is more and more internationally oriented, and education is increasingly faced with a culturally and linguistically mixed audience. This is particularly the case in Europe, where a huge number of nationalities, each having their own culture and often their own language, are on their way to a unified continent. Such a process is far from trivial, as is proven by the sometimes violent opposition between minorities and the majority in numerous countries (e.g., the "Macedonian problem" in the Balkans, the Hungarian minority in Romania, the position of Basques in France and Spain, the Ulster situation in Ireland).

The problem of cultural diversity is tackled in some cases by creating federal structures within the larger boundaries of a given country (e.g., Switzerland, Germany, and Belgium), with a tendency to give regional autonomy in a number of other countries (such as the United Kingdom, Italy, Spain, and France). It might seem contradictory in all these cases to support national identities, including cultural and linguistic ones, as part of the unification process, but it is probably the only solution that really works. Beside and within the European Union, a "Europe of the Regions" is strengthening accordingly, which has led to the publication of all official documents of the Union in all the countries' languages, as well as a policy permitting members of the European parliament to address the Union's assemblies in their native languages (Coulmas, 1991; Fishman, 1993).

This awareness of cultural identity has also largely influenced education, both on a national level (e.g., education in "regional languages" such as Gaelic, Welsh, Fries, and Catalan) and on an international one. Since its very origin, the European Union has promoted transnational education as a means to create transborder understanding by supporting the creation of European schools and European colleges (postgraduate education) and by the stimulation of staff and student exchange between educational institutions from various European countries (primarily on the university level, but increasingly extended to higher, secondary, and even primary education and vocational training). With increasing numbers of contacts, this physical mobility is gradually complemented and reinforced by virtual mobility. Due to European support programs, such as SOCRATES and LEONARDO in the field of education and training and others in the area of telematics research and development, which have special strands for distance education, trans-European networks for education and training have been established. In the framework of these networks solutions are being developed for coping with cultural and linguistic problems.

Most of the literature and research on the issue of cross-cultural differences in distance education investigates empirical difficulties regarding basic questions such as language, style, and attitudes, and then suggests various small-scale ways of improving the situation. The literature largely fails to deal with the social and cultural complexity of the conditions in which learning takes place and results in a narrowing of focus to how cross-cultural dimensions of learning are conceived.

In this chapter, the experiences in the transnational network of EuroPACE 2000* and in a number of European projects on education in a virtual environment are reflected. In these experiences, virtual instruction is considered to take place in a network-based environment, that is, a trans-European network of traditional universities for telematics-supported education and training. Although this network uses the Internet for communication and course delivery, it is not a virtual university in the sense of an electronic campus. Virtual instruction occurs through combinations of interactive (satellite) television, video-conferencing, Internet communication, computer conferencing, and even conventional mailing of prerecorded videotapes and written materials.

In the discussion that follows, the influence of cultural diversity on virtual instruction is analyzed in three steps. In the first step, focusing on the influence of culture on knowledge building and education, some reflections are offered on the definition of culture (as relevant to learning) and on the cultural embedding of knowledge and learning. This discussion is followed by a survey of the influence of cultural diversity on the use of technology. Illustrated for the European continent, it stresses specific factors that affect virtual instruction and translates these with respect to course and courseware design for transnational use. Language as one of the most influential identified factors is given special attention in the third part of the discussion. A plea is made to replace language policy in virtual networks by language management; that is, by an active approach toward language, and some specific guidelines for its use are suggested. Finally, there are concluding remarks on the open question of whether cultural diversity should be considered as a threat or rather as a challenge, maybe even as a possible asset for virtual networks and instruction.

*For more information on EuroPACE 2000, see http://www.europace.be.

THE INFLUENCE OF CULTURE ON KNOWLEDGE BUILDING AND EDUCATION

The Definition of Culture

The term "culture" refers in general to views, values, norms, expectations, and conventions for behavior that are typical for a specific society or community. In recent years, culture has become a favorite concept in the sociology of science and of higher education, where it is preferred by some authors to the concept of social system. Culture offered itself as a concept that is sufficiently wide and complex to cover all relevant traits (ranging from everyday life to cognitive and social structures) and that is also "naturally" linked to a concept of socialization. Culture is used in this broad sense to refer to communities that have different attitudes toward political and social issues, different cultural practices and preferences in their private lives, different social backgrounds, and so forth (Huber, 1990).

Cultural communities and their borders may coincide at least partly with national borders, and cultural differences do exist between countries; but they can be found as well between ethnic groups or language communities within a country. Language difference is often paralleled by cultural difference, and, on a macro level, language is one of the most important determining factors, if not the only determining factor, of cultural diversity. Cultural differences exist also on a micro level, ranging from disciplinary cultures in academic communities (Huber, 1990) to working environments (company culture, professionals versus the unemployed).

"Socialization" refers to processes of transferring culture through learning. Within socialization, the term "culture" refers to the meanings and understandings that are learned and shared in specific groups against the background of other cultures of class, community, and society (Verma & Entzinger, 1992). The transfer of information and knowledge (in other words, teaching and learning) not only takes place in a given cultural or cross-cultural framework, but also communicates cultural and social values. From this viewpoint, distance teaching and learning by means of communication technology offer specific challenges and opportunities that entail the creation of a multicultural society (Barrera, 1993). Important cross-cultural skills, such as tolerating ambiguity, being nonjudgmental, or developing empathy, can be cultivated (Reif, 1989). Computer-mediated conversations in teleconferences and videoconferences can be used to support this process.

However, people tend to communicate with those who share a similar outlook on life, a common language, compatible belief and value structures: in other words, similar cultural orientations. People's response behavior is thus predictable, which, in turn, makes the process of communication easier. Participants in such communication transactions share, to a great degree, a common pool of experience and cultural perspectives. As people tend to interpret others' behavior through their own framework of cultural norms, communication with someone who speaks a different language, possesses different values and belief structures, and maintains a different philosophical outlook on life may create misunderstanding and miscommunication and thus become frustrating. Because of the inevitable differences in cultural norms, even among partners in the same society, the idea of any perfect or unproblematic communications has to be questioned, even though one may be unaware of any difficulties. Such differences are likely to increase as soon as the objective ground for differences (such as linguistic, religious, and economic habits) becomes more obvious.

Culturally Embedded Knowledge and (Open Distance) Learning

Knowledge acquisition does not take place in a vacuum. Researchers in disciplines such as psychology, anthropology, the theory of science, and artificial intelligence have studied the relationship between knowledge acquisition and culture. The different theories agree that there are different ways of knowing attributable to the different cultural backgrounds of "knowers." As far as the Western schooling and learning tradition is concerned, some observations can be made in comparison with other traditions:

- The Western schooling tradition places emphasis on quantification and universal statements or universal truth.
- Western learners are led by orthodoxy and attend less to differences in practice; they emphasize general features at the cost of details; the Western learner learns to reason in a purely abstract, psychologically "unreal" world.
- The Western learner emphasizes authority rather than experience.
- Knowledge transfer focuses more on the data, or their elements as such, than on the process of transfer; the act of interpretation consists mainly in the integration of these bits and pieces into the uniform frame of the theory (Pinxten & Farrer, 1990).

Therefore, issues of knowledge transfer may be meaningfully explored only if social and cultural contexts are taken into account when designing learning technologies and methods.

With respect to (open) learning theory and practice, Strydom and O'Mahony (1993) warn of some major problems:

- One way of approaching the issue of cross-cultural differences in education is to focus on the empirical difficulties with respect to language, learning style, and habits that make cross-cultural cooperation difficult, and then to suggest various small-scale ways of improving the situation. This approach mostly bypasses the deep structural problem and concentrates only on its manifest form.
- A basic problem of any cybernetically constructed educational medium is the intrinsic tendency to stress the cognitive and individualistic dimensions of learning and to neglect the social learning that constantly occurs through cooperation. The absence in either the literature or the practice of a well-worked-out conception of open learning as a cooperative phenomenon that involves a whole range of shifting contexts of both pedagogical and

nonpedagogical nature results in a one-sided conception of learning. It neglects the significance of relevance structures that humans bring to any given learning situation and which depend on social-emotional structures of internalized motivation for their effectiveness.

- The transmission theory of education in its many variants is the dominant educational paradigm of industrial society. It is experienced that the model does not work any longer, due to the depth of social transformation in society. As a possible way out, educational techniques are changed while maintaining the core philosophy (the transmission ideology). This leads to a technicalization of the learning environment: Technology is treated as an instrumental frame that disburdens human beings by replacing action functions with technical artifacts and by connecting actions to technical systems (transmission, informatization). The role of the community of learners as initiators of their own contexts and mechanisms of technologically assisted learning tends to be neglected.

- There has been less of a concern with producing interactive systems designed around social action. The absence of a focus on social action has resulted in the sociocultural world being reduced to an environment rather than designing systems around criteria of relevance derived from the sociocultural context. Where human learning is the object of computer programs, its sociocultural conditions and mechanisms cannot be objectified as external. It is only by including the sociocultural dimension that learning technology research and practice can fully address the sociopedagogics of learning.

Advanced learning technologies are being and will be used, with all the pedagogical assumptions and institutional constraints connected to them, whether or not the sociocultural level is taken into account. Strydom and O'Mahony (1993) presume that if these technologies are successful (in the sense that they are widely used), they will have significant implications for shaping the form of culture that incorporates this kind of education. This kind of impact can be called "morphogenetic." Morphogenetic consequences of technology should not be taken into account after the fact; their possible implications should be reflected at its inception and thereby contribute to the fuller realization of existing potentialities.

What is true for learning and the learner is also true for teachers: The attitudes of teachers toward technology and pedagogical issues have to be considered. Research conducted by McInerney (1989) makes it clear that the introduction of technology into the learning environment has affected educators in the structure and nature of their relationships and in their approaches to the tasks they perform. While technology has led to advanced opportunities and increased effectiveness, it has also led to suspicion and mistrust between users and nonusers. McInerney observes that where computer enthusiasts are developing applications to perform work they consider important themselves, computing has led to an increased sense of autonomy and satisfaction. On the other hand, where computing has been controlled by the organizational hierarchy and employed in the service of organizational goals, users have sometimes functioned as technicians and have been placed under what they perceive to be considerable pressure.

Differences in attitudes toward the use of learning technology have been observed not only among individual teachers but also within different disciplines. Becher (1990) states that scholars and students in the framework of a given discipline or knowledge area learn to share its concepts and norms in the same way as people who are born and brought up in a particular national context learn to operate with the language and social practices of their country of origin. This leads to the existence of disciplinary "cultures" and subcultures of specialization.

Challis and Johnston (1994) conducted research on the perceptions of university staff about distance as opposed to traditional, face-to-face teaching. The researchers observed that perceptions of academics are value driven, with many evaluative statements suggesting that their perceptions of actual experiences had been influenced, if not conditioned, by some theoretical template of what a degree, a postgraduate experience, and even the nature of a university ought to be. In comparing the faculty of two disciplines, namely engineering and education, they found the most significant area of concern for the education faculty to be the student-tutor relationship. The distance learning mode was perceived to inhibit the development of personal relationships with students, thereby limiting the tutor's ability to broaden the student's view of the world. Distance learning was consequently perceived as an inferior method of teaching and learning. For the engineering faculty, the main focus was on the amount of planning and coordination that had gone into the production of the distance learning mode. Lack of student contact was identified as a problem but was generally related to academic issues.

CULTURAL DIVERSITY AND INFLUENCE ON TECHNOLOGY USE

Cultural Diversity in Europe

The historical boundaries of many European countries have merely been designed as an outcome of war and political power, rather than as an expression of the community cohesion of their inhabitants. Even in very recent history, great efforts have been made to acculturate divergent groups into the dominant language and culture of these countries. In spite of these efforts, the European nation-states have always retained within their political boundaries very substantial ethnic minorities, whose cultures vary significantly from that of the dominant state.

The process of European integration, which affects rules, regulations, and therefore people's daily lives to an increasing extent, has definitely decreased differences in life style and outlook. In certain cases, however, these differences may have been replaced by other cultural differences between groups of people within each of those countries. Another highly relevant trend in Europe has been the recent development of multiethnic, multicultural communities in which individuals of different and potentially conflicting cultures live in the same country, city, or street. This is the result of large-scale immigration from European, as well as non-European, countries (Verma & Entzinger, 1992).

As modern technology, media, international travel, and everyday intercultural contacts cause cultures to become closer, many differences seem to become relative and reduced to common factors. This convergence and mixing of cultures also generates defensive attitudes. Even Europe's unification process, expressed in common legislation, legal standards and administrative regulations, a common currency, and so forth, may reinforce the fear of not being able to locate oneself in a common European culture. Hence the concept of multicultural societies in a Europe that is becoming more and more integrated contains both anxieties and opportunities (Knapp, 1990). Such apparently contradictory tendencies are not surprising, because standardization and destandardization are becoming part of daily life.

Research on the possibilities of intercultural cooperation and the experience of existing projects show that linguistic differences are one of the most crucial factors hindering intercultural cooperation (Cohen & Miyake, 1986). But communication is not only determined by language: For example, differences in style of writing, presentation of arguments, loudness of speaking, body distance, and so forth are also culture bound. However, communication styles are only a single aspect of cultural factors that influence interaction between people. Work-related, family-related, leisure-related, and other values, norms, and conventions differ among European countries, and/or within one and the same country. For instance, job competence is assessed according to culture-specific concepts, as are expectations about appropriate leadership styles. It is not surprising that many other factors influence virtual instruction.

Factors Influencing Virtual Instruction

The application of information and communication technologies (ICT) and their success in education varies from country to country. Influential factors include

- The availability of the technology. The lack of ISDN technology in some countries (e.g., in Central and Eastern Europe) prohibits educators from using videoconferencing as an instructional or instruction-supporting device. Education has never been a reason to develop technology. On the contrary, educational use of a specific technology only became successful in most cases after technology conquered the larger consumer market (e.g., television, audio and video recorders, and computers). Even the case of the Internet is illustrative. Although its initial major popularity was in universities, Internet use boomed for instructional purposes only after it proved its effectiveness in the research area. Besides the cost factor—the educational sector lacks the money to invest in updating its technology at the pace that is dictated by the ICT companies—this situation clearly illustrates the subcultures of business, research, and education, with completely different values about quality and estimation of user needs.

- National and European legislation. Legislation previously restricted cable television in many European countries to conventional television broadcast, only opening cable TV for other uses (including education) within local, small-scale experiments (Van den Branden, Devoldere, & Tilley, 1993). With the Directive of the European Union (a kind of supranational bill), which ordered the "liberalization" of telecom services and operations from 1998 onward, cable operators are able to extend their activities in the educational field. However, again there are differences between countries that anticipated what is coming and began experimentation with the educational use of cable TV in real-life settings and others that are still defending telecom monopolies within their borders, thus excluding cable TV use.

- Specific constraints. Satellite technology is primarily used for educational purposes (eventually in conjunction with other media) in countries that need to concern themselves with reaching populations in isolated regions, over wide expanses of territory (such as Finland), or both. Similarly, cable TV is only feasible in regions or countries that are densely cabled (such as Belgium and the Netherlands). Acceptance by users of these media for educational use is largely influenced by this need.

- Financial constraints. In some cases (e.g., Central and Eastern Europe) and certainly on an institutional level, the application of technology relies on the availability of financial support that comes from external funding sources. The European Union has recognized this problem for some time and therefore strongly supports the use of educational technology on a project basis through a number of programs (e.g., the open and distance learning strands of Socrates, Leonardo da Vinci, Phare, Tempus, and Telematics Application programs). Participation in these programs is very unevenly distributed among European countries, again illustrating the different perception of their use attributable to cultural differences in the member states.

- Cultural differences as such. These authors' own research in the framework of the European Open University Network project, using the questionnaire that was developed by Lowyck, Elen, Proost, and Buena (1995), found cultural differences between larger European regions in the attitude toward telematics use. Inhabitants of Northern and Western European countries show significant preferences for studying with computers compared with students and professionals from Southern and Central/Eastern European countries, although all respondents want to maintain traditional education methods also. The Southern, Central/Eastern European people believe more clearly that a high level of educational competence is necessary to work with telematics, and they prefer working with computers in

> small groups. They also believe more distinctly that audio and visual information is necessary for the learning process. These findings are quite independent of the various expertise categories to which respondents belong (undergraduate, graduate and postgraduate, Ph.D. students, professionals): Differences in attitudes among countries are about equally reflected in each expertise category.

When questioned about their interest in using telematics links to communicate with top experts and peers, no significant differences between these expertise categories were found. All are very enthusiastic about using telematics and are expecting/ finding that telematics are not difficult to use for this purpose. Differences emerge when more detailed aspects are taken into consideration. Ph.D. students and professionals are the most motivated to use computers for learning. Graduates, and specifically undergraduates, are less motivated, as they consider study with this medium as demanding more investment of energy than conventional study does. All student categories, and specifically undergraduates, expect, however, that technology will improve their learning, whereas professionals are more hesitant on this point (preferring more traditional environments, including lectures or printed materials for their learning/training).

Gender differences were also found: European men prefer computer-based technologies significantly more than European women do, but no difference is noticed for audio and visual learning media. This is in contrast to other (American) studies, where no significant differences between boys and girls on general attitudes toward computers were found (Askar, Yavuz & Koksal, 1992).

On an institutional level, we find again a mixture of influential factors. Some of these are objective (e.g., the cost factor, the access to technology relying on external availability within the country, the availability of central technical support for users), but some are clearly linked to cultural issues.

EuroPACE 2000's experiences demonstrate a clear distinction between the experience with and attitude toward educational technology of both staff and students in the science and humanities faculties (confirming the Challis and Johnston,

1994, observations). In addition to this illustration of "subcultures," another observation may be added: Typically, the implementation of ICT in education is advocated both at the level of top management (recognizing the potential of ICT as a strategic issue in opening the market of continuing and lifelong learning, as well as in preparing the university and its pedagogy for the next decades) and at the basic level of teachers and tutors who experienced the benefits of ICT in their lectures and tutorials and became very enthusiastic. The difficult layer lies in between those two: the faculty management, the university's intermediate decision levels, and management levels (Edwards & O'Mahony, 1996).

Courseware Design for Transnational Virtual Instruction

A number of problems must be addressed when designing courseware that can be used for transnational virtual instruction. It is vital that examples and references should be considered by the learner as relevant to his or her own experience and expectations. Cultural biases can consequently affect the acceptability of courseware.

Problems may arise with spelling of words, the use of humor, the application of certain colors and graphic characters, and so forth. A possible solution to this problem is localizing or versioning, either by the course developers or through local adaptation at the user's level. A second solution, but normally also the more expensive one, is the specific development of courseware for the local market. Such courses should seek to incorporate local cultural material not only for its own value and accessibility but also to facilitate understanding of general concepts found in imported distance education programs (Weatherlake, 1995).

In addition, learning and teaching styles vary from one country or community to another because what is pedagogically acceptable in one may not be in another. A possible solution to this problem is for learners to choose their own route through a course and adapt the material so that it uniquely fits their own learning styles (Dixon & Blin, 1993). Collis, Parisi, and Ligorio (1995) suggest that, when adapting courses for trans-European telelearning, one has to choose a course content with cross-cultural or culture-neutral aspects. This results in two guidelines :

1. Choose course contents in which the cross-cultural aspects of trans-European participation are either of minimal relevance (thus highly specialized courses or courses relating to a common transborder phenomenon such as learning to use the Internet) or courses in which the cross-cultural aspects are integral to the content (such as courses preparing persons for internationally oriented work experiences).

2. Do not assume that course quality and usefulness will automatically improve by embedding communication and interaction. If these are not carefully planned, only extra problems from the cross-cultural perspective may be developed. For example, forcing learners to talk with each other in a common—foreign—language, such as in videoconferencing, may create more confusion than understanding and burden the learners.

Many of the students in virtual instruction environments are adults with busy lives, and part-time study is just a relatively minor part of their lives. Because teachers and course designers often come from conventional universities, they lack experience with mature students and tend to ignore the constraints of these students' wider social contexts (expectations of partner and family, demands of professional and social life, daily pursuits). The "subcultures" that are connected to these social contexts will, again, largely influence course experience and results.

LANGUAGE IN VIRTUAL INSTRUCTION

Because virtual instruction in Europe addresses primarily a transnational audience, language is probably the predominant cultural factor confronting all involved actors. Almost all international conferences on distance education in recent years have reported on language as a complicating factor in cross-cultural instruction and education (Lambert, 1998). Our own experience when evaluating courses and validating the functional models of a virtual university (Dillemans, Lowyck, Van der Perre, Claeys, & Elen, 1998) within EuroPACE 2000 are not different (Van den Branden, Sculley, Maes, & Van Hove, 1998).

The Concept of Language

The term "language" in this context does not refer to the broader concept of language as the collection of sign systems (e.g., electronic signs in computer use) or—in the more restricted sense—verbal communication (as opposed to nonverbal communication). Although these meanings of the term may also be significant for virtual instruction, what is reported here refers quite strictly to the communication difficulties that are created by using "a foreign language" (mostly English as the lingua franca) for instruction and support activities. Let us add that "foreign language" tends also to be, quite erroneously, reduced to foreign "national standard languages," which exclude so-called dialects, if not the full range of oral discourse activities and other varieties of discourse. But the very conflict among national languages is already so complex in itself that it deserves to be treated first of all as "the problem of language" in virtual instruction: The problem of language and/as discourse has hardly been explored yet.

The fact that the use of language(s) in communication is treated as a difficulty rather than simply an intrinsic aspect of communication within any cultural situation is indicative of the nature of the problem itself. Research on international communication has developed in the areas of business administration and management, social psychology, anthropology, and so forth, but with very erratic references to linguistics and with a strong emphasis on those kinds of (Saussurean) linguistics that leave "culture" (and discourse, or pragmatics) out of the debate (Janssens, Lambert, & Steyaert, in press). Consequently, language has generally been left out as an object of research on intercultural communication, with the exception of translation as a "(technical) service" (Janssens et al., in press). Hence, the linguistic component has generally been abandoned to applied linguistics and especially to foreign language teaching. Language has been treated as a technique, not as culture.

Language Policy Versus Language Management

Given the lack of a well-established research tradition, managers and political leaders have often looked for pragmatic (and political) solutions. It is frightening, however, that the same attitude can be found in educational environments. During the Online Educa Conference in Berlin (November 1995), the TELESCOPIA project suggested that the language problem in open and distance learning could be solved by imposing the use of one common language (that is, English), now possible because better methods for teaching English exist all over Europe, and by shifting in instruction from language to visual communication wherever possible. Such recommendations ignore at least two important considerations: (1) the obvious conflict between such options and the general claims in matters of cultural identity and language on behalf of the European Union and its member states, regarding advantages of differentiation in minorities (just like colonization, the lingua franca model imposes standardization quite unilaterally); and (2) the rich research tradition about the interaction between language and culture, and more specifically the research on visual communication (advertising, intercultural communication, semiotics), which rejects the assumption that visual communication would simply escape cultural differentiation. The so-called missionary stance, again, becomes the heart of the matter, while promoting simplification as a key to worldwide (economic) success.

In other words, the language question is often approached on an incorrect basis:

- Can we prevent language from being an obstacle?
- Is language an obstacle to efficient communication?

Such a defensive point of view prohibits those who plan ICT-based education from integrating the language question from the beginning into their planning, in the expectation that imposing a common language policy automatically will solve the problem. In a state-of-the-art overview on language policy versus language management, Jansen and Lambert (1995) concluded that naive individuals believe in the existence of perfect communication and that we must reject the assumption that all partners in international (virtual/distance education) networks have the same goals, expectations, and competences. In fact, the diversity of goals, expectations, and backgrounds is often the very reason why people like to study in a transnational context. It may even be the sine qua non of the learning process: We all want to learn from those who are different from us because they are supposed to be more "learned." Any assumption of homogeneity leads to the opinion that misunderstanding is an accident, instead of an inevitable component of any communication, for which language is largely responsible. Such perception implies that the overall view of communication is highly mechanical and not culture oriented. Therefore, language policies should be replaced by language management, which aims at avoiding mechanical solutions and replacing them with solutions based upon observation, options, goals, strategies.

Virtual societies—including the virtual instruction networks—represent a new kind of society. They can be characterized as societies in which the relationships among members become possible only through (verbal and other) communication. In their study on the language component in virtual networks, Cammaert, Lambert, and Van den Branden (1997) analyze the language component in traditional networks to establish whether its function can be transferred into virtual networks as well. Most traditional learning networks (e.g., learned societies) originated as national networks, as part of the educational establishment, and gradually became international by accumulation of national networks. Most of them promoted a lingua franca policy in that larger international contacts (meetings, conferences) were using a common language or some common languages (with translation), but bilateral meetings would use the language(s) of the partners involved. The larger the extension, the more languages might be used simultaneously. The organization Scholars in Translation Studies formerly used English, French, and German as linguae francae, but now that meetings are taking place in Central Europe, languages like

Russian, Czech, and so forth are under consideration as "official" languages of the organization. Similar approaches have been undertaken by UNO, UNESCO, and—the most extreme example—the European Union, in which all official languages of member states automatically become official languages of the Union itself (Fishman, 1993; Lambert, 1994, 1995, 1998).

The progressive way in which these societies evolved had effects on the language issue, too. As highly regarded, well-established networks, these societies were solicited by candidate members, who were prepared to pay the price of entrance in accepting the language policy. Comparable to interhuman relations in colonial situations, this policy was often not questioned by the newcomer, nor was it reflected upon by the network management (Cammaert, Lambert, & Van den Branden, 1997). With the shift from paternalism to democracy, the implicit opinion of new partners in international networks increasingly assumes that real partnership is incompatible with one-sided domination. This insight has not yet resulted in systematic application to the language question, except on certain levels of the European Union apparatus (Fishman, 1993). However, since the entire package of agreements between partners in a network needs to be negotiated, the question of language can (and should) be integrated into the general deal. Language then becomes part of the general management, which by definition implies the possibility of adapting the decisions and options to new needs and situations.

What applies to the traditional networks is also valid for virtual ones. Strategic planning of activities is needed, taking into account various practical aspects:

- Are there any reasons for planning monolingual/multilingual activities?
- Who decides, and what might be the consequences of the fact that x decides (instead of y)?
- Who has to use, at which moment, which language, where and with what aim?

Language management thus also involves a form of human resources management, and it is wrong to imagine that language can or could ever be unproblematic, even in so-called monolingual societies (Janssens, et al., in press; Lambert, 1998).

Guidelines for Language Management in Virtual Instruction Networks

Based on the previous discussion, the following practical guidelines are offered:

- All partners have to agree on the language policy to be followed. This matter has to be discussed explicitly beforehand and on an equal basis among the partners. The conditions for efficient communication should be clear to all partners from the start, and the partners must commit themselves to respect these conditions. This means that no language should be used that has not been agreed upon initially; if this does occur, the mutual confidence among the partners is likely to be damaged. Changes in the linguistic constellation should only be made if they are accepted unanimously by all partners.
- The management of languages should be built into the general communication strategy, which in turn should be based on the principle of feedback. The principle of integration entails that this discussion is part of the general discussion on the aims of the instruction program: What do the partners want to achieve with it, and what is the target audience? This discussion should be as open and multilateral as possible. In accordance with this, other decisions have to be made, for example about the additional learning resources, who will be involved, when and for what, and so forth. This open communication is bound to have a positive effect on the entire organizational process, which can thus be made more efficient and harmonious. In addition, the use of languages can be utilized as a marketing strategy toward new audiences.

- Special attention should be paid to the efficiency of the language used in telecommunications in the multicultural environment: a mixture of use of common language(s) for transnational communication and local language for internal communication, provision of translation (e.g., in Internet communication, or simultaneous translation in videoconferencing), dubbing and subtitling of prerecorded instruction, and so forth. The development of speech production programs, only one aspect of the mediatization process, deserves our full attention, not just because of its practical implications, but also because in its very basic principles it redefines the borders between language and discourse.
- It is very important that the actual functioning of these and other principles be systematically monitored in real-life situations by independent observers (researchers). A constant observation of the conscious and unconscious difficulties that occur in multilateral and multilingual communication is an absolute condition for preventing irritation and conflicts. For this purpose, sophisticated descriptive models have to be worked out (within frameworks such as descriptive translation studies, sociolinguistics, communication studies, and the like).

THE VirtUE AND THETA-DUNE CASES

Virtual University for Europe (VirtUE) is a project in the framework of the TEN ISDN program of the European Union, to promote the use of Euro-ISDN-based technologies (Van den Branden, 1998). The project finished a feasibility and pilot phase to prepare the launch of a European Tertiary Distance Education Network. This network is based on cooperation between traditional universities (involved through the European networks of EuroPACE 2000 and Coimbra Group and the Italian network Consorzio Nettuno), one open university (Fern Universität Hagen), technology providers (IBM and Alcatel Bell), and telecom operators (Helsinki Telephone Company and

Telecom Italia). The study addressed "on-campus" students (from undergraduate to graduate and Ph.D. level) and "off-campus" students at the postgraduate level (including continuing education and professional development). It aimed at the further development of the "virtual university" concept through three conceptual models of network-based educational services and is directed toward implementing this concept in a permanent operational network (VirtUE itself), including the necessary service provision, which uses a mixture of Euro-ISDN and other technologies (Internet, interactive television) and services. The project has entered a "deployment" phase: extension of the network from about 20 to 100 universities in a five-year period. Experiences and outcomes of the feasibility and pilot phase are reported below.

The three educational services models ("effective utilization models") that are elaborated and validated through trans-European pilots within the project period are virtual class and campus, flexible and distance education, and learning on demand.

Virtual Class and Campus

This model is based on internal communication among the network nodes (universities). Within the "virtual campus" model, subject-oriented subnetworks of universities are created to set up virtual classes in which the participating universities offer joint seminars and courses, as well as research communication and cooperation activities, to staff and students by means of ICT. The model was validated in the fields of the humanities (virtual class at the undergraduate level in human rights, European environmental law, and literature) and European Ph.D. seminars (in the fields of contemporary biomechanics, cosmology, computer vision, social representation and communication, dynamic system identification, and telecom engineering).

More concretely, the basic elements of virtual classes consist of transmitted lectures, usually taught to live audiences who are present, on the average, in five to six remote classrooms during transmission time. Each lecture is taught by one teacher—in the physical presence of a group of students at some point—and followed by all (remote) classes in the network. In the series of lectures, each lecture is typically taught by a different teacher (working at a different participating university in a different European country). By choosing the best content expert for each lecture topic, the students receive an outstanding "course," although each professor has to provide only one lecture or one module.

Some variants of this basic model will use partly pre-recorded lectures, demonstrations as part of the lecture, or both; others provide modules that are taught simultaneously by various professors, each residing in a different university while teaching. However, the model of the virtual class always implies that the students can communicate with the teacher and with their fellow students during the class and in between classes. This ongoing dialogue takes place through e-mail or computer conferences.

To enhance (synchronous) communication during the lectures, the basic technology used for the virtual class is ISDN multipoint videoconferencing. For the same reason, the number of participating sites (classes) is usually limited to eight. This number enables real communication and matches the available ports of many MCUs (conferencing bridges) currently in use.

Larger numbers of student groups (greater than eight) are either serviced in cascaded ISDN bridges or by using interactive television (satellite). Cascading can be considered when the course is taught to an asymmetrical audience: an "inner circle" of actively participating university classes (e.g., five to seven) that are involved in direct interaction through the videoconferencing system and an "outer circle" of participant groups (participating sites) on the cascaded bridge(s), which follow the lecture rather passively, only interacting with the teacher through asynchronous communication technologies (fax, e-mail, computer conferencing). The incoming comments and questions of these groups are passed to the lecturer (e.g., on a computer screen) to be dealt with during the lecture. The teacher then can invite an "outer circle" site to take the floor when the incoming communication is relevant to all learners. However, from a cost viewpoint, the use of a combination of satellite transmission for the delivery of the lecture with back-links for interaction (audio-links, e-mail, and computer conferencing, eventually fax and even videoconferencing) is preferable when the number of receiving sites increases.

Flexible and Distance Education

In this model, students remain at their workplaces, homes, local study centers (e.g., open universities), or company training centers. The model is used within VirtUE for continuing education and for professional postgraduate programs that may lead to professional advanced master's degrees.

The "electronic university on the Web" concept can be considered as one way among many to realize this model functionally; other ways include conventional open university course production and delivery combined with technology-supported tutoring, or "television universities."

The VirtUE pilots that validated this function are in the field of professional development in IT&T (Ketels, 1998). The pilot lectures and seminars are offered by interactive TV (e.g., satellite transmission, broadcasting) and (ISDN-based) videoconferencing, depending on the size and level of the target audience, the nature of the subject (e.g., the need for high-quality images), and the number, as well as dispersion, of the participating classes (reception sites). Videoconferencing and audio conferencing are also used for synchronous interaction between learners and teachers, whereas asynchronous learner support is enabled by the Internet and a dedicated computer conferencing system. Network management issues (e.g., scheduling, technical information) and support for teachers and tutors (course development, exchange of experience, and relevant expertise) use the computer conferencing system, as this is a protected environment.

The courses are again typically set up by networks of universities (and companies) to bring available expertise together. Each participating university develops and delivers the course modules, as well as accompanying study materials, in which it excels. All courses and study materials are pooled in the network to provide study support to independent home learners (or learners participating through study or training centers). The learners register for a course through the local university (study/training center) but may get support from different areas: local tutoring for more general aspects in combination with specialized tutoring on subject aspects by remote specialists. Course materials and remote tutoring are mostly provided in a lingua franca (English), whereas local tutoring may take place in the native language.

Learning on Demand

A trans-European university network is a distributed knowledge resource with available expertise (in materials and personnel) that is nearly unlimited: Any demand for learning can in principle be responded to. Within VirtUE, some elements of such a model were elaborated (e.g., competency testing and crediting through the network), leaving the real development of the model for the deployment phase. Guided tours in the field of "state-of-the-art computer sciences" are currently being developed for professionals who graduated some 5 to 10 years ago and need updating. This is one example of a provision for learning on demand.

THETA-DUNE is a joining of two similar projects (THETA submitted by EuroPACE 2000 and DUNE submitted by the European Open University Network, [EOUN]) in the framework of the Erasmus-Thematic Networks strand of the SOCRATES program (European Union). Thematic Networks aim at dissemination through collaboration of quality in European university education. In contrast with the other Thematic Networks, which are mostly discipline based, THETA-DUNE aims at the creation of a European Forum for discussion and dissemination of opportunities, conditions, and examples of best practices of technology-supported education in conventional and open universities.* Although the influence of cultural factors on (virtual) instruction in international networks is not the central focus of the activities, the issue is brought into discussion.

*For more information, see http://www.europace.be/project/theta/default.htm.

OBSERVATIONS

The intermediate results of both ongoing projects, specifically with respect to aspects related to cultural factors, are summarized below (Van den Branden et al., 1998).

Attitudes of Teachers and Students Toward Technology

There is a scale of attitudes toward technology, ranging from reluctance and resistance to enthusiasm. The attitudes are influenced on the negative side

- By fear of the unknown, by the expectation that technology use will add additional work to what conventionally is expected ("normal" teaching preparation, "normal" study assignments) and consequently will create a work overload.

- By opposition to the change of roles implied by technology. Teachers must shift from the role of knowledge communicators through lectures and seminars to the role of supporters of the students' learning (mainly based on self-instruction) and mediators of understanding by the provision of learning resources. Students are confronted with increased responsibility for their own learning process and outcomes.

On the positive side students (and teachers) welcome technology for

- Its supportive role in eliminating boring tasks (for example, calculus in problem solving),

- The opportunity to obtain fast and easy access to large learning and teaching resources,

- The possibility to become familiar with the tools that are of use outside education (in research, in daily life),

- The challenge of innovation that educational technology may create (e.g., introduction in a transnational context).

These attitudes are, however, culturally embedded:

- Students and teachers from the humanities are on average less familiar with technology and tend to question the advantage of technology use. It must be admitted, however, that once they have "taken the plunge" and immersed themselves in it, their attitude becomes mostly positive.
- Overall, students are very enthusiastic about the European dimension that technology can bring into their education. This is best demonstrated when a course deals with content that is culturally embedded, but even for culturally "neutral" information, a transnational discussion is experienced as very enriching.
- Students appreciate the opportunity to have direct access to experts (who are often foreign) and to expertise that is not available in the home university or organization. This observation is particularly valid for the postgraduate and Ph.D. levels. Such opportunities also confront students and teachers with (results of) differences (both as advantages and disadvantages) in the tertiary education concepts of various countries and may challenge universities to come up with innovative changes. However, positive attitudes are not eliminating justified criticism of technology and education.

Technology-Driven Versus Technology-Supported

Teachers and students are very hesitant about a technology-driven use of educational technology (technology overruling pedagogy). Education comes first and technology should offer an additional value to it or be omitted. They are very critical of courses in which content and pedagogy are subordinated to technology. They equally demand that the technology mix be functional to the teaching/learning process and not be determined by the needs of European industry to test equipment and services for educational use. This observation is indifferent to cultural background but is influenced by the still-existing lack of (technical) standards and availability of technological infrastructure, which hinder a full trans-European use of educational technology. Specifically, in Central and Eastern Europe, a tendency is noticed to accept lower quality as long as technology becomes available.

Investment by Universities

The use of ICT is relatively expensive. However, it is a common observation that universities are willing to make the necessary investment in hardware and software and are prepared to accept reasonable communications costs. Less fortunately, in a number of cases, the utilization requirements and their connected costs are underestimated or overlooked, with the consequence being that sometimes equipment is available without people being aware of it or that its use is hindered by a lack of technical support.

A similar failing in managerial attitude is encountered in that most universities are still reluctant to pay for courses produced by other universities or institutions, even if they are recognized as being of high quality. If courses are offered for free, participation increases immediately, proving the fact that this phenomenon is not caused by a "what-we-do-ourselves-we-do-better" attitude but by insufficient recognition of education as an economic reality. Large-scale development of a self-supporting virtual university for Europe may depend largely upon overcoming such attitudes.

Although these observations are more or less valid for all universities, the larger the university, the more the organizational culture tends to be rigid, with a more pronounced tendency toward these attitudes as a consequence.

Language and Cultural Factors

Although the previous points illustrate the existence of many "subcultures" in the university world (certainly in a transnational comparison but even within the same university), language and other aspects that are typically considered as culture bound, such as (differences in) prior knowledge, cultural subjects, attitudes toward culturally embedded topics, discussion and learning styles, and so forth, remain barriers to transnational educational networks.

Technology may contribute to overcoming some of these barriers. Specifically, the language factor could benefit from technology developments, for example, local organization of simultaneous translation while transmitting lectures and seminars, and in the future speech recognition combined with online automatic translation. Most participants (lecturers and students alike) are, however, insufficiently aware of these problems. Technology itself is not sufficient; it needs to be used and integrated. The mere awareness of the cultural and linguistic components may have no power on budgets; the equipment for simultaneous interpreting has generally been overlooked, even in very multicultural environments for videoconferencing. Native speakers of the lingua franca tend to forget that they must adapt the speed at which they talk; teachers and students use concepts in discussions that have different meanings in different countries; and so forth. Transformation of the language problem into a language management policy, which is set up from the very beginning as an agreement among participants and then maintained according to good management principles, is the only way to tackle the issue.

The solution for other cultural problems is less straightforward. Many of these issues are tightly connected with social relations among individuals, groups, and even nations, relations that are the outcome of spontaneous evolution or intentional actions of power creation and maintenance.

CONCLUSIONS

Cross-cultural issues have been studied largely throughout the world. Most often, however, the research focuses on basic factors (gender, social status, race, ethnic origin, age, language, learning style, and so forth) and measures the influence of these factors on outcomes of education (learning difficulties, grades, success in finding employment, and so forth). Studies that take the scope of the complex sociocultural reality and investigate its influence on transnational distance education are rare, although difficulties that arise when organizing this kind of distance education are recognized and reported. With virtual instruction becoming more popular, it can be expected that complaints and feelings of dissatisfaction will increase, unless proper action is undertaken. This action cannot be one of the last stages: If adaptation and localization of existing learning and instruction materials ever worked to overcome the problem in more conventional distance education, it certainly will fail in the virtual instruction environment, largely characterized by its synchronous as well as transnational nature.

The influence on education of cross-cultural factors should not necessarily be considered as negative: Users who participate in European virtual education projects express their enthusiasm (finding the transnational study experience interesting, enriching, and stimulating), as well as their problems with cultural diversity. The search for diversity and complementarity is often a decisive element at the very origin of partnerships and learning processes. It may be our strong tradition of conventional education that imposes the narrow idea of standard profiled audiences. A predominant element within this problematic area is the language factor. Students, teachers, tutors, administrators, and even technical staff are aware of the problem but fail to find or handle solutions. This can be explained partly as a consequence of the isolation of the linguistic factor from its more complex cultural background and by the tendency to reduce the language problem to a technical-mechanical phenomenon instead of situating it in the broader context of communication. The problem is more or less neglected by the use of a lingua franca or transferred to another level of solution (e.g., the suggestion to take language courses, on the assumption that these will enable participants to communicate efficiently). The idea that language must (necessarily) be an obstacle, can easily be turned upside down: It may be an obstacle for certain partners but become a strategic tool for others, namely those who know how to use it, as one of the (not yet) validated assets in most kinds of intercultural communication. In other words, many partners in international cooperation use the (linguistic) global model as an instrument of wishful thinking that protects them against better and more competitive partners: We are to be blamed when not taking any benefits from it. In any competition, complaints are interesting indicators of weaknesses and offer interesting suggestions for strategic options. As for the other aspects of virtual instruction (design, development, delivery, support, and so forth), a (total quality) management approach (Lambert, 1998) must be taken to cope with difficulties that are created by the cultural and linguistic diversity of the participants.

It remains remarkable that even recent reports and well-received publications in the field (e.g., European Round Table of Industrialists, 1997; Edwards & O'Mahony, 1996; Laurillard, 1993) omit or mention only implicitly the cultural factors and their influence. Most of the time they are dealt with as threats. The question is whether the time has come to share the enthusiasm of students and teachers, concentrate on the enrichment of cultural diversity, and tackle this diversity as a challenge on the way to communication among societies and improvement of the quality of education.

REFERENCES

Askar, P., Yavuz, H., & Koksal, M. (1992). Students' perceptions of computer assisted instruction environment and their attitudes towards computer assisted learning. *Educational Research Volume, 34*(2), 133–139.

Barrera, A. (1993, Fall). Distance learning: The challenge for a multicultural society. *Focus,* 4–14.

Becher, T. (1990). The counter-culture of specialisation. *European Journal of Education, 25*(3), 333–346.

Cammaert, G., Lambert, J., & Van den Branden, J. (1997). The language component in ODL. In D. Sánchez-Mesa Martinez, J. Lambert, D. Apollon, & J. Van den Branden (Eds.), *Crosscultural and linguistic perspectives on European open and distance learning.* TRANSCULT I (67–108). Granada, Spain: University of Granada Press.

Challis, K., & Johnston, R. (1994). Two cultures: The influence of academic discipline on staff perceptions of teaching and learning. *International Journal of University Adult Education, 33*(2), 15–28.

Cohen, M., & Miyake, N. (1986). A worldwide intercultural network: Exploring electronic messaging for instruction. *Instructional Science, 15,* 257–273.

Collis, B., Parisi, D., & Ligorio., B. (1995). *Becoming more flexible: Issues confronting the adaptation of courses for Trans-European Tele-learning.* Twente, The Netherlands: University of Twente.

Coulmas, F. (Ed.). (1991). *A language policy for the European Community: Prospects and quandaries.* Berlin: Mouton de Gruyter.

Dillemans, R., Lowyck, J., Van der Perre, G., Claeys, C., & Elen, J. (1998). *New technologies for learning: Contribution of ICT to innovation in education.* Leuven, Belgium: Leuven University Press.

Dixon, M., & Blin, F. (1993). Issues in instructional design for CAL: Problems and possible solutions. In S. A. Cerri & J. Whiting (Eds.), *Learning technology in the European communities* (pp. 725–733). Dordrecht, The Netherlands: Kluwer Academic Publishers.

Edwards, K., & O'Mahony, M. (1996). *Restructuring the university: Universities and the challenge of new technologies.* Geneva, Switzerland: Association of European Universities (CRE).

European Round Table of Industrialists. (1997). *Investing in knowledge: The integration of technology in European education.* Brussels, Belgium: Author.

Fishman, J. A. (1993). Ethnolinguistic democracy: Varieties, degrees, limits. *Language International, 5*(1), 11–17.

Huber, L. (1990). Disciplinary cultures and social reproduction. *European Journal of Education, 25*(3), 241–261.

Jansen, P., & Lambert, J. (1995). Language and/as intercultural strategy in open distance learning. In J. Van den Branden (Ed.), *Handbook of cultural factors in use of technology learning environments* (pp. 26–90). Heverlee, Belgium: EuroPACE 2000.

Janssens, M., Lambert, J., & Steyaert, C. (in press). *Vertalen en talen leren in het meertalige bedrijf: Organisatie-metaforen [Translation and language learning in the multilingual company: Organisation metaphors].*

Ketels, M. (1998). Bridging companies and universities for postgraduate training: Two large-scale case-studies. In A. Szücs & A. Wagner (Eds.), *Universities in a digital era. Transformation, innovation and tradition. Roles and perspectives of open and distance learning* (pp. 62–65). Budapest, Hungary: EDEN Secretariat.

Knapp, K. (1990). Common market, common culture? *European Journal of Education, 25*(1), 55–60.

Lambert, J. (1994). Ethnolinguistic democracy, translation policy and contemporary world (dis)order. In F. Eguiluz, & R. Merino (Eds.), *Transvases culturales: Literatura, cine, traducción* (pp. 23–36). Vitoria, Spain: Universitad del País Vasco, Departamento de Filologia Inglesa y Alemana.

Lambert, J. (1995). Literatures, translation and (de)colonization. In *The force of vision: Proceedings of the XIIIth Congress of the International Comparative Literature Association.* Tokyo: University of Tokyo Press.

Lambert, J. (1998, June). The trouble with language in ODL: State of the art, options, strategies. Paper presented at the 1998 EDEN Conference, University of Bologna, Italy.

Laurillard, D. (1993). *Rethinking university teaching: A framework for the effective use of educational technology.* London: Routledge Kegan Paul.

Lowyck, J., Elen, J., Proost, K., & Buena, G. (1995). *Telematics in open and distance learning: Research methodology handbook.* Leuven, Belgium: Catholic University of Leuven, Centre for Instructional Psychology and Technology.

McInerney, W. (1989). Social and organizational effects of educational computing. *Journal of Educational Computing Research, 5*(4), 487–506.

Pinxten, R., & Farrer, C. K. (1990). On learning. A comparative view. *Cultural Dynamics, 3*(2), 233–248.

Reif, L. (1989). Interkulturelles Kommunikationstraining: Konzepte, Ziele und Organisation [Intercultural communication training: Concept, nature, and organization]. *Personalführung,* (2), 175–177.

Strydom, P., & O'Mahony, P. (1993). Sociological questions in open learning standards and the learner environment. In P. Strydom & P. O'Mahony (Eds.), *Learning technology in the European countries.* Dordrecht, The Netherlands: Kluwer Academic Press.

Van den Branden, J. (1998). VirtUE: A virtual university for Europe. In A. Szücs & A. Wagner (Eds.), *Universities in a digital era. Transformation, innovation and tradition. Roles and perspectives of open and distance learning* (pp. 662–667). Budapest, Hungary: EDEN Secretariat.

Van den Branden, J., Devoldere, P., & Tilley, K. (1993). *International aspects on the use of cable TV for education.* Leuven, Belgium: Mediatek.

Van den Branden, J., Sculley, T., Maes, V., & Van Hove, C. (1998). *VirtUE: Validation report on the pilot network.* Heverlee, Belgium: EuroPACE 2000.

Verma, G., & Entzinger, H. (1992). Transferring knowledge in a cross-cultural perspective. In *Learning technology in the European communities* (p. 683). Dordrecht, The Netherlands: Kluwer Academic Publishers.

Weatherlake, S. (1995). Course design for a multicultural society. In D. E. Sewart (Ed.), *One world, many voices: Quality in open and distance learning* (pp. 186–190). Milton Keynes, England: International Council for Distance Education and The Open University.

CHAPTER 9

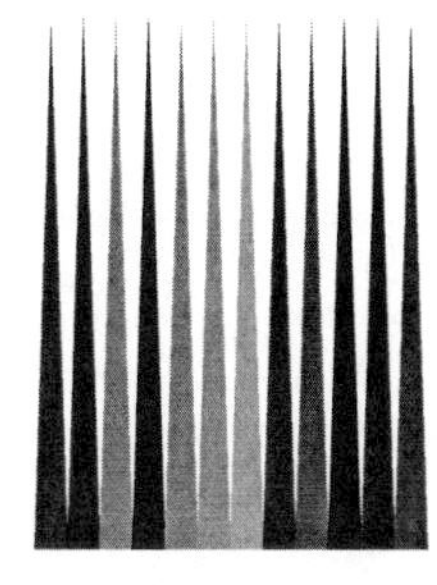

Distance Learning and Virtual Instruction

An Asian Perspective on a Culture of Simulation

Chen Ai Yen and Azam Mashhadi
Singapore

INTRODUCTION

Around the world, distance learning over the Internet or by means of other communication and information technologies is growing at an astonishing pace. The distinction between "distance education" and "traditional education" is fast disappearing with the increasing use of these new technologies. As the use of distance learning or telematics in education grows, the question arises of whether there are inherent limitations to the use of such an approach. Should instruction at a distance ultimately only be a component of a course? What are the roles of experience, language, and culture with respect to learning in an electronic or simulated learning environment? These questions are explored in this chapter.

THE FUTURE OF INTERACTIVE DISTANCE LEARNING

Although many national distance education programs are at present primarily print based, with broadcast media coming in second, the future for interactive distance learning lies in the much-hailed electronic networks, in which there is a "seamless networked learning environment" where the learner interacts with other learners, teachers, subject experts, libraries, the Internet, and so forth, in both real time and non-real time (Chute, Sayers, & Gardner, 1997, p. 75).

Chute et al. (1997) usefully summarize the two types of communication technologies used in electronic networks:

> Synchronous communication technologies, such as desktop video teleconferencing and interactive group video teleconferencing, enable live, real-time interaction between instructors and learners. Instructors, subject matter experts, and learners see and hear one another at all sites and engage in interaction similar to face-to-face classroom interaction. Asynchronous communication technologies, such as e-mail, multimedia databases, virtual libraries, and the Internet, support non-real-time interactions and access to vast information resources at a time and place convenient to learners. (p. 76)

The use of such electronic networked learning environments does hold out the promise of enabling the process of education to become more accessible, effective, and cost efficient. It is important, however, not to be overwhelmed by the associated technology and to realize that despite its potential, that technology is not a universal panacea. Increasingly, the term "virtual learning" is being used. But what does this mean? In one sense, it refers to the use of synchronous and asynchronous communication technologies in powerful and flexible learner-centered networks. In another sense the term is an oxymoron, because for learning to occur, learning has to be "real." Virtual learning, therefore, presumably refers to the use of electronic networked learning environments to achieve real learning or understanding among students.

The future of effective distance learning, telematics, or both depends on the full exploitation of the dominant claims made by distance learning enthusiasts. All point to the power of telematic learning environments in facilitating and enhancing learning. Among the often-mentioned strengths are (1) interconnectivity among people, sites, disciplines, institutions, and nations; (2) interactivity within the electronic machines, systems, software, and hardware; (3) immediacy of feedback; (4) integration of subjects, curricula, and the products and processes of technology; and (5) increasing accessibility to larger numbers of individuals. However, unless this power is properly harnessed and used, with programs being appropriately designed to further facilitate a student's learning, distance learning will be no better than its predecessor, correspondence learning.

EXPERIENCES OF VARIOUS DISTANCE AND ONLINE LEARNING MODES

Teaching inherently involves directing the learning of the student or novice. In the future, students will have greater responsibility and autonomy in influencing their own learning, but the teacher will still set the direction (influenced by time, space, resources, and curriculum constraints) and try to build a structure for the novice's learning (Scardamalia & Bereiter, 1996). Teachers in Asia, even those functioning in "traditional" environments, have some ideas, some freedom and responsibility to choose what to teach and how to teach a subject, a skill, and a procedure. Decisions are continuously being made about the what, the why, and the how of teaching irrespective of the kinds of technology and materials available.

The early distance education delivery systems were mainly print based. These correspondence courses were effective in providing information to students at a distance, unable to attend educational institutions; however, they lacked immediate two-way communication and interactivity. The growth of the

Open University in the United Kingdom in the 1970s, in particular, resulted in a change in the model. Study at the level of the university became increasingly available to working people, and broadcast media (television and radio) were used to bring education into the home (see Harry, Keegan, & Magnus, 1995). As McIsaac (1996, p. 4) points out, models of distance education reflect national policies. Korea has a cable television channel dedicated to distance learning. Britain's Open University has worked closely with the BBC in broadcasting its courses. In China, there is a huge distance education program that broadcasts nationally, while France uses satellite video transmissions.

To better illustrate how various distance learning modes are being used in the East, the experiences of particular individuals and the research literature are combined to form a few hypothetical case studies (see Zhao, 1995). These stories of Ranee in India, Yong in China, and Chu Fung in Singapore are used to highlight some of the common concerns regarding the problems and challenges of distance learning and virtual instruction.

Ranee, a middle school language teacher in India, enrolled in a correspondence language course in the Punjab. She found that, although there were times when she would have liked immediate feedback from her tutor, the time delay between letters did give her time to reflect and carefully compose her replies. Working on her own, without interaction with other students, was a lonely experience; discussing ideas with other people would have enriched the experience. On the whole, however, she found that the correspondence course did cause her to reflect and illuminate her teaching methods. She also learned to be more precise in her expressions in writing, which in a strange way seemed to help her lesson and unit planning and classroom communication.

Yong, an electrical engineer in Guangdung Province, China, learned new skills about water and flood control in a telecorrespondence course offered by the Beijing Broadcasting University. The use of radio and television, rather than just text, made learning more enjoyable and the material more digestible. But there was only a one-way communication, from the tutors/lecturers to the learner. Feedback from tutors was still a slow process, and access to libraries with relevant information was difficult. Yong found the midcourse workshop in Guangzhou most useful as he interacted with the other course participants face-to-face and received direct instruction and immediate feedback from provincial tutors and his classmates. He was able to clarify some misconceptions about flood control and felt that he could put his learning to good use upon his return to the counties under his charge.

Chu Fung was upgrading his computer skills in a virtual college course at the Singapore Polytechnic that utilized the latest Web technology. With his advanced computing diploma from the same polytechnic, received two years earlier, Chu Fung had no problem learning basic concepts and techniques about computer animation from the virtual college. Even though access to the virtual college was not as immediate or as fast as anticipated, Chu Fung was pleased that he could learn at his own pace and talk to his lecturers sometimes through e-mail or the chat facilities. He was, however, frustrated by not being able to consult readily with course lecturers online. The increasing number of students accessing the virtual college's 39 courses resulted in reduced transmission rates. Even the implementation of Singapore ONE's broad bandwidth might not solve the "traffic problem." Chu Fung's questions about the more difficult concepts and intriguing problems remained unanswered. With a heavy work schedule, Chu Fung found many advantages in being a distance learner and in having ready access to resources at his own pace, but he still appreciated face-to-face communication in tutorial and lab sessions with his peers and tutors.

As these cases illustrate, despite the fact that the promise of any new technology seldom matches the reality of its implementation, the use of electronic networked learning environments does hold out the promise of making the process of education more accessible, efficient, and cost-effective. However, there are limitations to each of the above technologies, because none of them is able to reproduce exactly the situation of two people meeting face-to-face or the teacher interacting with a group of students in the classroom. The sensory information that flows between individuals, for instance, consists not just of words but of all the nuances of body and facial language. To enhance the efficacy of e-mail, for instance, "emoticons" (such as the smiley face :)) were developed to simulate emotional nuances. This, however, is only virtual emotion and not the real thing.

Real-time videoconferencing can provide virtual face-to-face interconnectivity and interactivity, but it still has a number of physical constraints. Teleconferencing is still limited by the slow frame rate of transmission (Jacobs & Rodgers, 1997; Sankar, Ford, & Terase, 1997). Jacobs and Rodgers (1997), for instance, in describing the experience of a trans-Europe project involving the use of videoconferencing for remote interactive tutorials, mention the constraints of the number of students that can be identified on a television monitor, the quality of the video signal, and the lack of perfect synchronization between the sound and the speaker's lips. In our Asian experience, we have found that subtle facial and body gestures can be obscured in a videoconference link.

In online courses, because time to formulate questions is not limited, students can reflect on the information presented (Black, 1997). Whitelock, Brna, and Holland (1997), however, point out that there has been little empirical work on the effectiveness of virtual reality environments in promoting conceptual learning. Most previous research has demonstrated their usefulness for drill and practice "contextually welded" experiences (for example, in the acquisition of sensory-motor skills). Clift, Thomas, Levin, and Larson (1996), describing the experience of using electronic networks with student teachers, concluded that telecommunications technology is most helpful when the student does not need or want sustained dialogue (for example, when exchanging information). In times of emotional stress, prospective teachers want the visual reassurance of face-to-face communication. The benefits of using e-mail in undergraduate teaching (e.g., submitting and returning assignments) are reported on by Pitt (1996), but they are not as useful for seminar courses, which require sustained argument over a period of time. Harkrider and Chen (1998), in their qualitative inquiry into reflection by student teachers in Singapore on classroom practice using e-mail and a virtual "chat" environment, point out the merits of a "structured" dialogue and the importance of using socially and culturally sensitive language. They found that if dialogues were well-planned ahead of time, sensitivity to others was assured, and if ground rules were established, the dialogue "would be purposeful, smooth flowing and community-building" (p. 6).

One of the most exciting aspects of the information and communication revolution is how it facilitates collaboration or partnerships among learners, not just within the same community but particularly across geographical boundaries, gender, age, ethnicity, and disciplines (Gaines & Shaw, 1996). This can be clearly seen in the creation of chat groups, and multiuser domains (MUDs) and multiuser object oriented domain (MOO). The main characteristic of chat groups is the immediate transmission of typed messages between members, a form of electronic dialogue. A MUD is a software program that accepts "connections" from multiple users across the Internet. A MOO is a MUD built using object-oriented technology that makes it easier for a learner to create new objects.

The first MOO based on a virtual school in Singapore, called SkooWOO, was launched in October 1996 (Looi, 1998). Two other online learning communities were created in 1997. The first was ScienceALIVE!, a project involving 10 secondary schools that were chosen as the demonstration schools in the IT Master Plan in Education. In ScienceALIVE!, students from different schools formed a project team to research a science topic and published their findings as a virtual science exhibit. IT instructors from the Educational Technology Division of the Ministry of Education provided facilitation for the project teams to work together. Content experts from the National Institute of Education, Nanyang Technological University, and the Singapore Science Centre were also involved in serving as science experts to guide and help the students. This community of students, teachers, IT instructors, content experts, and technical experts interacted in face-to-face meetings as well as online using ScienceALIVE! An offspring of the ScienceALIVE! project is SpaceALIVE! This ongoing project involves students from schools in six SEAMEO countries (Brunei, Indonesia, Malaysia, Philippines, Singapore, and Thailand) doing research projects on the topic of transportation. Yet another online learning community is HistoryCity, a virtual community modeled on Singapore in the second half of the nineteenth century. Children can "make history" by being residents of that era, collecting and trading period items, and using them to create interactive dioramas. They have access to many different parts of old Singapore, from Chinatown to Commercial Square to Little India. These are simulated learning environments that have been specially developed as research and development projects sensitive to the culture and language of the people of Singapore and the rest of Asia.

The development of current and future technologies is fueled by a desire to develop and produce a true artificial or "virtual reality" that can ultimately reproduce in full all five sensory modes (Russell, 1997). However, even if such an artificial reality could be achieved, it is not just the limitations of the existing technologies that can lead to misunderstandings but the very nature of concepts themselves. Concepts exist within a web of meaning that is mediated by the cultures to which individuals belong (Vygotsky, 1989). The role of culture, the experiential basis of learning, and the nature of electronic learning environments are examined in greater detail below.

EXPERIENTIAL LEARNING AND THE ROLE OF CULTURE IN DISTANCE LEARNING

An inherent feature of commonsense thought is the assumption that its tenets arise directly from experience. However, an integral aspect of what "common sense" is involves the conclusions arrived at by a mind that is filled with presuppositions (Geertz, 1993). In other words, observation is "theory laden," and an individual's observations are influenced by any prior theory or "conceptual framework" developed on the basis of previous experience. The philosopher Thomas Kuhn (1977) argued that the relative importance of a "fact," its relevance, and even whether it counts as a fact at all, depend on the view of the world and the standards contained in a disciplinary framework. All knowledge is, therefore, embedded within a historical, cultural, and social framework.

The philosopher of language Ludwig Wittgenstein (1953) has provided an example of this interpretive "point of view" with his conceptual analysis of two uses of the word "see." Suppose that a person is looking at a line drawing that he or she sometimes sees as a rabbit and sometimes as a duck's head (the long bill of the duck being where the rabbit's long ears are). In one use of the word "see," this person is looking at exactly the same object; yet he or she sees it as two different objects without being able to show that difference to someone else by drawing it. Wittgenstein argued that "seeing as" (the second use of the word "see") is not part of perception. "Seeing as" is the result of the interpretation of perception.

David Hwang, best known as the playwright who wrote *M. Butterfly,* recently premiered a new play, *Golden Child,* in Singapore. The play explores the dilemmas faced by a Chinese man, who has three wives, on the eve of his conversion from Confucianism to Christianity. The audience at the premiere consisted of both Asians and Westerners. How members of the audience interpreted the play depended on their own previous physical, emotional, intellectual, and spiritual experiences, the culture(s), for instance, in which they grew up. Similarly in education, the tabula rasa conception of the learner has come to be replaced by the concept of the learner who brings to the classroom or lecture theater a complicated body of personal knowledge and understanding (Ausubel, 1963). During lessons, examples used to illustrate a concept may convey a markedly different meaning to various students, the net result being that the actual outcome may well be different from that intended.

An appreciation of the role of culture in education is essential, because it leads researchers to a deeper and more valid understanding of the nature of student learning. The anthropological conception of culture is not to think of, say, societies as having cultures in an object sense. Societies do not possess a culture, societies *are* cultures (Bate, 1994). Particular cultures may have particular "worldviews" or basic underlying assumptions (Hofstede, 1983; Pepper, 1942). At the risk of stereotyping or overgeneralizing, there are fundamental differences between Western and Eastern philosophical, religious, and cultural traditions. Western culture's sense of reality, for example, has been shaped to a large extent by a mechanistic worldview, a viewpoint that still dominates the school curriculum (Doll, 1989; Gough, 1989). Eastern culture's sense of reality seems to be more holistic, a view that takes into consideration the interdependent relationships of living things and the environment, the natural and human elements, and their mutual shaping in the construction of meaning. Williams-Green, Holmes, and Sherman (1997, p. 5), reviewing the literature on the philosophical assumptions underlying various cultures, conclude that there is a general tendency in the West to emphasize and value independence; the rights of the individual; and straightforward, purposeful interpersonal exchanges. In stark contrast, people from non-Western traditions are seen to emphasize more cooperation, group harmony, intuition, and reflection.

People interpret the information they receive from the senses via sets of beliefs they have about the world. These theories of the world are sometimes referred to as paradigms or worldviews. Proper, Wideen, and Ivany (1988) define a worldview as "a person's set of beliefs, held consciously or subconsciously, about the basic nature of reality and how one comes to know about it" (p. 547). In acting as a shield against bewilderment, one of the paradoxical features of worldviews is that their interpretative power creates unavoidable "blind spots" in the individual's perceptions. Theories of the world provide frameworks within which to organize information received from the senses, but in the process they also limit what can be perceived because of the inherent assumptions that underpin them (Marzano, 1994). Worldviews "tell" individuals and groups what to do and what to expect in a situation without the need for deep philosophical consideration. There is an interdependence of language, thought, and reality. The world is known not as it is but as it is mediated through symbolic systems, primarily linguistic, by which it is experienced and represented.

A major source of differing understandings may lie in the differing assumptions held by individuals about the underlying nature of reality and the particular structure of thought and language used to describe and communicate that reality. For example, typically in everyday language the speaker stands outside the "thing," regarding it as an object of consideration (Haste, 1993). The dualistic subject-object style of thinking may well carry with it an overwhelming bias about the way the individual comes to develop a worldview.

The experiential basis of learning is emphasized by a philosopher of education, John Dewey (1933), who referred to basic personal beliefs as a product of "original learning" and suggested that "learning ... is not primarily cognitive." Wittgenstein (1953) similarly suggested that "the propositions describing this world-picture might be part of a kind of mythology. And their role is like that of rules of a game; and the game can be learned purely practically, without learning any explicit rules" (p. 22). Garrison and Bentley (1990) combine arguments by Dewey, Wittgenstein, and Kuhn to propose that "the world picture cannot be rationally learned" (p. 20).

In other words, if communication is regarded as an exchange of ideas through the use of symbols, the symbols are not the words themselves but some elements of common human experiences with which the words are associated. Wittgenstein (1953) distinguished between "first language," which is essentially experiential and tacit, and "second language," which is expressed through the translational medium of the first. An examination of personal metaphors may reveal an individual's worldviews in ways that literal language cannot. Taylor (1984) extends Wittgenstein's suggestion that language is personally constructed from experience and suggests that metaphor is a basic component of language: "Metaphor is the basis of the conceptual systems by means of which we understand and act within our world" (p. 5).

The individual makes sense of the world through language and the process of active interaction with other individuals. Metaphors or mental models form the basis for assumptions taken for granted about the world. For example, there is a primacy of the metaphor of dualism in Western culture. The world is made sense of in terms of either/or, in terms of polarities (e.g., atomistic-holistic, linear logic-intuitive, harmony-mastery, rationality-intuition). Real change occurs when there is a profound change in the underlying metaphor of the nature of the world. If there is more than one valid alternative perspective, a monolithic or absolutist position is untenable. Metaphors provide models for explanation and can transform meaning. As Haste (1993) points out in a discussion of the sharing of common metaphors, "Metaphors provide frameworks within which we are able to think, and to communicate. Metaphors are components of lay social theory which set the agenda for the way we will conceptualize the issues, and for the solutions we will find" (p. 43).

The Western dualistic or commonsense "relative" world consists of a collection of discrete objects, interacting causally in space and time (Reichenbach, 1951). In contrast, as argued by the philosopher David Loy (1986), much of Asian philosophy constitutes a radical critique of thinking as it is considered to usually occur: "Another nonduality, the nondifference of subject and object, is a crucial—perhaps the crucial concept for several of those Eastern systems which criticize reasoning/conceptualizing particularly Mahayana Buddhism, Advaita Vedanta, and Taoism" (p. 294). The implication is not that people in Asia think nondualistically, but that in the Asian cultural tradition(s) there are underlying systems of philosophy that are fundamentally different from the Western historical and philosophical tradition. Language is not "just" a technical matter to be factored into the program of instruction; it is an integral aspect of culture (Smith, 1991). Culture itself cannot be objectified as just another factor to be programmed into designing a distance learning course. Language, culture, and learning are closely knit in Confucianist thinking and teaching. The inherent nature of electronic learning technology and the role of metaphorical mental models in shaping learning are described below in more detail. The inseparable links between language, culture, and education are also explained.

THE NATURE OF ELECTRONIC LEARNING ENVIRONMENTS

A sociologist of science, Sherry Turkle (1997), recalls, "When I first studied programming at Harvard in 1978, the professor introduced the computer to the class by calling it a giant calculator" (p. 76). Since that time there has been a significant cultural change in the understanding of computers, from a "culture of calculation" to a "culture of simulation": "The computer is a simulation machine. The world of simulation is the new stage for playing out our fantasies, both emotional and intellectual" (Turkle, 1997, p. 81).

Computer simulations enable students to think actively about complex phenomena as dynamic systems and to gain experience in manipulating a system whose underlying assumptions are not understood or may even not be true (Mellar, Bliss, Boohan, Ogborn, & Tompsett, 1994; Turkle, 1997). Microworlds, such as a collaborative computer simulation for exploring Newtonian physics (Cockburn & Greenberg, 1995), have been shown to have an intuitive appeal in promoting discovery and exploratory learning. The criticism often made is, of course, that students learn more about computer reality but less about the "real world." Computer microworlds, however, are not "passive"; they do more than transmit information. A key goal and challenge of virtual instruction is, therefore, that students become not just fluent users of simulations (that is, the software and hardware) but also wise and apt in understanding the nature of simulation itself.

People invent technology, but technology also shapes people. A similar sentiment was expressed by Marshall McLuhan (1994) in the 1960s, when he coined the phrase, "The medium is the message." What he meant was that, contrary to popular assumption, communication networks are not transparent; in conveying messages the medium does shape the meaning of the message. Television does not just present events that occur, it determines what the viewers see and how they interpret the events (Woolley, 1992, p. 127). Technology appears to make everything transparent but is, in fact, conveying and shaping both private and public understanding. McIsaac (1993) points out that often media, materials, or services are inappropriately transferred without sufficient recognition of the recipient cultural setting.

Gutenberg's development of the printing press resulted in a move from an oral to a written culture. The development of an electronic culture likewise will arguably have a transformative effect on both people and societies (Birkerts, 1994). Rud (1997, p. 30) summarizes the argument by Birkerts about electronic mediated language leading to (1) a form of language erosion due to the loss of subtle uses of language (e.g., irony) by the requirements of distant, easy, and quick communication; (2) a flattening of perspective attributable to a lack of a historical perspective; and (3) the diminishment of the private, interior self as individuals become part of a system that is transparent and where duration is replaced by immediacy. Whether these predicted consequences will or do actually occur should be investigated by the educational research community, which itself is only beginning to come to terms with interactive, multimedia technologies.

THE IMPORTANCE OF METAPHORICAL MENTAL MODELS AND LANGUAGE

The importance of culture in the use of language and the role of metaphor, with respect to networked learning environments, can be illustrated by a few examples. In China, the concept of the computer is expressed or translated as an electronic calculator. This definition carries with it connotations of the old Western conception of the computer. It implies an operating system or a machine that operates in a quantifiable, observable, or measurable way. In Hong Kong, Singapore, and Taiwan, however, the concept of the computer is expressed in Chinese symbols meaning electronic brain. The latter expression for computer has connotations that imply greater flexibility and power. Similarly in Taiwan, the concept of software is expressed as meaning a soft piece. In China, the term used means a soft organism. The term used for software in China carries with it a greater suggestive or imaginative power. In Taiwan, the term for the Internet refers to "the net within the web," while in China the term used indicates a cooperative network. The term used in China, therefore, has a greater potential for indicating the power and usefulness of the Internet for international cooperation. The appropriate choice of metaphor underlying a particular concept and the appropriate use of language have consequences for how a particular technology is perceived and, therefore, fruitfully used.

In using technology for education nowadays, much effort is being made to ensure that it is more than merely conferring literacy, whether of the textual or visual kind. Instruction in virtual learning environments must, of necessity, be more than multiple interactive conduits of information; it must involve well-designed communication and pedagogical systems that motivate thinking and learning. What the education of the future will require is that we, the professional teachers, learn not merely "how to think and solve problems"; we must also learn "how other people think and solve problems" (Eoyang, 1997). Effective instructional systems should be so designed that learners are provoked and prepared to think not only for themselves but also for and through others.

CRITICAL INSTRUCTIONAL DESIGN PRINCIPLES

Just as the attributes of communication technologies for distance learning are often cited as promises, so these attributes should also be the basis for the design of Web-based or network-based courses for distance learning. Unless the Web-based courses are so designed that they are easily accessible and technically user-friendly, the participants of distance learning courses will soon be too frustrated and disillusioned to continue using them. User friendliness is related not only to the design of courses but also to the nature and quality of technology available, such as the navigational power of the Internet for bringing about interconnectivity; buttons and forms for facilitating interactivity; the bandwidth for enhancing immediacy; and the ease of integration of different subjects, concepts, and skills.

CONCLUSIONS

Learning Is Situational and Culturally Mediated

In a simulation or virtual learning environment, there are fundamental assumptions underlying the worldview(s) being promoted either explicitly or implicitly. An essential metacognitive skill that students need to develop is to understand the nature of virtual learning environments, not simply to become fluent in their use.

Bearing in mind the importance of experiential learning and that learning is culturally bound, instruction at a distance should ultimately only be a component of a course. "Face-to-face" communication arguably still remains the most efficient and powerful form of communication. The critical factor for consideration is choosing at just which point in the information flow, or the structure of knowledge, or the course of communication, the distance learning should take place, even if it is in a virtual learning environment, such as desktop videoconferencing among several groups of learners.

Critical Instructional Design Principles for Distance Learning

The tremendous power and potential of the communications and information technologies are shaping and will continue to shape the educational process in the future, but the limitations and the inherent nature of technologies shape the message or information that is transmitted to students (and teachers). Even if the significant elements of instructional design for distance learning, such as accessibility, interconnectivity, immediacy, interactivity, and integration, are considered and incorporated into courses, the quality and nature of learning are largely determined by the individual's experience of cultures and technologies.

The interpretation of information and the generation of knowledge will be dependent on the existing conceptual frameworks of the learner, frameworks that will be culturally mediated. The particular metaphors underlying concepts (e.g., electronic calculator versus electronic brain) serve to stimulate or limit the human imagination. The success of the marriage of technology and the culturally mediated ways in which technology is perceived will, in the end, determine the success of telematic courses, virtual instruction, and distance learning.

REFERENCES

Ausubel, D. P. (1963). *The psychology of meaningful verbal learning.* New York: Grune and Stratton.

Bate, P. (1994). *Strategies for cultural change.* Oxford: Butterworth-Heinemann.

Birkerts, S. (1994). *The Gutenberg elegies: The fate of reading in an electronic age.* Boston: Faber & Faber.

Black, J. (1997). *Gray areas* [Online]. Available: http://www.news.com/SpecialFeatures/0,5,8353,00.html. (Accessed March 19, 1999).

Chute, A. G., Sayers, P. K., & Gardner, R. P. (1997). Networked learning environments. *New Directions for Teaching and Learning,* No. 71, 7583. Used with permission of Jossey-Bass Publications.

Clift, R. T., Thomas, L., Levin, J., & Larson, A. (1996). Learning in two contexts: Field and university influences on the role of telecommunications in teacher education [Online]. Paper presented at the American Educational Research Association Conference. Available: http://www.ed.uiuc.edu/tta/Papers/AERA96-Learning-in-2-contexts/index.html. (Accessed March 19, 1999).

Cockburn, A., & Greenberg, S. (1995). TurboTurtle: A collaborative microworld for exploring Newtonian physics [Online]. Paper presented at the Conference on Computer Support for Collaborative Learning. Available: http://www-cscl95.indiana.edu/cscl95/cockburn.html. (Accessed March 19, 1999).

Dewey, J. (1933). *How we think.* Boston: D. C. Heath.

Doll, W. E. (1989). Foundations for a post-modern curriculum. *Journal of Curriculum Studies, 21*(3), 243–253.

Eoyang, E. C. (1997). Hong Kong and the human trinity: Language, education, culture. *Asian Thought and Society, 22*(66), 242–248.

Gaines, B. R., & Shaw, M. L. G. (1996). *Implementing the learning Web* [Online]. Available: http://ksi.cpsc.ucalgary.ca/articles/LearnWeb/EM96Tools/. (Accessed March 19, 1999).

Garrison, J. W., & Bentley, M. L. (1990). Science education, conceptual change and breaking with everyday experience. *Studies in Philosophy and Education, 10,* 19–35.

Geertz, C. (1993). *Local knowledge: Further essays in interpretive anthropology.* London: Fontana Press.

Gough, N. (1989). From epistemology to ecopolitics: Renewing a paradigm for curriculum. *Journal of Curriculum Studies, 21*(3), 225–241.

Harkrider, N., & Chen, A.-Y. (1998). Design considerations for Web-based reflective inquiry. Unpublished manuscript.

Harry, K., Keegan, D. J., & Magnus, J. (Eds.). (1995). *Distance education: New perspectives.* London: Routledge Kegan Paul.

Haste, H. (1993). *The sexual metaphor.* London: Harvester Wheatsheaf.

Hofstede, G. (1983). The world view orientation relativity of organizational practice and theories. *Journal of International Business*, Fall, 75–89.

Jacobs, G., & Rodgers, C. (1997). Remote teaching with digital video: A trans-national experience. *British Journal of Educational Technology, 28*(4), 292–304.

Kuhn, T. S. (1977). *The essential tension.* Chicago: University of Chicago Press.

Looi, C. K. (1998). Online learning communities. Manuscript submitted for publication.

Loy, D. (1986). Nondual thinking. *Journal of Chinese Philosophy, 13,* 293–309.

Marzano, R. (1994). When two worldviews collide. *Educational Leadership, 51*(4), 6–11.

McIsaac, M. S. (1993). Economic, political and social considerations in the use of global computer-based distance education. In R. Muffoletto & N. Knupfer (Eds.), *Computers in education: Social, political and historical perspectives* (pp. 219–232). Cresskill, NJ: Hampton Press.

McIsaac, M. S. (1996). Learning for the future [Online]. Keynote address presented at the First International Distance Education Symposium, Ankara, Turkey. Available: http://seamonkey.ed.asu.edu/~mcisaac/future/paper.htm. (Accessed March 19, 1999).

McLuhan, M. (1994). *Understanding media: The extensions of man.* Cambridge, MA: MIT Press. (Originally published 1964).

Mellar, H., Bliss, J., Boohan, R., Ogborn, J., & Tompsett, C. (1994). *Learning with artificial worlds.* London: Falmer Press.

Pepper, S. C. (1942). *World hypotheses: A study in evidence.* Los Angeles: University of California Press.

Pitt, M. (1996). The use of electronic mail in undergraduate teaching. *British Journal of Educational Technology, 27*(1), 4550.

Proper, H., Wideen, M. F., & Ivany, G. (1988). World view projected by science teachers: A study of classroom dialogue. *Science Education, 72*(5), 547–560.

Reichenbach, H. (1951). *The rise of scientific philosophy.* Berkeley: University of California Press.

Rud, A. G., Jr. (1997). Musty paper, blinking cursors: Print and digital cultures. *Educational Researcher, 26*(7), 29–32.

Russell, A. L. (1997). Nonexpert conceptions of virtual reality. *Journal of Research on Computing in Education, 30*(1), 53–66.

Sankar, C. S., Ford, F. N., & Terase, N. (1997). Impact of videoconferencing in teaching an introductory MIS course. *Journal of Educational Technology Systems, 26*(1), 67–85.

Scardamalia, M., & Bereiter, C. (1996). Engaging students in a knowledge society. *Educational Leadership, 54*(3), 6–11.

Smith, J. E. (1991). Interpreting across boundaries. In R. E. Allinson (Ed.), *Understanding the Chinese mind: The philosophical roots* (pp. 26–47). Hong Kong: Oxford University Press.

Taylor, W. (1984). Metaphors of educational discourse. In W. Taylor (Ed.), *Metaphors of education* (pp. 4–20). London: Heinemann.

Turkle, S. (1997). Seeing through computers: Education in a culture of simulation. *The American Prospect, 31,* 76–82.

Vygotsky, L. S. (1989). *Thought and language.* Cambridge, MA: MIT Press.

Whitelock, D., Brna, P., & Holland, S. (1997). *What is the value of virtual reality for conceptual learning? Towards a theoretical framework* [Online]. Available: http://www.cbl.leeds.ac.uk/~euroaied/papers/Whitelock1/. (Accessed March 19, 1999).

Williams-Green, J., Holmes, G., & Sherman, T. M. (1997). Culture as a decision variable for designing computer software. *Journal of Educational Technology Systems, 26*(1), 3–18.

Wittgenstein, L. (1953). *Philosophical investigations.* Oxford: Blackwell.

Woolley, B. (1992). *Virtual worlds.* London: Penguin Books.

Zhao, Y. (1995). China: Its distance learning system. In K. Harry et al. (Eds.), *Distance education: New perspectives.* London: Routledge Kegan Paul.

CHAPTER 10

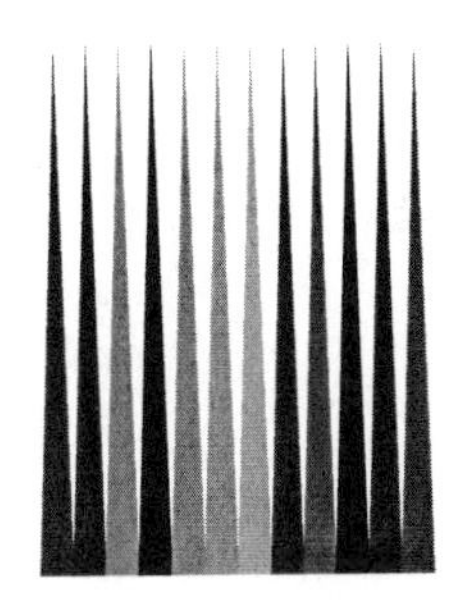

Use of Information Technology in Education

Present State and Future Prospects in Japan

Takashi Sakamoto
Japan

THE ADVENT OF AN ADVANCED INFORMATION AND COMMUNICATION SOCIETY

Today's society can be said to have entered into a new age of social revolution. This is characterized as an "information revolution," comparable in scale to the civil and industrial revolutions of the past. The Japanese Headquarters for the Promotion of the Advanced Information and Communication Society (1995), an organization headed by the country's prime minister, recently issued an article entitled, "Basic Policy for the Promotion of the Advanced Information and Communication Society." This article defines today's society as being "based on a new socioeconomic system that realizes the unrestricted creation, distribution, and sharing of information and knowledge produced from human intellectual activity; and that harmonizes life, culture, industry, economy, nature, and the environment as a whole" (p. 1). Education is naturally geared into this system.

The Meaning of Information in Social Life

The advent of the advanced information and communication society, a historical phenomenon propelled by scientific and technological progress, will engender a radical change in the course of our civilizations' development in the coming years. Specifically, the form in which information is exchanged between people will be severely altered.

Because words provide the basis for the exchange of information, they are of vital importance for life in human society. Words convey the outbreak of danger, lessons, the art of living, and so forth. Of course, words are also essential vehicles for the process of thinking. In many cases, information flows from those who know something or who have authority to those who do not. Even after written language was invented and recorded on stone or bamboo, the subject matter consisted mostly of accounts of the lives of great people or the lessons they left for posterity. In most cases, the person receiving the information read and interpreted the meaning of the written words. The verbal and textual communications imparted in the Analects of Confucius, religious or philosophical scriptures, stories, songs, and proverbs were a truly effective means of conveying knowledge and authority. People interpreted the meanings of texts, mulled them over, and disseminated their new insights by means of education. With the birth of the printing press, written materials became mass-produced, and the content of written texts became more closely associated with authority and knowledge. Even today, an author is viewed as an authority in possession of intellectual content that is to be imparted to others.

Conversely, those commonly regarded as "ordinary people" read the information as "receivers" or learners and utilized it in their lives. Opportunities for these people to send written information outward were usually in the form of correspondence or diaries, and before literacy education prevailed, even these forms of writing were the privilege of only the educated. Even today, people primarily acquire their perspective on world knowledge from media such as books, newspapers, or magazines.

With the coming of the age of radio, those with messages to transmit were widely seen as individuals of wisdom and authority, and it was perceived as an important task for the average person as a learner to take in information related to his or her own life. At the outset of the television age, too, participation on the part of the general public was infrequent, and appearance in the media once again represented authority. This tendency still persists; to appear in some types of programs evokes an impression of authority. The same applies to the cinematic medium, but because very few people have the resources for creating a movie, the perception of authoritativeness is much greater. Ordinary people, again, are merely passive observers who watch the movies to absorb an interpretation of the meaning of life.

In conventional distance education, until recently learners were receivers who were to read and understand the information sent via media such as books, radio, or television. If they were ever placed in a position where they could send information, this took at best the form of a compulsory assignment or report. Recently, however, this aspect of the world of these "ordinary people" has undergone great changes.

Information Receivers Become Information Senders

New tools for expression, such as cameras, videorecorders, word processors, and computers have appeared, and their use is now widespread. As a result, populations at large, which had hitherto been restricted to receiving information, now have the capability to send information at their disposal. The individual can easily transmit words, voice, sound, still images, and moving video images. Today, business people habitually create and transmit information using multimedia tools and word processors, and small children can draw pictures on their computers that may win prizes in competition with middle school students or older competitors. To cite one striking example, a first grader in Japan created a multimedia work, recorded it on a floppy disk, and subsequently won a prize from the Minister of Education, Science, Sports, and Culture. One pupil currently in primary school even creates "multimedia poems."

The process of creating, altering, and disseminating new information has seen great changes. Originally people who drew, sang songs, and played musical instruments transmitted the messages they had created in the same way in which they communicated the spoken word. Often this process required considerable time and effort. Using a computer, however, people are easily able to draw pictures or to compose music. Moreover, the works they create can be modified or duplicated at any time, and mistakes can be instantly undone with the click of a mouse. This can be contrasted favorably with the difficulty of erasing "real" painting or traditionally written music scores and, therefore, of realizing a drastically new idea in those older media.

The prevalence of word processors heralds the rapid approach of the "information-sending" society. In the past, ordinary individuals could only impart their knowledge to those nearby. Today, if a school is linked to a network, one individual can disseminate a message all over the world. In this way, the written medium as a source of information has expanded to multimedia. We can selectively receive data from media through reliable databases, and now we can also send multimedia information. In a real sense, we are at a great turning point in the history of our civilization.

As the twenty-first century progresses, the selection, understanding, utilization, creation, and transmission of information using multimedia will become more and more natural. The process of transmitting via media that integrate characters, images, videos, voices, and sounds over networks will become as commonplace as the telephone is today. Although text-based information will continue to play the most important role in the communication of multimedia data, the reading of written texts alone will be insufficient. Communication with graphics, pictures, photographs, tables, and moving video will be of importance both in learning environments and in everyday life.

Learners in the impending advanced information and communication society will have to possess not only the skills of reading, writing, and understanding information through media such as radio or television, but also those of retrieving and utilizing multimedia information and of self-sufficiently creating and transmitting multimedia work.

In receiving information from media, there are of course a few new responsibilities to be learned and reflected upon. It is important, for example, to bear in mind that we must not allow ourselves to be misled by the bewildering quantity of information. We need to arm ourselves with the ability to identify and distinguish between genuine and biased information, as well as the ability to maintain a grasp on reality without relying too much on the mediated representations and perceptions conveyed by the information we absorb. Also, we have to be able to gather and select real information independently. In sending information, we should be careful not to invade the privacy of other people. We should not use or create biased or erroneous information, and we must respect the intellectual property rights of information produced by others. To act responsibly, learners will need to truly understand the importance of information for life in society.

NEW PERSONNEL TYPES NEEDED IN MODERN SOCIETY

Characteristics of a Work Force Prepared for the Information Age

With the rapid changes in our society, the scientific and technical knowledge and skills obtained in school education will soon lag behind the levels of advances in the world "outside." To catch up with these social changes, particularly to play a role in the active construction of this society, lifelong learning will be essential. In this regard, the Subcommittee on Educational Content in the Central Council for Education introduced the term "self-education ability" in its interim report (1983). The elements of this ability include study motivation, study method, and a spirit of inquiry into life. Since this report was issued, many schools have been actively researching how to stimulate motivation and ability to self-educate.

Serious challenges face children and young adults who wish to obtain and develop this ability. They will need to set up a personalized objective, select the educational content, establish a study process, and study and evaluate their progress independently. Consequently, a review of one's educational goals, content, and study process is essential, and improvements must be made if necessary. Additionally, because the study content must be constantly renewed, the self-study method is far beyond the average child's capacity to control. Thus, in many cases in the school educational stage, teachers prepare the educational goal or content, while the order of study and study method are left to the pupil, and the pupil's so-called self-learning ability is thus cultivated.

The individual in this dawning Information Age will need to be competent in independently utilizing the outcomes of technology in modern society. It will become particularly important to equip students with skills for using technology as an effective means for self-education or for self-study.

Economic organizations hope that educational circles will turn out personnel well prepared for the new age. A number of useful documents discuss this concern:

1. The special committee for education of the Japanese Federation of Employers' Associations (Nikkeiren) issued a report (1995) listing five desirable characteristics for people in the new age: (1) rich character and vision, (2) originality and creativity, (3) the ability to identify and solve problems, (4) the ability to adapt to globalization, and (5) leadership abilities.

2. Another paper, published by the Federation of Economic Organization (Keidanren), also suggests that "the ideal personnel for the future society of this country will be active, highly responsible, and creative" (1996, pp. 1–2).

3. The Committee "Vision for the 21st Century" of the Japan Teachers' Union submitted its final report on April 12, 1995. This report proposed a series of traits, not unlike those cited above, desirable in the children to inhabit the twenty-first century, including (1) the ability to adapt to social changes in active and creative ways; (2) the ability to live as a global citizen while fostering local and traditional culture; and (3) the ability to form new civil communities in cooperation with others, while also preserving, if not fostering, the independence of the individuals living within those communities.

This last quality is in accord with the direction that the *Standard Course of Study* (Ministry of Education, Science, Sports, and Culture, 1989) stresses: development of a willingness to study by oneself and the ability to adapt to social change, the perfection of teaching of basic contents, and the enrichment of education for cultivating one's individuality. It also corresponds to those elements of the *Standard Course of Study* that place great emphasis on interest, willingness, and a positive attitude toward subject matter; logical thinking ability and capacity for judgment; and self-expression.

Above all, the *Standard Course of Study* values the ability to actively contribute toward constructing modern society. This new direction is a reflection of what is now expected of Japanese industry. After straining to catch up with the advanced nations of the West in terms of scientific and technological development, industry in this country is now expected, with the advent of the new century, to contribute more actively to the world with leadership and originality.

Passive groups of personnel engaged simply in processing the orders passed down from superiors have proven ill equipped to adapt to the upheavals in the advanced Information Society and will be unable to take on this societally constructional role. Thus, Japan, a country resolutely working to become one of the world's scientific and academic leaders in the twenty-first century, will have to revise its models for more relevant personnel profiles to prepare new personnel who are appropriate to the tasks ahead.

Qualifications for Information-Oriented Persons

Faced with the advanced information communication society, the next generation, the creators of society in the twenty-first century, will need to equip themselves with the following six qualities/abilities to positively utilize, create, and transmit information: (1) information literacy, (2) full awareness of the value of information, (3) an information-oriented sensitivity, (4) respect for the morality of information, (5) mastery of information skills, and (6) an ability to participate in an information network. These six qualifications are described below:

1. "Information literacy" is an understanding of the mechanism, role, and theory of information technology.

2. "Awareness of the value of information" is a recognition of the importance of information, as well as the adverse effects it can have on daily life. An awareness and understanding of both the positive and negative sides of information, as well as an ability to assess the authenticity of information, will be essential.

3. To have "an information-oriented sensitivity" is to have a rich appreciation of the concepts of truth, virtue, and beauty; namely, to appreciate and feel the delicacy, complexity, and relevance of certain types of information, such as the beauty of flowers, the precious nature of humanity, and the glory of love.

4. If one possesses "respect for the morality of information," one will refrain from misusing information technology. This entails respect for intellectual property rights and the privacy of others and a refusal to disseminate bogus or biased information that is potentially confusing to society; in other words, one will work toward the establishment of a moral ethic.

5. "Mastery of information skills" means just that: the skill to use information technology.

6. Participation in an information network involves the exchange of information and assistance and cooperation with many people through information networks in business and in everyday life.

An information-oriented person in the future not only must be equipped with the skills to use a computer self-sufficiently but must also have a good balance of these six qualifications.

GOVERNMENTAL POLICIES AND THE 15TH CENTRAL COUNCIL FOR EDUCATION

Headquarters for the Promotion of the Advanced Information and Communication Society

On February 21, 1995, the Headquarters for the Promotion of the Advanced Information and Communication Society, headed by the prime minister, set out its "Basic Policy" document. Based on this, in August the Ministry of Education, Science, Sports, and Culture published guidelines on informatization in education, science, culture, and sports (1995). The guidelines proposed the following concrete measures.

Primary and secondary school education

- Programs for improving computers and related equipment, and promotion of intelligent school facilities;
- Diffusion of software and the research and development (R&D) of good software;
- In-service teacher training and teacher education to equip teachers with the basic knowledge and skills related to utilization of computers;
- Research on methods of education using advanced communication networks based on technologies such as fiber optics;

- Establishment of a center equipped with a national-center function, providing general information on education and culture.

Higher education

- Improvement of information facilities and improvement of network environments, including intraschool LANs and utilization of a communications satellite;
- Improvement of educational and research organizations for graduate schools, faculties, and departments;
- Improvement and extension of the University of the Air throughout Japan;
- R&D and promotion of new educational methods and educational forms utilizing communication satellites, fiber optics, and so forth;
- Multimedia support for private universities and specialized colleges;
- Supply of information on university/college life and admission information using advanced communication networks.

Social education

- Improvement of supply of information for lifelong education;
- Informatization of libraries and museums;
- R&D for learning methods using new media;
- A variety of learning opportunities in local communities;
- Enhancement of the qualifications of leaders in social education.

Science

- Enhancement and speedup of scientific information networks and expansion of international connectivity;
- Improvement of intraschool LANs, such as introduction of an ATM network system;
- Improvement of scientific informational databases;
- R&D of new systems, such as an electronic library system; expansion of the National Center for Science Information, and others, that play a central role in the promotion of science information distribution.

Culture

- Improvement of information systems providing information related to the possession of cultural assets and art objects, and improvement of cultural administration of local government and art groups;
- Development of information and materials for Japanese language study, using an advanced informational communications network to support Japanese language learners within and outside Japan.

Sports

- Improvement of the system providing information on local sports activities;
- Promotion of R&D on scientific training methods using multimedia, and establishment of a national center dealing with information on sports science;
- Promotion of research on training methods and teacher education using communications media.

Using these lists as a basis, it is clear that promotion of the utilization of multimedia has become a national policy in education, science, culture, and sports.

After the appointment of committee members on April 10, 1995, the 15th Central Council for Education was presented with a list of questions by the minister of education on April 26, 1995, centering around the following three topics: (1) the ideal state of education and the respective roles and collaboration of schools, households, and local communities; (2) the training to cope with the abilities and aptitude of each student and improvement of the connections between different levels of schools; and (3) the optimum way of accommodating societal changes such as internationalization, informatization, advances in science and technology, and so forth.

The ideal method for education in the multimedia age is included in the third topic. Although Japanese education has so far proven effective, it has turned out not to be fully effective in keeping up with the swift changes society has been undergoing. Reform in education aimed at coping with environmental issues, advances in science and technology, internationalization, and so forth is greatly desired.

After more than a year's discussion, the 15th Central Council for Education issued a report in July 1996 emphasizing the active promotion of educational informatics. The report (Central Council for Education, 1996) recommends the following forms of activity: (1) the systematic implementation of informatics education, (2) qualitative improvement in school education through the use of informational communications networks, (3) the construction of the "New School" to handle the advanced information communication society, (4) overcoming the less desirable components of informatization, and (5) enhancing balanced human beings.

Task Force on Utilizing Multimedia in Higher Education in the Twenty-First Century

A Ministry of Education task force was formed under the title "Utilizing Multimedia in Higher Education in the 21st Century." In July 1996, it issued a report that emphasized promoting the use of satellite and Internet technology in higher education and utilizing new information communications technology for distance teaching and learning in higher education institutions.

To introduce innovative educational methods at higher education institutions, the necessity for a Central Research and Development Institute was agreed upon, and the National Institute of Multimedia Education (NIME) was designated as the organization possessing these functions. The Central Institute, it was argued, should have three main functions: (1) coordination of educational use of communications satellites (CS), (2) assistance in terms of educational improvement in each higher education institution, and (3) R&D on multimedia and Internet use in higher education.

USE OF INFORMATION TECHNOLOGY IN SCHOOL EDUCATION

100-School Networking Project

Vying with the National Information Institute in the United States to promote the informatization of society, the Ministry of International Trade and Industry (MITI), in cooperation with related ministries, announced the implementation of the advanced informatization program in June 1994. Under the program's so-called 100-school networking project, the Information Processing Promotion Agency publicly invited schools to participate in a 100-pilot-school program with the Center for Educational Computing, and 1,543 schools applied. Schools selected comprised 30 A-Group schools, that is, schools with advanced policies and skilled teachers with good performance records; and 70 B-Group schools, that is, schools capable of actively establishing plans and participating in the network project. In addition to these 100 schools, 2 American schools (1 added to each group) and a number of specially designated schools and hospitals were also added, bringing the total to 111.

The information collected by these schools included messages from the U.S. president, data on earthquakes, video from the weather satellite *Himawari,* and information on admission into schools of higher grade. As far as transmission of information is concerned, some schools are currently sending information on works of art and music, local contamination levels and status, and natural monuments within and outside the country.

Various types of information are exchanged among the schools. Students communicate with the middle schools they graduated from or exchange messages about manners and customs, seasonal and natural topics such as cherry blossoms, and original pictures and music. The programs planned for joint study include rainfall levels, air pollution, water pollution, water shortage, the altitude of the sun, flying in the route of the hooded crane, greeting words, dialects, manners and customs, local products, commodity prices, and cooperative creation of relay-style novels and scripts. In the area of network conferencing, discussion among foreign schools is planned centering on fashion, culture, and customs. At present, videoconferences among schools and joint research on subjects such as acid rain and the germination of pumpkinseeds have been started.

In many schools, information exchange with foreign schools was also conducted. After the three-year experiment, researchers summarized the accomplishments and challenges of the project as follows (Conference to Introduce Results from the 100-School Networking Project, 1998).

Educational effectiveness

- Creation of new educational modes
- Creation of new teaching methods
- Cultivation of new scholastic achievement
- Experience of national and international exchange
- Feeling and awareness of mutual relationship with foreign societies via information technologies

- Interest in information technologies and understanding of their social functions
- Discovery of enjoyment through self-expression and in creative activities
- Enhancement of comprehensive cognition and skills
- Recognition of the importance of curriculum development
- Substantial understanding of evaluation and innovation of evaluation methods
- Actual understanding of collaboration and cooperation and formation of positive attitudes toward these
- Achieving knowledge in diversified fields
- Understanding and skill formation with respect to computer software
- Enhancement of problem discovery and awareness of problems

Educational problems

- Informational ethics (privacy, intellectual property, copyright, informational etiquette)
- Difficulties in achieving systematic and academic knowledge
- Workload for preparing teaching
- Necessity of enhancing informational literacy in teachers
- Difficulties of balancing Internet and traditional classroom teaching
- Interruption of teaching due to technical problems
- Handling the obsolescence of resources caused by drastic changes in information technologies
- Problems in collaborative organization in schools

- Costs of implementation
- Difficulties in teaching in terms of time distribution, redundancy, and load
- Necessity of integrating students who are at different levels of achievement
- Difficulties of evaluation

Konet Plan, Satellite, and DVD

In 1996, Nippon Telegraph and Telephone Corporation (NTT) launched its "Konet Plan," a consortium with the aim of providing 1,014 schools with a network environment that would support e-mail exchange, collection of information, and World Wide Web home page design and transmission. This marked the true arrival of the multimedia age in the schools. However, not every school in Japan will enjoy the benefits of this project. Basically, in regular classes, pupils must get accustomed to a combination of various media (a so-called media mix) and be able to actively and intelligently use a variety of educational materials, overhead projectors, broadcasts, printed materials, models, and other physical objects. Multimedia can only be put to effective use after students have obtained this experience. Unless pupils have the adequate ability to gather, store, retrieve, create, and express information freely and independently without the provision of an actual computer in the classroom, simply bringing in a computer and connecting it to a network will not ensure effective use of multimedia networks. It is important to combine new media with conventional ones.

In this project, better videoconference systems were simultaneously introduced. Compared to the low quality of CUseeMe in the 100-school networking project, more effective information exchanges are attained. At the moment, the number of schools with an Internet connection is very small, with only 18 percent of all schools being equipped in 1998. However, many useful activities are in evidence in such advanced schools.

Education via satellite is especially beneficial for schools in isolated areas. Children in 17 pairs of sister schools in isolated areas learned subjects from teachers in urban schools using a videoconferencing system, in addition to exchanging information. Similar activities have been undertaken between schools on isolated islands and in urban schools via communications satellite (Ministry of Education, Science, Sports, and Culture, 1998).

GENERAL TRENDS

The NIME conducted a survey on the use of new technologies in universities in Japan in 1995 (Kikukawa, 1997). Data were collected from 87 national universities out of a total of 98, from 40 out of 54 public universities, and from 301 out of approximately 450 private universities.

According to the survey results, national universities were, generally speaking, more advanced in the use of new technologies than public and private universities. Although the use of videoconference systems, multimedia CAI, and home-page presentations was not very widespread, national universities were still more positive in the use of their applications compared to public and private universities. Unfortunately, staff training was entirely neglected at Japanese universities.

In the 22 most advanced universities, the use of a computer network, the research into and development of multimedia instructional materials, and R&D applied to instructional methods utilizing new media were more common than other activities. The use of satellite, VOD, and videoconferences was still rare at the university level.

SPACE COLLABORATION SYSTEM

In October 1996, the NIME established a Space Collaboration System (SCS) and became the SCS Hub station (Ministry of Education NIME, 1998). One hundred ten national higher education institutions, including 85 national universities, 14 national colleges of technology, and 11 national research institutes, will have 133 very small aperture terminal (VSAT) stations at the end of the 1998 fiscal year.

The main goals of the new system of SCS are (1) the promotion of a new model of higher education, through cooperatively produced seminars, team teaching, symposia, and so on, by means of simultaneous and interactive image communication among remote universities and higher education institutions; and (2) the promotion of research tasks, such as developing educational methods and content through the use of various kinds of media.

The influence of SCS seems to be strong, judging from the participation of leading traditional universities in the project, because distance education in the past generally had been conducted by a group of open universities. Moreover, communication satellites are utilized for in-service teacher education and adult education.

CONCLUSIONS

Systems Functions

As mentioned above, educational technology has been proceeding with conventional study on the improvement of education. Above all, progress in the field of effective use of information technology has been remarkable and has had a vast effect on education.

For one thing, information technology works both as an equalizer and an amplifier. As information technology enables everybody to obtain information from every part of the world, it functionally realizes equal educational opportunities, and in that sense it serves as an equalizer. Moreover, it increases the volume of information to be collected and saves time, and thus it functions as an amplifier. However, different levels of skill in using information technology might result in gaps in the information collection or learning progress in education.

Second, information technology contributes to generalization, as well as specialization. Information technology enables all people to share informational subject matter, thus contributing to the generalization of common education. Moreover, it facilitates the systematic collection of specialized information, which in turn constitutes a significant contribution toward specialization.

Third, information technology contributes to both diversification and individualization. Thanks to information technologies, education is diversified and individualized and can facilitate the collection of a variety of types of information from law, economy, literature, science, medical science, and art. By learning selectively, students can develop their own individuality.

Utilization of Information

Advanced information technology is also effective in terms of utilizing information. In the first place, as each information source provides unique and distinctive information, we can collect broader information than that previously available, and we can utilize local cultural information or specialized information supplied by schools and educational institutions. It is also an approach to excellence. A great deal of cutting-edge information can be made available, so if we are selective enough, we can approach excellence in a given field.

Another positive effect is the elimination of redundant activities. As we can gather broad information, we can eliminate production of duplicate information. Information can be produced even in distributed cooperative efforts.

Finally, the use of information technologies is helpful in publicizing schools' outcomes and activities. Each institution, organization, and individual can publicize its distinctive features worldwide on a home page. This is expected to be far more effective than distributing brochures within limited areas.

Development of Mental Faculties

Utilization of information technology contributes to cognitive development. First of all, the power of probing into, expressing, and transmitting information is formed through the repeated experiences of collection, selection, editing, creation, and transmission. In addition, information literacy is developed. Through the rich experiences of information handling, the six qualifications of an information-oriented person can be developed.

Contribution Toward Internationalization

With the completion of the formation of an advanced information communication society, distinctive network education systems can emerge. When all education-related facilities are connected through networks and provide unique information in the forms of databases, home pages, or direct transmission throughout the world, the entire globe will have formed into a single-network educational information system. Systems for admission, graduation, or obtaining qualifications will be more flexible, and a society in which people can learn freely will be realized.

It is urgent that we establish effective curricula for advanced information and communications technologies (ICT) and that we develop all our citizens' abilities to utilize multimedia or Internet information as a source of basic education. Educational technology can contribute to this process in many areas.

REFERENCES

Central Council for Education. (1996). *The model for Japanese education in the perspective of the 21st century.* Tokyo, Japan: Ministry of Education, Science, Sports, and Culture.

Committee "Vision for the 21st Century." (1995, April). *Toward the new century of open education.* Tokyo, Japan: Japan Teachers' Union.

Conference to Introduce Results from the 100-School Networking Project (Phase 2). (1998). *Center for educational computing.* Tokyo, Japan: Author.

Federation of Economic Organization (Keidanren). (1996, March). *For the development of creative personnel: Desired educational reform and business involvement.* Tokyo, Japan: Author.

Headquarters for the Promotion of the Advanced Information and Communication Society. (1995). *Basic policy for the promotion of the advanced information and communication society.* Tokyo, Japan: Author.

Japanese Federation of Employers' Associations (Nikkeiren). (1995, April). *University education and industry for the new age.* Tokyo, Japan: Author.

Kikukawa, K. (1997). *Research survey on the present state and perspectives of higher education utilizing multimedia.* Chiba, Japan: National Institute of Multimedia Education.

Ministry of Education National Institute of Multimedia Education. (1998). *Operation of the Space Collaboration System toward a multimedia society.* Chiba, Japan: National Institute of Multimedia Education.

Ministry of Education, Science, Sports, and Culture. (1989). *Standard course of study.* Tokyo, Japan: Author.

Ministry of Education, Science, Sports, and Culture. (1995). *Guidelines on the adaptation of information technology in education, science, culture, and sports.* Tokyo, Japan: Author.

Ministry of Education, Science, Sports, and Culture. (1998). *R&D project for multimedia use in isolated schools.* Tokyo, Japan: Author.

Subcommittee on Educational Content, Central Council for Education. (1983, October). *Progress report on discussion.* Tokyo, Japan: Central Council for Education.

Task Force on Utilizing Multimedia in the Higher Education of the 21st Century. (1996). *Utilizing multimedia in the higher education of the 21st century.* Tokyo, Japan: Ministry of Education, Science, Sports, and Culture.

Index